UNDERSTANDING THEORIES
AND CONCEPTS IN
SOCIAL POLICY

Also available in the series

Understanding social security (second edition)
Issues for policy and practice
Edited by **Jane Millar**

"This updated second edition brings together some of the leading writers in the field to provide a critical analysis of the recent changes to the social security system."
Dr. Liam Foster, Department of Sociological Studies, University of Sheffield
PB £21.99 (US$36.95) **ISBN** 978 1 84742 186 9 **HB** £65.00 (US$99.00) **ISBN** 978 1 84742 187 6
344 pages February 2009
INSPECTION COPY AVAILABLE

Understanding equal opportunities and diversity
The social differentiations and intersections of inequality
Barbara Bagilhole

This book challenges the official discourse that shapes the debates on Equal Opportunities and Diversity (EO&D) at national, regional and European level.
PB £21.99 (US$36.95) **ISBN** 978 1 86134 848 7 **HB** £65.00 (US$99.00) **ISBN** 978 1 86134 849 4
272 pages April 2009
INSPECTION COPY AVAILABLE

Understanding social welfare movements
Jason Annetts, Alex Law, Wallace McNeish and Gerry Mooney

The book provides a timely and much needed overview of the changing nature of social welfare as it has been shaped by the demands of social movements.
PB £19.99 (US$35.95) **ISBN** 978 1 84742 096 1 **HB** £65.00 (US$99.00) **ISBN** 978 1 84742 097 8
304 pages June 2009
INSPECTION COPY AVAILABLE

Understanding human need
Hartley Dean

"Hartley Dean's book certainly meets a need: he expertly summarises debates over what human needs are, how they relate to happiness and capabilities, and what they entail for human rights and social policies. An invaluable book." Ian Gough Emeritus Professor of Social Policy, University of Bath
PB £21.99 (US$34.95) **ISBN** 978 1 84742 189 0 **HB** £65.00 (US$89.95) **ISBN** 978 1 84742 190 6
240 pages February 2010
INSPECTION COPY AVAILABLE

Understanding social citizenship (second edition)
Themes and perspectives for policy and practice
Peter Dwyer

"A second edition of this excellent book is most welcome. Dwyer's understanding of social citizenship is second to none and this new edition provides an updated discussion and assessment of all the practical and theoretical issues that students need to know about this important area of study." Nick Ellison, University of Leeds
PB £19.99 (US$32.95) **ISBN** 978 1 84742 328 3 **HB** £65.00 (US$85.00) **ISBN** 978 1 84742 329 0
280 pages June 2010
INSPECTION COPY AVAILABLE

For a full listing of all titles in the series visit www.policypress.co.uk

www.policypress.co.uk

INSPECTION COPIES AND ORDERS AVAILABLE FROM:
Marston Book Services • PO Box 269 • Abingdon • Oxon OX14 4YN UK
INSPECTION COPIES
Tel: +44 (0) 1235 465500 • Fax: +44 (0) 1235 465556 • Email: inspections@marston.co.uk
ORDERS
Tel: +44 (0) 1235 465500 • Fax: +44 (0) 1235 465556 • Email: direct.orders@marston.co.uk

UNDERSTANDING THEORIES AND CONCEPTS IN SOCIAL POLICY

Ruth Lister

First published published in Great Britain in 2010 by
The Policy Press
University of Bristol
Fourth Floor, Beacon House
Queen's Road
Bristol BS8 1QU
UK

t: +44 (0)117 331 4054
f: +44 (0)117 331 4093
tpp-info@bristol.ac.uk
www.policypress.org.uk

North American office:
The Policy Press
c/o The University of Chicago Press
1427 East 60th Street
Chicago, IL 60637, USA
t: +1 773 702 7700
f: +1 773-702-9756
e:sales@press.uchicago.edu
www.press.uchicago.edu

Reprinted 2011

British Library Cataloguing in Publication Data
A catalogue record for this book is available from the British Library.

Library of Congress Cataloging-in-Publication Data
A catalog record for this book has been requested.

ISBN 978 1 86134 793 0 paperback
ISBN 978 1 86134 794 7 hardcover

Cover design by Qube Design Associates, Bristol
Front cover: photograph kindly supplied by www.alamy.com
Printed and bound in Great Britain by Hobbs, Southampton

FSC
MIX
Paper from
responsible sources
FSC C020438

Contents

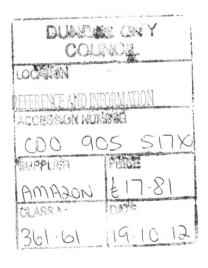

Detailed contents

List of boxes

Acknowledgements

Saul Becker asked me, more years ago than I care to remember, whether I'd like to contribute a volume to the Understanding Welfare series, based on the theory module that I teach at Loughborough University. I'm very grateful for the opportunity that this has provided me to write this book and for Saul's patience, guidance and support as well as his reading of the penultimate draft at a particularly busy time. I'm also very grateful to The Policy Press and the editors who have worked with me, especially Emily Watt, for their patience – I know that there were times when they wondered whether the book would ever see the light of day! Thanks to my dear friends Brid Featherstone and Jim Kincaid for reading the draft chapters and for their positive and helpful comments; to John Clarke for his guidance on the book's overall contents and structure; and to Dominic Wring for his advice on Figure 1.1. Thanks too to Liz Fowkes for her practical help.

To the memory of Jo Campling –
a much missed member of the
social policy community.

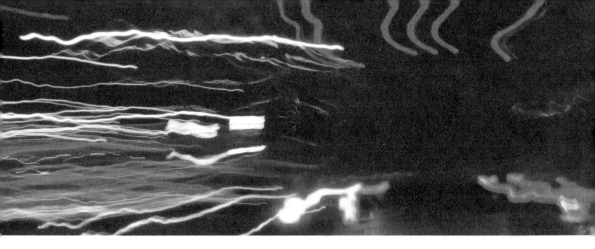

Introduction: laying the groundwork

Theory can appear far removed from the stuff of everyday social policy: health care, housing, social care, social security, poverty. Students are often nervous of an apparently abstract subject, which does not obviously relate to their everyday lives in 'the real world'. As the implementation of social policy becomes more managerial and 'evidence-based', with the key test being 'what works', politicians too are more suspicious of arguments rooted in political ideology, demanding instead 'hard facts'. One purpose of this introductory chapter, therefore, is to try to persuade you of the relevance and value of theory to the study and practice of social policy. The chapter will also lay some conceptual foundation stones and guide you through the rest of the book. It is thus divided into three main sections:

* Theory: what and why?
* Conceptual foundation stones
* Outline of the book.

Theory: what and why?

I spent the first half of my adult life working for a British campaigning charity, the Child Poverty Action Group (CPAG). When I became an academic, I was initially rather sceptical about the value of 'Theory' with a capital 'T'. What help was theory to tackling poverty and ending injustice? It seemed too abstract and frankly sometimes impenetrable so that reading it could be like wading through treacle. I say this not to put you off (after all I want you to read this book!) but to acknowledge that many of us come to theory with some trepidation.

However, I have come to realise theory's value. Yes, it can be more difficult than simply reading descriptive material, but it can also be very rewarding

– providing new insights and helping to make sense of that descriptive material. Facts don't speak for themselves: they have to be interpreted and can be interpreted in different ways depending on the theoretical framework used, explicit or implicit. Likewise current political and policy debates can better be understood if put in theoretical context. Indeed, in retrospect I can see how when I worked at CPAG we were operating with theories even if we did not articulate them as such. Implicitly we were drawing on theories of: what caused poverty; what should be done about it; the impact of government policies. And these in turn drew on some of the theoretical concepts explored in this book, notably social justice, equality, need and citizenship. At the same time, the governments with which we engaged were also drawing implicitly or explicitly on the kind of theoretical perspectives outlined in Chapter One and the concepts explored in Part Three.

O'Brien and Penna's description of theory (see **Box 0.1**) gives a good sense of what it is about at the level of both everyday practical action and more abstract generalisation.

Box 0.1: O'Brien and Penna on the nature of theory

Theory is not simply a word-game, conducted in a complex linguistic system and abstracted from reality by academic professionals. Theory is a dimension of action in so far as it gives direction and meaning to what we do. All people, separately and collectively, hold theories about the way the world works. Some of these theories are little more than vague hypotheses about what will happen if we act in a certain way in certain situations and what we expect from others in those situations. Some of the theories we hold are more complex and express our understandings of the workings of the economy or of... the distribution of social roles at home, at work, and in other contexts. In this sense, theories are generalisations about what exists in the world around us and how the components of that world fit together into patterns. In this sense also our theories are 'abstractions' – they generalise across actual situations our expectations and suppositions about the reasons why certain patterns exist and how we should deal with them.

Source: O'Brien and Penna, 1998, p 3

So, theory helps us to:

- Make sense of the world we live in from the level of everyday interaction through to the wider society and government policies and even international developments.
- Make connections between different social phenomena and policies. For example, there are various theories about the relationship between women's position in the labour market and the unequal gendered division of labour in the home, which means that they are still responsible for the bulk of care and housework. Implicit in policies designed to improve women's labour market position will be theories about whether the main levers for change lie in the labour market itself or in the home.
- Put specific issues and policies in a wider context. For instance, the significance of the treatment by the police of the murder of the black teenager Stephen Lawrence could not be understood without a theory of police practices and racism in the wider society, and such theories informed the subsequent Macpherson Inquiry.
- Question the assumptions underlying social policies and political programmes. For example, as we will see in Chapter Five, the equation of social inclusion with paid work by a growing number of governments reflects particular dominant theories of social inclusion and of society, which are contested by some observers.
- Adopt a more critical and sceptical stance towards what is presented as common sense – 'what everybody knows'. 'It's just common sense' is a claim often made by politicians to preclude further debate. As Clarke and Cochrane advise, 'social scientists need to stand back, to view common sense or "what everybody knows" from the perspective of a stranger' (1998, p 15). Theory helps us to do that (as we will see, in particular, in Chapter Five).

Helpful here is a distinction between two types of welfare theory, categorised by O'Brien and Penna (1998) as 'social' and 'normative'. *Social* theories ask 'how', 'why' and 'what' questions. They are concerned with understanding how we came to where we are; why things are as they are; and where we may be going. They often look at the interconnections between different forms of change – economic, social, cultural and political. So to take again the example of women's labour market position, social theories seek to explain it with reference to developments in the labour market itself (economic); the extent to which the domestic gender division of labour is or is not changing (social); shifting attitudes towards women's roles (cultural); and the impact of feminism and trade unionism (political). Social theories inform and are informed by empirical research (see ***Box 0.2***).

> ### Box 0.2: The role of theory in health inequalities research
>
> In an account of a UK research programme into health inequalities, Hilary Graham points to two broad theories used to 'explain how socio-economic position might exert its influence on health' (2004, p 81). The first holds that 'past socio-economic circumstances hold the key to understanding the socio-economic gradient in adult health' (2004, p 81). The second contends that current circumstances are a more significant determinant. The two theories were tested by the research programme. The conclusion reached was that 'theories emphasising early and later life influences offer complementary rather than competing explanations of health inequalities' (2004, p 81). Graham draws the following policy implication from this new theoretical understanding, rooted in empirical evidence: interventions targeted on the early years are important. But so too 'are the long-established welfare services that influence life chances and living standards across the population: education and social security, healthcare and personal social services, social housing and public transport', together with employment and fiscal policies that address inequalities in income (2004, p 82).

Normative theories ask how things could or should be and what could get us there. They are aimed at changing norms (including of behaviour), attitudes, the organisation of institutions such as the labour market and patterns of responsibility for welfare as between individuals and families, the state, the private and voluntary sectors. So, for instance, social security or welfare policy in the UK, the US and a number of other countries reflects a particular normative theory about human behaviour. This holds that claiming social security for any length of time creates undesirable 'welfare dependency' (see Chapter Five). Policy therefore aims to prevent this by encouraging or requiring claimants to seek paid work. Or, with reference to women's labour market position, there are a range of normative theories as to what women's position in the labour market should be. For instance, some normative theoretical positions hold that gender equality requires women to hold an equal position with men in the labour market. Others place greater emphasis on mothers' childcare responsibilities and the role of part-time work in facilitating these. An alternative normative theory emphasises the need for fathers to take more responsibility for childcare as pivotal to gender equality. Each normative theoretical position has different implications for: the attitudes and behaviour of women and men and also employers; the organisation of the labour market itself; and a range of policies from parental leave to working time.

Both social and normative theories inform **welfare ideologies**. At its broadest, ideology simply refers to 'a set of values and beliefs held by individuals, groups and societies that influences their conduct' (George and Wilding, 1994, p 5). However, welfare ideologies as they operate in the political sphere are more than that. George and Wilding (1994) identify four main features (see ***Box 0.3***).

Box 0.3: George and Wilding on the features of welfare ideologies

Welfare ideologies provide:

- 'a view of the world', especially of human nature and of the relationship between state and society;
- 'a critique of existing socio-economic systems';
- a vision of the ideal society;
- some guidance as to how to get there (the ideal) from here (the existing).

Source: George and Wilding (1994, p 6)

George and Wilding's account of welfare ideologies should not be interpreted to mean that those who run or benefit from the existing socioeconomic and political system do not operate with an ideology. They do, but often present it as 'common sense', dismissing critical positions as 'ideological'. This underlines how theory has political consequences. Theory is used implicitly (and sometimes explicitly) both by dominant groups to justify the *status quo* or their preferred variant of it and by marginalised groups to challenge the *status quo*. The ways in which marginalised groups, organised through social movements, use theory to challenge the *status quo* will be explored in Chapter Nine.

Box 0.4: An example of the implicit use of theory in political debate

Question: Have a look at these two statements. The first is a motion put down by the Conservative Opposition in the UK Parliament for a debate on 'social policy and the relief of poverty'. The second is an edited version of the Government's amendment to the motion. Think about how George and Wilding's four features of welfare ideology are expressed in them; the ways in which the statements implicitly apply both social and normative theory; and the differences and similarities between the statements in terms of the underlying theories upon which they draw.

> This House notes with concern the fact that the United Kingdom comes bottom of a league table of 21 rich countries in a recent UNICEF study of child well-being, has one of the worst drug problems in Europe, has low levels of social mobility, has higher rates of family breakdown than many other European countries and has more people living in severe poverty today than there were in 1997; regrets that sufficiently effective action has not been taken to deal with these problems; recognises that a shared sense of social responsibility is the basis for a more effective response to multiple deprivation and for more effective solutions to the problems of social breakdown; and urges politicians of all parties to join together in an attempt to support families, provide new routes into work, enable people to escape from addiction and indebtedness and to enable voluntary organisations and social enterprises of all sizes to increase their invaluable contribution. (Motion moved by Oliver Letwin MP)
>
> This House notes that since 1997 employment has risen to the highest level ever..., the number of workless households has fallen, the number of children in workless households has fallen, the number of children in non-decent homes has been cut by 1.4 million, child poverty has fallen by 600,000, pensioner poverty has fallen and educational attainment has risen for pupils from all social classes...; further notes that this has happened because of a sustained strategy..., which includes the New Deal programme, Tax Credits, the National Minimum Wage, Sure Start, a National Childcare Strategy, programmes to improve parenting, Educational Maintenance Allowances and record investment in public services; and urges politicians of all parties to recognise the benefits of these reforms and not undermine them, support all children and work together to tackle the social challenges that the UK still faces through continued investment, engagement of individuals and communities, work with the voluntary sector and through an approach which recognises that the best way to build a fair society is through providing opportunities for all citizens, not just the few, to meet their aspirations. (Amendment moved by Edward Miliband MP)
>
> Source: *House of Commons Hansard*, 11 July 2007, cols 1510, 1521

It is important to stress at this point that there is no clear 'right' or 'wrong' theory in this context. The theories that inform social policy are not like natural scientific theories which can be tested. Some social theories might be better than others at helping us to understand social realities; theories may differ in how much light they throw on various social phenomena. Also, there can be debates and disputes *within* particular theoretical perspectives.

So you do not need to feel that you must line up behind any one theory. It is best to try and approach the various theoretical perspectives and concepts with an open mind. Which normative theories you adopt will depend on your own values and beliefs. Likewise, while I aim to be even-handed in my presentation of the various theoretical positions, inevitably my own values and beliefs, forged in anti-poverty and feminist campaigning, will colour my interpretation of them to some extent.

Conceptual foundation stones

Constructing theory is rather like building a wall. Just as a wall is made up of bricks so a theory is composed of a number of concepts. Part Three will explore some of the key concepts used to build theories in social policy. In addition to these, there are a number of conceptual foundation stones, underpinning the wall of theory, which we will explore briefly here, as follows:

- the **individual** in terms of identity, the idea of the welfare subject and beliefs about human motivation and behaviour, which underpin theories and policies;
- the interplay between individual human **agency, structural** constraints and opportunities and **culture**;
- the **state**, **nation** and **nation–state**; and
- the **transnational** and the **global**.

The individual

Who is the individual at which social policy is directed? This might seem like an odd question. Whereas in the past it is one which would probably just have been taken for granted, now the individual is the subject of theorising in at least three main ways in relation to identity, the 'welfare subject' and motivation and behaviour.

First, the question of **identity** has been at the heart of debates around postmodernism and social policy (Taylor, 1998; Hunter, 2003). Postmodernist theory has questioned the very notion of the individual as an autonomous agent with an essential self. Instead, we are all deconstructed into a mass of multiple, shifting identities. We will explore this idea in more detail in Chapter Three and see how social policy theorists have contributed to thinking about different aspects of identity. We will see there that the idea of multiple and shifting identities is now part of mainstream political debate. This is in part both a reflection of and reaction to forms of identity politics, which appear to privilege single identities, such as of ethnicity or religion, over others as the basis for political action.

At the same time an understanding of the fluid nature of social identity helps us to see how, when policy is framed with reference to particular groups such as young people, 'the poor' or motorists, it speaks to only one of many identities with which members of these groups might identify. Looking at it 'from above', when people are treated by politicians or the media as if they have only one identity or they are encouraged to think of themselves in that way or appeals are made to a particular identity, we need to question the political interests that are involved. Similarly there may be a gap between how certain groups are identified in public debate and how they see themselves. For example, research shows that people referred to as living in poverty do not necessarily identify themselves as 'poor' (Lister, 2004a). I drive a car but that does not necessarily mean that I think of myself as a 'motorist' in whose name appeals for more roads or cheaper petrol, with which I disagree, are advanced; and even those who identify with the label of 'motorist' are also typically pedestrians or public transport users at times. But it is rare for the identity of 'pedestrian' or 'public transport user' to be invoked in political debate.

Looking at it 'from below', when marginalised groups mobilise around a single identity it can be a crucial step in contesting injustice, but there are dangers too in suppressing the differences within groups. So, for instance, women achieved enormous progress through coming together in the women's movement in the late 20th Century. Yet differences around 'race', sexuality, (dis)ability, age and social class soon punctured the single identity of 'woman' around which the movement had coalesced.

Implicit in this discussion about identity is the idea that identity is something that is not simply 'given' but that the individual creates and identifies with: 'the self is seen as a reflexive project, for which the individual is responsible. We are, not what we are, but what we make of ourselves' (Giddens, 1991, p 75). This idea of the individual creating her or his own biography draws on the sociological theory of 'individualisation' (Beck and Beck-Gernsheim, 2002). Translated into policy, the theory emerges as assumptions about the extent to which individuals are able to make choices, for instance to be full-time workers, which are not necessarily in line with the realities of their lives, particularly in the case of women (Lewis, J., 2004; Lewis and Bennett, 2004). In turn, these issues raise wider questions about the relationship between 'agency', 'structure' and 'culture' to which we will return shortly.

In an essay on the complex processes involved in identity formation, Rick Muir points out that a 'key source of identity is the organisational life of society' including state institutions (2007, p 12). This brings us to the second relevant form of theorising about the individual. In the context of welfare institutions, the problematisation of the idea of individual identity has given rise to the notion of the '**welfare subject**'. The welfare subject is 'constructed' by those in power, for instance as a consumer/customer, a client, a patient, a claimant, a citizen. Students, for example, are increasingly constructed or talked about as customers; citizens are constructed as consumers of services. (The notion of social construction will be discussed in Chapter Five.) New Labour's first welfare reform Green Paper spoke of 'the rise of the demanding, sceptical, citizen-consumer' (Department for Social Security, 1998, p 16). In response, social policies are increasingly aimed at encouraging and satisfying this 'citizen-consumer'. This citizen-consumer is, in turn, invoked to justify the 'marketisation' of welfare services, in other words the treating of users of welfare as if they were consumers of services, bought in the private market rather than people with needs, which society has a responsibility to meet. How welfare subjects are constructed may have implications for identity and behaviour as ***Box 0.5*** explains.

Box 0.5: The welfare subject

'The point to emphasise here is that the way in which people are named affects their own and others' expectations of them in specific sites: so, for example, being a "customer" positions a person within discourses and practices of health professionals and institutions in a different way to being a "patient" would' (Lewis, 1998c, p 64).

Question: Think about your last contact with a health professional. Did you think of yourself as a 'patient' or a 'customer'? What difference, if any, do you think it makes?

At the same time welfare subjects also construct themselves in interaction with welfare institutions. Empirical research suggests some resistance to being named as a customer or consumer in dealings with public services. Instead, people still tend to identify with 'service specific terms' such as patient or service user or to identify themselves as a member of the public or local community (Clarke et al, 2007, p 128). Gail Lewis (1998c) writes about 'new welfare subjects' who have challenged the ways in which they have been treated by welfare institutions and have demanded recognition of their needs as they define them. An example would be the challenge to the medical model of disability by the disabled people's movement (see also Chapter Six and Chapter Nine).

While discussion of multiple identities and welfare subjects is relatively recent, social policy theory and practice have always to some extent involved an account of individual **motivation and behaviour**. In the past, this was rarely made explicit, but today it is the subject of theoretical and political debate. The importance for policy is underlined by a paper produced by the UK Prime Minister's Strategy Unit, entitled *Personal Responsibility and Changing Behaviour: the state of knowledge and its implications for public policy*. The paper is based on the premise that 'nearly all public policies rest on assumptions about human behaviour' (Halpern and Bates, 2004, p 3). Furthermore, the motivation behind the paper is to enable government to *change* personal behaviour more effectively by drawing on a range of theories of behavioural change.

The paper notes that 'the most simple theories see people as rational economic actors' motivated purely, or at least primarily, by economic calculations of self-interest and financial advantage (Halpern and Bates, 2004, p 14). While the authors acknowledge that 'real human psychology is more complicated' (2004, p 14), involving cultural and other factors, many social policies seem to operate with just such a model of 'economic rational man' (Taylor-Gooby, 2009). The model is derived from neoclassical economics. However, it has been challenged by another school called behavioural economics, which draws on psychology. According to behavioural economics a number of factors other than economic advantage also influence human behaviour including what other people do and a desire 'to do the right thing' and to act in line with our values and other people's expectations of us (Dawnay and Shah, 2005). Behavioural economics has been taken up by politicians in recent years, particularly in the popular guise of 'nudge' (Thaler and Sunstein, 2009). The essence of the idea of 'nudge' is that policy can be used to steer or 'nudge' individuals into changing their behaviour. 'For the nudger, the state needs to get the messages right and provide low-level incentives and costs to promote the right kind of behaviour' (John et al, 2009, p 367).

An example of the limitations of the 'economic rational man' model (which does not derive from behavioural economics) is provided by a social policy study of lone mothers. The authors, Simon Duncan and Rosalind Edwards, take as their starting point the 'particular notion of personal motivation, based on a neo-classical concept of individual economic rationality' that underpins North American and British policy designed to increase lone mothers' labour market participation (1999, p 1). They argue on the basis of their findings that:

> it is socially negotiated, non-economic understandings about what is morally right and socially acceptable which are primary

> factors in determining what is seen as rational behaviour – calculations about individual financial costs and benefits are secondary. (Duncan and Edwards, 1999, p 118)

They suggest the notion of 'gendered moral rationalities' (1999, p 3) to capture the way in which rational choices have a moral as well as an economic element. So, for example, lone mothers' choices in relation to paid work will reflect not just an economic calculation but also what they think is the right thing to do as a mother. Duncan and Edwards found that such beliefs are in turn affected not just by what government and the wider society says but also by what friends, family and neighbours believe is right. Such beliefs are part of what has been called 'gender culture', which helps to shape women's and men's actions, particularly with regard to paid work and care (Pfau-Effinger, 1998; Kremer, 2007).

Policy-makers' beliefs about what motivates both recipients of policy and those who implement it have been analysed by Julian Le Grand. He argues that:

> Policy-makers fashion policies on the assumption that those affected by the policies will behave in certain ways and they will do so because they have certain motivations.... [There has been] a fundamental shift in policy-makers' beliefs concerning human motivation and behaviour. People who finance, operate and use the welfare state are no longer assumed to be either public spirited altruists (knights) or passive recipients of state largesse (pawns); instead they are all considered to be in one way or another self-interested (knaves). (Le Grand, 1997, pp 155, 149; see also Le Grand, 2003)

The shift in perceptions of welfare providers from 'benevolent guardians of the public interest' or knights to self-interested knaves is associated with 'public choice theory' (Hindmoor, 2006, p 85). Public choice theory, which originated in economics, has been highly influential in recent decades and will be discussed in Chapter One in relation to its impact on political ideologies. With regard to users, to some extent social security policy in Britain has always treated claimants as potential knaves out to defraud or exploit the social security system. Nevertheless, it is possible to discern more generally the shift in beliefs to which Le Grand refers.

The shift reflects underlying perceptions of human nature and motivation. For many years British social policy was strongly influenced by Richard Titmuss (see **Box 1.2**). His belief in people's fundamental altruism 'underpinned his conviction that welfare could be reformed so as to provide a framework which fostered and channelled that altruism' (Deacon and Mann, 1999, p 418; see also Deacon, 2002; Land, 2008). Such a view of human nature has been challenged in recent years, most notably by US New Right theorists (see Chapter One). In the UK, the New Labour politician Frank Field deliberately challenged 'the ascendancy which the role of altruism was seen to play in welfare' (1997, p 33). 'Mankind was (and is)', Field argues, 'capable of acts of extraordinary altruism, but altruism is generally secondary to self-interest. To place self-interest at the centre of the discussion ... is simply basing welfare policy on realistic assumptions' (Field, 1997, p 30; 1996, p 19).

> **Question:** Based on your own experiences and what you know of others, do you agree with Field that altruism is generally secondary to self-interest?

From a postmodernist perspective, the very idea of a fixed human nature is nonsense. It is not, however, necessary to subscribe to postmodernism to question claims about human nature being essentially either self-interested or altruistic. If you just think about your own motivations, you will probably conclude that the issue is rather more complex than that and that the extent to which you put yourself or others first depends in part on context. In relation to social policy, the welfare state itself represents an important part of that context. Welfare states vary in the extent to which they appeal to individual self-interest on the one hand and a sense of solidarity with others or altruism on the other. The more that politicians appeal to us as self-interested knaves and frame policies in those terms, the more likely it will be that self-interest will govern our responses by legitimating it as 'human nature' (Hindmoor, 2006). This is something that Titmuss understood when he wrote that

> the ways in which society organizes and structures its social institutions – and particularly its health and welfare systems – can encourage or discourage the altruism in man; such systems can foster integration or alienation, they can allow for 'the theme of the gift' – of generosity towards strangers to spread among and between social groups and generations (1971, quoted in Land, 2008, p 54)

Agency/structure/culture

This passage from Titmuss also illustrates how social policy is concerned with the interaction between agency (individuals' choices and actions that flow from 'the altruism in man'), structure (social institutions) and culture ('the theme of the gift'). Traditionally social policy theory has tended to focus on structure. Increasingly, though, it has acknowledged the importance of agency and culture, as hinted at earlier in the discussion of the individual.

Structure, agency (and power)

Alan Deacon has played an important role in placing the question of agency on the social policy agenda. He provides a helpful definition of **agency** and its relationship to **structure** (see *Box 0.6*).

Box 0.6: Defining structure and agency

Social structure: The pattern of social arrangements within a society or social group. There is no agreement among social scientists as to what are the most important elements of the social structure. Some commentators and theorists point to social divisions based upon class, gender, ethnicity, sexuality or disability, some to economic and political institutions, some to the family and local communities of place, ethnicity or faith. In general a structural account or explanation is one which emphasises the ways in which human behaviour is shaped and constrained by social structures, as opposed to explanations that emphasise the importance of agency.

Agency: The capacity of individuals to operate independently of the social structure. One of the central questions in sociology has long been the extent to which human behaviour should be understood as constrained or determined by social structure, or as purposive and involving the exercise of choice and judgement.

Source: Deacon (2002, pp 138, 135)

Question: How far do you think your own life-choices have been shaped by your position in society? Has that position provided you with opportunities or obstacles? How have you responded to those opportunities and/or obstacles? Think of someone from a very different background to yours and then try and imagine how they may have faced a different set of opportunities and/or obstacles in making decisions about what to do with their lives.

Social policy's earlier privileging of **structure** over agency meant that it tended to look for the causes of social problems in economic institutions (notably the labour market); social institutions (notably the failures of the welfare state or, from a feminist perspective, the oppressive impact of the family on women); and/or political institutions (notably government (in) action). Simultaneously it analysed individuals' situations with reference to their positioning in the hierarchies of social class, gender, 'race', sexuality or disability or their position in the life-course rather than with reference to their own choices and actions. This reflected both an analysis, which identified elements of the social structure as responsible for social ills, and a political stance, which regarded any attribution of cause to individual behaviour as akin to 'blaming the victim' in the face of deep structural inequalities (Deacon and Mann, 1999; Deacon, 2004). In Le Grand's classification, individuals were thereby regarded as 'pawns'.

The 'revival of interest in human **agency** within both sociological and social policy debates' (Deacon and Mann, 1999, p 413) reflects a number of developments: the sociological theorisation of individualisation, discussed earlier; the growing influence of psychology; and a shift in the nature of the political debate about welfare, which originated in the US (Deacon, 2002, 2004). This shift involved a focus upon 'dependency rather than upon poverty or inequality, upon changing people's behaviour rather than upon changing the distribution of resources. In short, the focus is upon agency rather than structure' (Deacon and Mann, 1999, p 423). The new focus heralded the displacement of the welfare 'pawn' by the welfare 'knave' and also by the 'queen' or the 'active' rather than 'passive' welfare subject with 'a measure of control over and responsibility for' her own life (Le Grand, 2003, p 14, Williams, 1999).

As this account indicates, in social policy the agency-structure question has been played out most clearly and controversially in the literature on poverty and welfare reform. As David M. Smith observes, the result has been attempts 'to squeeze the complex processes that produce and reproduce poverty' into a theoretical framework, which privileges either agency or structure, 'to the detriment of a fuller understanding of how these processes interact' (2005, p 41). An alternative approach is to respect the agency of people living in poverty as creative human beings – or 'queens' – rather than represent them as helpless and hopeless 'pawns', whilst paying due regard to the ways in which that agency is constrained by their material position (Lister, 2004a). A related contemporary development in the theorisation of agency-structure in social policy is a focus on resilience (see **Box 0.7**).

Box 0.7: Resilience: an example of the interplay between agency and structure

'The notion of resilience refers to the process of withstanding the negative effects of risk exposure, demonstrating positive adjustment in the face of adversity or trauma, and beating the odds associated with risks' (Bartley, 2006, p 4). With regard to poverty, a focus on resilience attempts to 'identify factors and capabilities within families and hard-pressed communities that help them "beat poverty" – that is to cope with, or to get by despite living in, poor circumstances' (Bartley, 2006, p15; see also Young Foundation, 2009, Ch 11). Researchers who have worked with the notion of resilience acknowledge that emphasising the agency associated with resilience should not, however, mean losing sight of the structural forces that can undermine resilience or at least constrain it. As Mel Bartley observes, 'we cannot expect individuals to develop resilience all by themselves: this could put us in danger of "blaming the victim" instead of investigating underlying obstacles and barriers' (2006, p 5).

In another context – that of children caring for parents with HIV and AIDS – Evans and Becker write that 'the concept of resilience emphasises people's strengths in coping with adversity and their agency in engaging with protective factors that may help to reduce their vulnerability' (2009, p 19). Their study demonstrates the ways in which structures, in the form of support services, can both undermine and strengthen agency.

The example of the poverty and resilience literature illustrates the more general point made by Deacon and Mann that the choices involved in the exercise of agency are not 'free floating of any structural restraints' (1999, p 413). Rather than viewing agency and structure as in opposition to each other, social policy and sociological analysis is increasingly concerned with the interaction of the two. In fact, this is not such a new position. It was, after all, Karl Marx (1852/2007) who long ago observed that 'people make themselves but not in circumstances of their own choosing'.

This position is underpinned by two different understandings of **power** (another important conceptual foundation stone) identified by Lukes (1974/2005) and by Giddens (1991, pp 211-14). Lukes describes power in its more general sense as 'being able to make or to receive any change, or to resist it' (2005, p 69). It is a capacity. Exercising power represents the expression of agency. Giddens (1991, p 214) writes about the power of 'self-actualisation', which he dubs 'generative' power. The more restrictive meaning of power, which Giddens calls 'hierarchical', refers to the ability of one group or individual to exert their will or agency over others. It is 'explicitly relational and asymmetrical' (Lukes, 2005, p 73). I have argued elsewhere with reference to women's citizenship, that 'people can be, at the same time, both the subordinate objects of hierarchical power relations *and* subjects who are agents in their own lives, capable of exercising power in the generative sense' (Lister, 2003a, p 41). However, it is also important to be aware of how powerlessness can crush agency or result in it being exercised in destructive ways, as the extract in *Box 0.8* explains.

> ## Box 0.8: Paul Hoggett on agency
>
> There is a danger that social policy develops a lop-sided model of agency which is insufficiently sensitive to the passionate, tragic and contradictory dimensions of human experience. A robust account of the active welfare subject must be prepared to confront the real experiences of powerlessness and psychic injury which result from injustice and oppression and acknowledge human capacities for destructiveness towards self and others. (2001, p 37)

Culture

The interaction between structure and agency has to be understood within the context of **culture**. It is, however, only relatively recently that social policy has engaged explicitly with the question of culture. Definitions of culture used in social policy typically refer to shared values and beliefs, which legitimate particular social and institutional practices and forms of individual behaviour (Baldock, 1999; Kremer, 2007). John Clarke (1999), the main exponent of 'the cultural turn' in social policy, has identified three main ways in which the notion of culture is used in social policy analysis and practice:

- *As a 'marker of difference'* (Clarke, 1999, p 72). As such it 'becomes a strategic resource to be deployed in struggles around politics and policy' (Clarke, 2004, p 33). Thus, for example, minority ethnic groups have argued, with varying degrees of success, that welfare state services need to take account of different cultural traditions. However, welfare states vary in the extent to which they subscribe to a model of 'multi-culturalism' (see Chapter Two). Moreover, many important issues for social policy today – around for instance language, marriage and dress (particularly women and girls' wearing of the veil) – are caught up in wider political debates about the implications of multi-culturalism for social cohesion and gender equality (Lister et al, 2007).

- *As a source of explanation.* The earlier reference to the competing explanations of poverty, rooted in structure or agency, was incomplete, as there is also a vein of explanation which attributes the persistence of poverty to cultural attitudes among those living in poverty. This 'culture of poverty' refers to a set of values and beliefs different to those held by the majority and to 'a way of life which is passed down from generation to generation along family lines' (Lewis, 1967, p xxxix). The idea of a 'culture of poverty' was most influential in the US, where it originated, but it can also be discerned in references by British policy makers to a 'cycle of disadvantage' and a 'poverty of aspirations'. Clarke (1999, p 77) uses the poverty debate to illustrate how culture is used as an alternative to structure to explain social problems.

    More broadly, cultural factors are now recognised also in comparative analysis as contributing to explanations of policy differences between welfare states (van Oorschot, 2007). Some analysts point too to how the same policies can have different effects in different kinds of welfare state because 'cultural values and ideals...influence the degree to which policies are accepted by the population and their impact on social practices of individuals' (Pfau-Effinger, 2005, p 12; Kremer, 2007). So, for instance, variations between countries in the number of lone mothers who move into the labour market in response to welfare to work policies partly reflect the dominant 'gendered moral rationalities' and 'gender culture' referred to earlier.

- *As a 'practice' that produces meaning.* This approach to culture is at the heart of social policy's 'cultural turn' spearheaded by Clarke. In contrast to the more dominant view of culture 'as possession', which, he argues, treats 'cultures as undifferentiated, closed and undynamic systems', within the cultural turn culture is 'actively constructed by social agents' through their everyday practices (2004, p 34). This shifts attention in social policy analysis to the changing meanings that various actors attach to their actions and to the social world in which they perform them. Thus, 'all social action is – at the very least – mediated by culture' (Clarke, 1999, p 79). To take the example of lone mothers again, the meaning attached to being a 'good mother' can vary not just between different countries but also within countries, between different regions, neighbourhoods and social groups.

The state, nation and nation-state

As this discussion suggests, cultural analysis provides an important lens for understanding state policies and their impact. The state represents a key foundation stone of social policy because it plays a pivotal role in the provision, funding and governance of welfare and in the maintenance of law and order and regulation of behaviour.

Political scientists who study the state tend to describe it as an abstraction, difficult to define. Its abstract nature lies in the fact that it is distinct from the government of the day and from the officials who staff it, even though it is politicians and officials who carry out the state's functions and who represent the 'human' face of the state at both national and local level. Nevertheless, we all encounter the state in very concrete ways on a daily basis. To paraphrase Christopher Pierson (1996), while it might be difficult to define, we recognise the state all right when it requires us to send our children to school at a certain age, goes to war in our name, bans or polices an anti-war demonstration, sends us a tax demand or provides us with benefits or pensions when we are unable to undertake paid work. What these examples illustrate is how the state has the authority and power to: make and enforce laws; raise taxes and distribute the proceeds; and propagate wars. The term 'welfare state' refers more specifically to those of the state's functions that promote the welfare and social protection of its members through a range of benefits and services.

There exists a wide range of theoretical positions on the nature of the state and its functions (discussed in, for instance, Pierson, 1996; Hay et al, 2006; Cudworth et al, 2007). The state is also characterised in numerous ways today, for example 'the social investment state' (Giddens, 1998; Lister, 2003b); 'the enabling state' (Miliband 1999); 'the managerial state' (Clarke and Newman, 1997). We will be looking briefly at some of the positions taken on the state in Parts One and Two. One of the critical issues if not *the* critical issue, which divides the ideological perspectives discussed in Chapter One is the answer to the question 'what is the proper role of the state?' Where should the boundaries lie between state and individual or family responsibility for welfare? What is the proper relationship between the state and the market, where goods and services are exchanged for money, reflecting the balance of supply and demand? What is the appropriate relationship between the state and the third or voluntary sector, which increasingly is delivering services on behalf of the state? To provide a more concrete example: who should take primary responsibility for the care of older people unable to look after themselves – their family, the state, a voluntary organisation? In practice, it is often a combination of the three that provides the care and then questions arise as to the most effective and appropriate relationship between each of the three and how the care should be funded.

These kinds of interrelated questions lie at the heart of contemporary political debates about welfare. The nature of the state also divides the various theoretical perspectives discussed in Chapters Two and Three. Is it a benign, neutral force or is it serving capitalist/patriarchal/racist/ interests? Is it an instrument of regulation and social control and/or of environmental destruction more than a source of welfare? Or is it, as postmodernists might argue, more complex than each of these positions suggests, so that it is not possible to identify a single monolithic state serving a single set of essential interests?

Traditionally social policy tended to take for granted the state as the main source of welfare. However, from a variety of theoretical and ideological perspectives the role of the state is now questioned and more attention is paid to other providers of welfare – families, the market and the voluntary sector. Nevertheless, we cannot ignore the state, for it still holds the ring. As Gamble and Wright put it:

> Whether the ideal is a neo-liberal free market society with only a minimal state, or a social democratic society with an active and enabling state, there is still the need for a state to underpin and sustain that society, to decide what matters can be left to individuals, and what matters the state itself needs to undertake. (Gamble and Wright, 2004, p 6)

The state also lays down the rules governing who may enter its territory and who may become a citizen, symbolised in the issuing of a passport. The territorial dimension of the state provides the link to the **nation**, as in the '**nation–state**'. According to Fiona Williams (1989), nation, together with family, has been a central theme in the development of welfare provisions. Historically, and today in emergent nation-states, the welfare state has played an important role in nation-building through helping to create a sense of collective national identity and citizenship (Williams, 2008; see also Chapter Seven). In Britain, for instance, the National Health Service is often held up as a symbol of the nation; in Sweden the welfare state symbolises a view of the nation as the 'People's Home'. Social, economic and immigration policies are frequently justified as being in 'the national interest' and, as we shall see in Chapter Three, increasingly social policy is being yoked to the overriding goal of national economic competitiveness.

Box 0.9 sums up the traditional view of what that hyphenated construction the nation-state represents.

> ### Box 0.9: John Clarke on the traditional view of the nation-state
>
> 'The "container" conception of the nation-state saw a people, united in culture, occupying a clearly defined space, whose collective identity was expressed in national politics, working through national institutions that delivered collective security and progress to the people of the nation' (2005, p 410).
>
> 'The nation-state is a foundational concept for social policy, and its provenance, applicability and stability are largely taken for granted within the subject. The nation-state provides the unacknowledged conceptual background for most national studies of social policies, politics and ideologies'(2004, p 82).

However, like the state itself, the nation-state is losing its taken-for-granted quality. Clarke describes the process as 'the contemporary destabilisation of the apparent unity of people, place, nation and state that underpinned the nation-state/welfare state formations of the post-war period' (2005, p 412). This destabilisation is the result of a number of contemporary developments including: the reshaping of the boundaries of nation-states, notably in Central and Eastern Europe and Germany; pressures for greater regional autonomy within nation-states and in the UK for the greater autonomy of its constituent nations (with significant implications for social policy); large scale migration flows; and the pressures of globalisation.

Beyond the nation-state: the transnational and the global

Despite the 'destabilisation' to which Clarke refers much social policy analysis continues to operate within the containers of nation-states: either individual nation states or comparisons between nation states. It is thus premature to write the obituary for the nation-state as a key building block of social policy. Nevertheless, in the face of globalisation in its various forms, there is also growing recognition that social policy in any one society has to be understood in a transnational and global context.

The idea of the '**transnational**', according to Clarke, represents a valuable conceptual tool in social policy analysis: 'It draws our attention to processes that work *in and across* nations' through the flows of capital, people and culture (2005, p 414; emphasis in original). Indeed, these very processes contribute to the nation-state's destabilisation. The idea of the transnational also helps us to see globalisation 'not as a disembodied external condition' but as 'materialised *within and across* nation-states (Clarke, 2005, p 409, emphasis in original). An example is provided by 'global care chains': a process by which women from poorer countries provide care in households in wealthier countries, often leaving their own children or older relatives to be cared for by others in their homelands. Nicola Yeates argues that such processes require social policy to integrate 'transnational dimensions… and the international context… into their conceptual and theoretical frameworks' (2005, p 232; see also Lister et al, 2007).

The meaning, extent and impact of **globalisation**, including on the autonomy of nation-states, are all highly contested. A working definition is provided in *Box 0.10*.

Box 0.10: What is globalisation?

According to Rob Sykes (2008), the term globalisation has been used most commonly

> as a generic term to refer to a variety of economic processes, such as an increasing internationalization of the production and exchange of goods and services, the deregulation of financial transactions, the spread of free trade on a world-wide scale, and the restructuring and relocation of productive activities between different regions of the world…. In the field of social and cultural analysis, globalization has been associated with a massive increase in the availability and circulation of information especially through the spread of the internet, with a greater interconnectedness between societies so that distances in both space and time seem to be shrunk through telephonic communication…; and with a threat to traditional cultures and social cohesion coupled with cultural homogenization, or so-called 'Macdonaldization', via the spread of global brands and products. (Sykes, 2008, pp 430-1)

Social policy analysis is particularly interested in the extent to which globalisation is driving changes in welfare states (Sykes et al, 2001; Sykes, 2008). 'Strong' theories of globalisation typically associate it with the demise of the nation-state and welfare state retrenchment. They are akin to structurally deterministic accounts, which allow little space for the autonomy or agency of governments in individual nation-states. Such deterministic accounts have, though, been criticised. Yeates is in the forefront of social policy analysts of globalisation who argue for 'a more nuanced account', which recognises the importance of how individual nation-states manage globalisation and how globalisation has itself created the space for new forms of resistance and contestation (1999, p 372, 2001, 2002; see also Chapters Four and Nine).

Yeates argues also for a 'global governance perspective', which takes on board the multiple institutional levels shaping policy in individual nation-states: from local through regional or sub-national to national government and above that to supra-national levels such as the European Union and beyond to the United Nations (UN) and other international bodies. This brings us on to the terrain of what is now known as '**global social policy**'.

Bob Deacon, who has done more than anyone to map out the terrain of global social policy, suggests that it can be characterised as 'global social redistribution, global social regulation and global social rights' (2005, p 437; Deacon et al., 1997). In other words, the objects of national social policy are inscribed at the international level too. The difference is that the institutional mechanisms for achieving these objectives are located in international governmental organisations such as the UN, the International Labour Organisation and the World Bank. These are mirrored by increasingly strong networks of non-governmental organisations (NGOs) and global activists who are sometimes described as an emergent 'global civil society'.

Box 0.11: Thinking about global social policy

Irving et al invite us 'to think imaginatively about how the classical concerns of social policy with social need, equality and citizenship, altruism, reciprocity, choice and efficiency translate at the global level' (2005, p 478).

Question: Can you think of examples of how some of these concerns are expressed at global level and of any particular organisations and/or campaigns promoting them?

Although Chapter One of this book and many of the examples used to illustrate the relevance of theory are grounded in the particular context of the UK, a number of the theoretical perspectives and concepts, such as anti-racism, environmentalism, citizenship and social justice, are key to global social policy also. Moreover, they help to illustrate the interrelationship between global and national social policy (analysed by, for example, Jordan, 2006).

Outline of the book

Social policy has been described as a 'magpie' subject, picking ideas from a range of social science disciplines (Dean, 2006). You may already have spotted references to economics, sociology, psychology and political science. This volume exemplifies how social policy draws on a range of theoretical sources in its analysis of 'the ways in which societies provide for the social needs of their members through structures and systems of distribution, redistribution, regulation, provision and empowerment' and of 'wider structural and cultural issues' (QAAHE, 2007, p 2). Any book on theory is to some extent selective. The theoretical perspectives and concepts covered in this volume are selected to help to make sense of the political, social, economic and cultural environments in which social policies are developed and of the values underpinning the policies.

The book is divided into three parts. The first two cover theoretical perspectives or ways of thinking; the third covers the concepts or ideas that, as explained earlier, make up theory. Parts One and Two help to frame Part Three, as the concepts covered in the latter are often the subject of contestation between different theoretical perspectives.

Part One deals with theoretical perspectives played out in the political arena, which means that they all have a normative component. Chapter One provides a brief overview of the key elements of the dominant political ideologies that have shaped post–Second World War social policies in Britain: the middle way, democratic socialism, the new right (and more generally neo-liberalism) and the third way and beyond. Although the explicit focus of this chapter is Britain the political ideologies (sometimes under different labels) have also informed social policy elsewhere. This is followed in Chapter Two by an introduction to the main theoretical perspectives that have provided a political critique of dominant political ideologies: Marxism, feminism, anti-racism and environmentalism.

The dividing line between the first two parts is to some extent arbitrary in that Part Two discusses theoretical perspectives as an analytical tool and the perspectives covered in Chapter Two represent analytical as well as political and normative critiques. Nevertheless, arguably it is the political and normative nature of their critique that provides the common thread between the perspectives discussed in Chapter Two. The analytical perspectives which make up Part Two are also critical, in the sense that they have contributed to the rethinking of the subject of social policy, but they are not typically deployed directly in political debate. Chapter Three looks at post-Fordism and postmodernism, which are two related theoretical interpretations of the contemporary economic, political, social and cultural context of social policy. The postmodernist perspective is also dominant in Chapter Four, the focus of which is the various theoretical perspectives that interpret the welfare state as a force of social control, discipline and regulation rather than a source of welfare and well-being. Social constructionism, the subject of Chapter Five, is also influenced by postmodernism. It explains the social constructionist approach to social problems – the stuff of social policy – and, as illustration, deploys this approach to discuss the various ways in which the problem of poverty has been constructed.

In Part Three we turn to three sets of theoretical concepts which are fundamental to social policy. Chapter Six deals with needs, the concept that many argue stands at the heart of social policy. The chapter introduces the various positions taken on the question of whether needs should be understood as universal or relative to particular contexts. It uses the notion of a 'politics of needs interpretation' (Fraser, 1987) to explore the ways in which needs are framed by different actors; the process of claims-making; and the central role played by competing constructions of need in the formulation of social policies. The chapter also refers to the related concepts of well-being and capabilities. Chapter Seven turns to the contested nature of the interrelated concepts of community and citizenship (which link back to the earlier discussion of nation), including more traditional and critical constructions of the concepts. It provides an overview of contemporary theorisations of citizenship and the ways in which they inform social policy, particularly in relation to rights and responsibilities. The final substantive chapter, Chapter Eight, takes three key concepts from political theory – liberty, social justice and equality – and analyses their meanings and relevance for social policy.

The concluding chapter returns to the theme of the relevance of theory to social policy and social politics. It does so by looking at how some of the theoretical perspectives and concepts covered have been deployed by social movements fighting for 'recognition' and 'redistribution'. The disability movement is used as a particular example.

Summary

- Theory helps us make sense of social policies and to put them in a wider context.
- Theories are used both analytically to understand social phenomena and normatively to effect change. Both kinds of theory inform welfare ideologies.
- Key conceptual foundation stones underpin social policy theorising: the individual; agency, structure and culture; the state, nation and nation-state; the transnational and the global.
- The individual is the subject of theorising in social policy with regard to identity, the 'welfare subject' and motivation and behaviour.
- There has been a shift in social policy analysis with increased focus on agency and culture relative to structure.

- The state plays a pivotal role in the provision, funding and governance of welfare and in the regulation of behaviour.
- The welfare state plays an important role in nation-building.
- The relationship between the state, nation and nation-state has become increasingly fluid.
- Social policy in any one society now has to be understood in a transnational and global context. This represents the terrain of 'global social policy'.
- Social policy theory draws on a range of social science disciplines.

Further reading

Some of the points raised about the nature of social policy theory are discussed in greater depth in **George and Wilding (1994, Ch 1)** and **O'Brien and Penna (1998, Introduction)**. A good brief introduction to many of the conceptual foundation stones can be found in *The Student's Companion to Social Policy* **(Alcock et al, 2008)**. The 'welfare subject' is discussed in **Hughes and Lewis (1998)**, while the assumptions made about human motivation and behaviour in social policy are explored by **Le Grand (1997, 2003)**, **Halpern and Bates (2004)**, **Deacon and Mann (1999)** and **Deacon (2002)**. The last two references also provide a helpful account of the agency-structure debate. **Clarke (2004)** introduces the 'cultural turn' as well as exploring the changing relationship between state and nation. **Van Oorschot (2007)** provides a rather different perspective on culture and social policy. An account of theories of the state can be found in **Pierson (1996)** and **Cudworth et al (2007)**. The global perspective on social policy is explored in **Deacon et al (1997)**, **Yeates (2001, 2008)** and a themed issue of *Social Policy and Society* **(2005)**.

Part One

Theoretical perspectives in the political arena

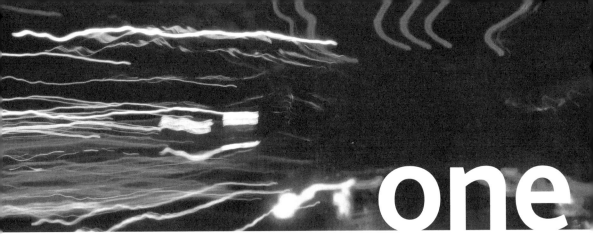

Dominant post-war ideological perspectives: from 'middle way' to 'third way' and beyond

The subject of this chapter is the ideological perspectives that have guided British governments in the era following the Second World War and that have therefore shaped post-war social policy. Broadly, *middle way* and *social democratic* governments shaped and executed the post-war welfare settlement until the advent of the *new right*, which dominated for nearly two decades following the election of Margaret Thatcher as prime minister in 1979. The *third way* represents the ideological label that New Labour used to describe itself when it came to power in 1997. Although the term has fallen out of favour the third way's essential characteristics continue to inform New Labour's philosophy. Moreover, it could be said that, in response, the Conservative Party has developed its own version of the third way.

This chapter provides a brief introduction to these ideological perspectives. It places each of them in historical context and outlines the key elements in their thinking. It pays particular attention to the position they take on the role of the state and the nature of individual motivation. Other aspects of their thinking will emerge in Part Three through discussion of the concepts. First, though, the chapter places these ideological perspectives in the wider context of traditions in political thought.

Ideological threads

Although this chapter is explicitly British in its focus, the ideological perspectives it covers are not unique to Britain, even if the labels that describe them are not necessarily those used more widely. Moreover, these perspectives are informed by broader political ideologies or traditions, which are translated into government in varying ways in different countries.

These run like threads – sometimes quite separate, sometimes intertwined – through the ideological perspectives discussed in this and, to a lesser extent, the next chapter and also inform the concepts discussed in Part Three.

The three main Western political traditions are: *liberalism, conservatism* and *socialism*, each of which has spawned many sub-strands. The most important of these today is liberalism's offshoot: *neo-liberalism*. Another important, although less influential, offshoot of liberalism is *libertarianism*. *Communitarianism*, a more recent political ideology, stands in opposition to liberalism and its offshoots. A brief guide to these ideological threads is provided in *Box 1.1* and *Figure 1.1*.

> ## Box 1.1: The key ideological threads of Western political thought
>
> ### Conservatism.
> Conservatism is typically described as a pragmatic approach rather than a fixed ideology based on an abstract set of principles. As such it is able to mutate according to cultural, historical and political context. Nevertheless, it represents an influential political ideology, in the sense of the term used in the Introduction. It has shaped the philosophies and policies of right-of-centre governments throughout the Western world including, in Britain, the philosophy of the 'middle way' (described in this chapter). As the name implies, conservatism favours tradition over change. It is premised on a pessimistic view of human nature as inherently imperfect. It therefore believes in strong, authoritative government but with the state playing only a limited role in welfare. It places great emphasis on the family, private property and the nation and views society as an organic, moral community. Because it sees people as being unequal in their abilities, it approves of hierarchy and inequality. Its most influential contemporary mutations have been the new right (discussed later) and neoconservatism: a moralistic, nationalistic, pro-market and big business and anti-welfare stance promulgated in the US (and the driving force behind the invasion of Iraq). Béland and Waddan argue that 'paying close attention to the nature of conservative ideas improves our understanding of social policy development in the United States' (2007, p 768).
>
> ### Socialism
> Socialism is the antithesis of conservatism and represents the original inspiration behind left-of-centre politics. It is premised on an optimistic view of human nature as cooperative and creative; human beings are therefore seen as capable of self-government through the principle of popular sovereignty. Socialism's motivating principle is social equality (discussed in Chapter Eight). From this stems a fundamental critique of capitalism and the inequality, exploitation, social class divisions, competitive individualism and materialist values that it generates. In its

place, socialism argues for the common ownership of the means of production and distribution and for societal responsibility to meet the needs of all its members in recognition of human interdependence. While united in their opposition to private provision, socialists differ as to whether welfare is better provided by the state or through self-help organisations such as cooperatives. In Britain the former view became dominant in the 20th Century. Socialists also differ in the extent to which they want to tame capitalism through reformist means or overthrow it through revolution. Such differences reflect different strands of socialism: the two most important are democratic socialism or social democracy (examined in this chapter) and Marxism (discussed in Chapter Two). Socialist philosophy is internationalist (that is it believes its principles should apply to humanity as a whole, regardless of national borders) even if governments, which have described themselves as socialist, have not always pursued internationalism in practice. Across Continental Europe, most notably Germany, there has been a resurgence in avowedly socialist political parties at the beginning of the 21st century. They are challenging the dominance of more centrist social democratic parties (Clark, N., 2008). There has never been a strong socialist movement in the US, where the word is often used as a term of political abuse by those on the right.

Liberalism

The essence of liberalism lies in the overriding priority it gives to the individual. Individuals are regarded as free, rational and moral beings worthy of equal respect. Liberty (discussed in Chapter Eight) is the overriding value of liberalism and it is regarded as a universal value applicable to all human beings. This leads to a belief in the free market and private property, together with a limited state. The state should not interfere with individuals' liberty and rights other than to protect others from harm and safeguard their freedom. However, like conservatism and socialism, liberalism does not represent a single, unified political philosophy. 'Classical liberalism', dating back to the 16th century and re-born in 'neo-liberalism' and 'libertarianism' today, emphasises a minimal role for the state. 'Social liberalism', which developed in the late 19th and early 20th centuries and shaped the post-war welfare settlement, accepts the state's role in welfare. It is regarded as necessary for equality of opportunity and the freedom of all in the 'positive' sense of ensuring all members of society have the resources necessary to exercise their freedom (an idea, which is explored in greater depth in Chapters Seven and Eight). Liberalism does not fit neatly into the left-right political spectrum and, in modified form, can be bracketed with some strands of both conservatism and socialism. Thus, although liberalism has not been formally represented in government through a Liberal Party in Britain since the beginning of the 20th century, its principles have shaped many aspects of government. Today, the extent to which both New Labour and Conservative parties do or do not embrace liberal principles is an important dimension of political debate (see, for instance, Collins and Reeves,

2008). Moreover, 'the basic language of liberalism – individual rights, liberty, equality of opportunity – has become the dominant language of public discourse in most modern democracies' (Kymlicka, 1995, p 484).

Neo-liberalism

Neo-liberalism represents a reaction against the social liberalism that dominated in the 20th century and a return to classical forms of liberalism. It is thus distinguished by hostility to the state in the field of welfare and by the lauding of the private market sector and private domestic sphere over the public sector as a source of welfare. The market is regarded as the most efficient producer and allocator of resources and the state's role should be confined to providing the necessary framework for the market and private property and to protecting the liberty and security of the individual. In this limited role it is a strong state. As with liberalism itself, the liberty of the individual represents the core value of neo-liberalism, but it works with a rather more negative view of human nature. Emphasis is placed on individual agency – expressed in the form of either 'rational economic man' or moral responsibility (Green, 2003). Neo-liberalism, as promoted by right-of-centre thinkers and politicians, has been enormously influential at a global level in the late 20th and early 21st century (Ellison, 2008).

Libertarianism

Libertarianism represents the logical extreme of liberalism's prioritisation of individual liberty and autonomy and its suspicion of the state. Its rejection of the state, or its confinement to a minimalist role, in virtually all spheres of life is more radical than that of liberalism or even neo-liberalism. US libertarians, for example, have argued for the complete abolition of the welfare state. Libertarians regard individuals as the rightful owner of whatever they gain with their own talents or through free exchange and as free to do what they like so long as they do not directly harm others. Libertarians are thus opposed to taxation, economic regulation, immigration controls, censorship and the criminalisation of behaviour such as drug-taking, prostitution and speeding on the roads. Libertarianism is most commonly associated with far right-of-centre politics. Nevertheless, there are also libertarians on the left who share a belief that the state has no right to interfere in individual behaviour. Some of this group can also be described as anarchists who distrust all forms of authority as oppressive (Goodwin, 2007). Conversely, many on the right do not go along with libertarianism's refusal to countenance a role for the state in regulating individual behaviour, particularly in areas of sexual morality. We return to libertarianism in the discussion of liberty in Chapter Eight.

Communitarianism

As a political school of thought, contemporary Western communitarianism represents a response to what its adherents perceive to be the excessive individualism of liberalism and neo-liberalism. It is the community and the common good rather than the individual and his or her autonomy that stand at the heart of communitarianism. Communitarians believe that individuals are social beings, embedded in national and local communities. As such their responsibilities towards fellow members of the community are emphasised over their rights and it is proper for community members to judge each other's behaviour. 'Communitarians pay special attention to social institutions', such as families and schools, which 'form the moral infrastructure of society', helping to inculcate values (Etzioni, 2006, p 82). Although the term 'communitarianism' is not widely used in public debate, 'communitarian terms became part of the public vocabulary in the 1990s, especially references to assuming social responsibilities to match individual rights' (Etzioni, 2006, p 83). In particular, communitarianism has influenced the third way and today it is possible to identify both 'left' and 'right' versions of communitarianism (White, 2009).

Figure 1.1: Traditions of Western political thought

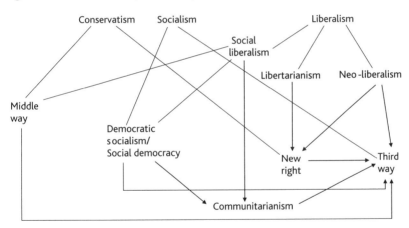

The middle way

The term 'the middle way' was coined in 1938 by Harold Macmillan in *The Middle Way*, which charted a path between classical liberalism and socialism, and which has been described as a 'classic exposition of the case for Tory collectivism' (Pinker, 2008, p 71). Although it had little impact on official Conservative (sometimes called Tory) thinking at the time, Macmillan went on to become Conservative Prime Minister in the 1950s. The middle way then became associated with the approach taken by his brand of conservatism, which was dominant in the Conservative Party for most of the post-war period until Margaret Thatcher came to power in 1979. It was, however, not only conservatives who subscribed to the middle way: key social liberal thinkers such as William Beveridge and Maynard Keynes, who were the architects of the post-war welfare settlement, also contributed to the middle way and provided its intellectual backbone. Indeed, the idea of the middle way inspired social democratic politics in Sweden and was effectively implemented there in the post-Second World War era, albeit in a more collective, pro-state social democratic form than the middle way embraced by British Conservatives, described here.

Thus, although the middle way is sometimes treated as synonymous with post-war Conservatism it draws on the social liberal as well as conservative traditions of political thought. George and Wilding sum up its mongrel nature:

> The Middle Way perspective on the role of the state in welfare is distinct but ill-defined. It embraces a range of thinkers with differing views but who are united in the conviction that it is both necessary and possible to graft measures of state welfare on to capitalism and soften its rough edges. (1994, p 46)

George and Wilding's description points to the essential pragmatism of the middle way's position with regard to the state. This reflects a broader pragmatism: the middle way is hostile to overtly ideological approaches – of both left and right – that promise utopian solutions. Instead it steers a middle course, which emphasises balance and gradual social improvement (George and Wilding, 1994). Rather than grand visions, it emphasises particular social goals such as supporting 'the family' in its traditional form, as the cornerstone of society and social order, and it focuses on tackling specific social problems. Remember, though, as pointed out in the Introduction, that pragmatism is itself an ideological position in some ways, in that it accepts the broad *status quo*. Thus, while the middle way is anti-ideology, it still represents an ideology in its own right, albeit an 'ill-defined' one.

The middle way's attitude to both the market and the state can be summed up as 'yes, but'. Rodney Lowe dubs middle way thinkers as 'reluctant collectivists' who regard the market 'as the best practical mechanism for ensuring individual initiative and hence political freedom, economic efficiency and social justice; but its flaws are recognised and thus the need for a judicious degree of state intervention' (1993, p 18). Just how much intervention is a pragmatic judgement made in response to the particular circumstances of the time.

As Lowe's characterisation of 'reluctant collectivists' suggests, proponents of the middle way believe in the free market as the basis of the economy. Nevertheless, they acknowledge that the market cannot be left to its own devices and that it therefore needs to be regulated. Moreover, some of its social effects, most notably poverty, need to be mitigated. For the middle way, the state thus has an important role to play in tempering the market's effects. The middle way also believes in promoting equality of opportunity in the sense that people should not face barriers, such as in the education system, so that everyone has the same opportunities even if both starting and finishing points remain unequal (see Chapter Eight).

At the same time, as the 'reluctant collectivist' label implies, the middle way is equivocal about the state's role in the provision of welfare (George and Wilding, 1994). There is anxiety that a strong state will expand to crowd out other sources of welfare, reduce efficiency, put strains on the economy and lead to over-centralisation. There are also fears that it could undermine personal responsibility and self-reliance, and thereby weaken the family. The traditional family is regarded as the basic unit of society, which must be supported. A state that places too much emphasis on rights, especially social rights, could weaken citizens' sense of obligation to society and prioritise the individual too much over the wider community (see Chapter Seven). The middle way is suspicious of what it sees as a tendency for a strong state to develop ideological blueprints and move beyond the simple alleviation of poverty to attempts to promote greater equality and more radical redistribution of income and wealth.

What this adds up to is a willingness to use the state in the provision of welfare, but within clear limits and in partnership with other welfare providers, as explained in ***Box 1.2***.

Box 1.2: The middle way and welfare providers

The middle way sees the state as part of a pluralist, mixed economy of welfare (although that is a more recent term), in partnership with private and voluntary forms of provision. The middle way's belief in a mixed economy of welfare is driven by: 'a faith in a public-private partnership as the ideal mode of provision, by a genuine belief in voluntary organisations as part of the fabric of the good society, by a keen sense of the ultimate responsibility for the state for social welfare and at the same time of its uneven capacity to meet the varieties of human need' (George and Wilding, 1994, p 68).

Overall, therefore, the state is seen as a fairly neutral instrument which can be used to good ends, but which must not be allowed to become overweaning, as this could then have negative effects. The state must work for the good of the whole community, promoting stability, social cohesion and national unity. This position is reflected in the label 'One Nation' Conservatives, adopted by some of those who identified with the middle way brand of conservatism. In the post-war period, the main concern was to avoid class conflict. However, implicit in middle-way conservatism was also a view of the nation and of immigrants to it shaped by 'nationalism [and] colonial superiority [which] had been … mobilizing themes during and after the war' (Williams, 1989, p 89).

The middle way did not operate with an explicit view of the individual and human nature/motivation. The individual was seen as essentially a social animal, connected to others through a web of interdependence (George and Wilding, 1994). Again, the middle way was pretty pragmatic: it viewed the providers and users of welfare more as knights and pawns than as knaves. Indeed Le Grand describes the British welfare state between 1945 and 1979 as a period when the 'knights [were] rampant' (2003, p 4), and although this was more a reflection of social democracy, it was not challenged by middle way Conservatives.

In terms of policy, the middle way sought a balance between economic and social policy so that one should not be subservient to the other (George and Wilding, 1994). As well as the mixed economy approach, with its emphasis on partnership with the voluntary and private sectors, the middle way pursued a pragmatic and shifting mix of universalist and means-tested programmes. In this it attempted to balance its commitment to 'one nation' with potentially socially divisive targeting of resources on the worst off. George and Wilding identify:

> a basic ambivalence about universalism and selectivity but Middle Way thinking has certainly changed through time to a greater concern, in a more affluent society, about the costs and effectiveness of universalism and to an in-principle belief in selectivity but with doubts about what it might mean if pressed beyond common-sensical limits. (1994, p 57)

Social democracy/democratic socialism

The terms 'social democracy' and 'democratic socialism' are often used interchangeably to describe the political philosophy of the Labour Party for most of the 20th century. There is, nevertheless, a subtle difference of emphasis between the two, with the latter placing greater weight on socialist goals (as outlined in **Box 1.1**) and the former on democratic means. Social democratic is the label typically applied to centre-left European political parties and today the Nordics, notably Sweden, represent the archetypal social democratic welfare state.

Our focus here is the influence of social democratic thinking on British politics in the 20th century. According to Rodney Lowe, despite the predominant influence of the two middle way thinkers, Beveridge and Keynes, following the Second World War:

> it was the ideals of the democratic socialists which gave the British welfare state its unique international reputation. At home these ideals also infused the welfare legislation of the 1945–51 Labour governments and provided the logic for further advances which Conservative ministers struggled to refute. (Lowe, 1993, pp 18–19)

Key thinkers were R.H. Tawney (pre-Second World War) and Richard Titmuss and Anthony Crosland (post Second World War); the first two in particular have been influential in the development of social policy theory. Leading contemporary social democratic theorists include David Marquand and Raymond Plant. (See ***Box 1.3***.)

Box 1.3: Key social democratic thinkers

R. H. Tawney (1880-1962) was a Christian socialist historian whose thinking was enormously influential on the Labour Party, particularly in the first half of the 20th Century, and also on other key social democratic thinkers. His work, particularly *Equality* (1931/1964), is still cited today as an inspiration by those who want to see a more equal society. *The Blackwell Dictionary of Social Policy* sums up his thinking: 'Tawney castigated capitalism for its unethical lack of social purpose and function. He advocated the redistribution of economic and social power to working people and the creation of remoralized, co-operative solidaristic communities so that the equal worth of all citizens could be upheld. He was a strong supporter of universal welfare services which, he believed, would bond people together' (Alcock et al, 2002, p 254; see also Deakin and Wright, 1995).

Richard Titmuss (1907-1973) was Professor of Social Administration at the London School of Economics for two decades until his death. He dominated the development of social administration as a subject and had considerable influence on wider social policy debates; his thinking still provides a touchstone for many social policy analysts. Influenced by Tawney, he was, like him, a moralist. He was highly critical of the market and made the case for state welfare and social policy to counter its divisive tendencies. He is remembered in particular for: his defence of universal services as a force for social integration; his analysis of 'the social division of welfare', which broadened the analysis of welfare beyond state provision to include fiscal welfare provided through the tax system and occupational welfare provided by employers; and his belief in the role of the state in promoting altruism, as discussed in the Introduction. (See also Wilding, 1995; Alcock et al, 2001; Deacon, 2002, Ch 1.)

Anthony Crosland (1918-1977) was a leading Labour politician who was in the Cabinet in the 1960s and 70s. His most important work was *The Future of Socialism* (1956). According to Raymond Plant, it 'provided the most articulate synthesis of social democratic thought in the post-war period and provided both a political analysis and strategy which inspired many, not only of his own generation but also the one that followed him. Equality was at the heart of Crosland's view of social democracy' (1996, p 165).

David Marquand (1934-) and Raymond Plant (1945-) are two contemporary thinkers in the social democratic tradition who have contributed to public debates about the role of the state, liberty, democracy and citizenship in particular (see also Miller, 1995 on Plant). Plant has provided one of the most incisive social democratic critiques of the new right (see, for instance, Plant, 1990). Marquand is a leading social democratic critic of New Labour and in particular of its neglect of the public realm and of liberty. In an essay on the state of social democracy (2006), he calls for a return to the kind of vision offered by Tawney and Titmuss.

In contrast to the pragmatic approach of the middle way, democratic socialism is explicitly ideological: it is 'a set of political ideas that suggest that the goal of socialism is achievable through the means of parliamentary democracy' (Sullivan, 1999, p 105). Thus it embraces an explicit commitment to socialism but also to democratic means of achieving it. The animating ideals of social democracy are those of the French Revolution: equality, liberty and fraternity (although the last is better expressed today in more gender neutral terms such as fellowship or solidarity). Equality and liberty are explored in Chapter Eight. The importance of fellowship to democratic socialism is underlined by George and Wilding, who point out that 'it dominates the writings of both Tawney and Titmuss, particularly in relation to social policy' (1994, p 99). 'Fellowship', George and Wilding explain, 'implies love for one's neighbour; a free gift for a stranger; altruism as well as self-interest; the good of the community as well as individual interest' (1994, p 99). Its emphasis on community can shade into a communitarian ethos and has implications for social democratic conceptualisations of citizenship (see Chapter Seven).

Social democratic thinking is distinguished by a negative attitude towards the market and a positive attitude towards the state. It has been suggested that if 'anything is to qualify as the credo for social democratic theorists it must be the belief that capitalism can and must be managed, in some sense, by the state' (Cudworth et al, 2007, p 119). While social democracy seeks to accommodate capitalism and accepts that the market has a part to play in a capitalist economy, its opposition to the market is grounded in the belief that it is:

• socially unjust because it is based on principles of profit rather than need;
• undemocratic in the way in which it concentrates economic and thus political power in a few hands; and
• unethical because it encourages self-interest and greed.

Antipathy towards the market is matched by belief in the power of the state. In power, this translated into use of Keynesian economic policy in order to regulate the market and the development of the welfare state in order to counteract the market's negative effects. The state was used to stimulate the economy both by social investment, for instance through education, and by increasing the purchasing power of people on low incomes as part of the state's wider role in promoting full employment.

To some extent, use of the welfare state to soften the impact of the market, particularly through the elimination of social distress and hardship, was consistent with the middle way. However, social democrats went further. They also saw the state as a means of creating a fairer and more equal society. Only the state can do this and thereby promote genuine freedom for the powerless through the redistribution of income, wealth and power. As Tawney (1931/1964) put it, freedom for the pike (a powerful big fish) is death for the minnows (powerless little fish); therefore, in the name of liberty, the state has to create greater equality to increase the power of the minnows relative to that of the pike.

The welfare state's role in promoting the democratic socialist value of fellowship through 'altruism and social integration' is expounded most 'passionately and vividly' in the work of Titmuss (George and Wilding, 1994, p 82). Titmuss also identified a further justification for state welfare: the need to compensate for diswelfares or 'the consequences and costs of economic growth and of scientific, technical and social change' (1968, p 157). Most notable is the adverse impact on people who lose their jobs as a result of technical change.

Unlike supporters of the middle way, democratic socialists are hostile, to a greater or lesser degree, to what we now call 'the mixed economy of welfare', as they believe the state should play a dominant role. Titmuss, in particular, opposed it on the grounds that it is divisive and inegalitarian, benefiting the better off at the expense of the worse off. The role of the voluntary sector is regarded as marginal to that of the state. What this all adds up to is an essentially benign conception of the state as a force for progress and social improvement. This in turn has reinforced a positive view of Britain's role in the post-imperialist world, as spelled out in **Box 1.4**.

> ## Box 1.4: Social democracy, the nation and the family
>
> Fiona Williams explains the relationship between social democracy's attitudes towards the welfare state and the nation in the mid-20th century: 'As the Empire began to fall away, the welfare state became central to the reconstruction of post-war Britain and brought a new order – of social justice and egalitarianism – that attempted to replace the old imperial ideal in sustaining national cohesion' (2008, p 162). However, these ideals were rarely in practice extended to embrace black immigrants from the former colonies who helped to staff the welfare state. Nor were they applied to relations within 'the family', which was generally seen as a cohesive unit headed by a male breadwinner supported by a wife responsible for childcare and housework (see Chapter Two).

Social democrats' enthusiasm for the state, underpinned by their commitment to the values of equality and fellowship, was reinforced by a benign understanding of human nature and motivation, which, as discussed in the Introduction, was most explicit in the work of Titmuss. Returning to Le Grand's knights, knaves and pawns: 'Democratic socialists assumed that the state and its agents were both competent and benevolent. It followed that ... those who operated the welfare state could be trusted to work primarily in the public interest: they were knights not knaves' (2003, p 5). Taxpayers were also believed to be knightly, or at least potentially so. It was thus

> assumed that the better-off would not only co-operate in collectivist enterprises such as national insurance and social services out of enlightened self-interest, but also willingly acquiesce in the payment of redistributive taxation that helped the disadvantaged, either because they empathised with the latter's plight or because they saw it as part of their civic responsibility to do so. (Le Grand, 2003, p 6)

Recipients of welfare services were regarded as essentially passive pawns without agency, 'who were supposed to be content with a universal, often fairly basic, standard of service' (Le Grand, 2003, p 6). They were expected to be patient, grateful, and to trust the professionals, in other words to act the deferential welfare subject described in the Introduction. Social security claimants, however, were also seen as potential knaves with agency, who were out to cheat the system. With this one exception, Le Grand concludes that 'it is not implausible to describe the bundle of implicit assumptions concerning human behaviour that characterised the rest of the democratic socialist welfare state as one designed to be financed and operated by knights for the benefit of pawns' (Le Grand, 2003, p 7).

These social democratic ideals and assumptions translated into a commitment to universal welfare services and benefits on the grounds that they foster integration and altruism: benefits and services confined to 'the poor' were seen as divisive and prone to become poor benefits and services without the support of the middle classes. Redistributive taxation was seen as necessary to achieve greater equality as well as to pay for decent welfare provisions.

The new right

Both the pragmatic middle way and the centre-left social democratic approaches to welfare came under challenge during the 1970s, which ended with the transformation of the political landscape following the election of the new right Conservative Party under Margaret Thatcher. This transformation was a response both to a gloomier economic environment and a reaction to what was perceived as an ever-expanding, paternalistic welfare state creating a nation of 'pawns'. A year later Ronald Reagan's election as President of the US cemented the advent of the new right era. The ideological impact of what came to be known as 'Thatcherism' and 'Reaganomics' continues to shape politics on both sides of the Atlantic (Katwala, 2009).

Two thinkers stand out in terms of their influence on the British (and also American) new right: Friedrick Hayek (who was especially influential on Margaret Thatcher) and Milton Friedman (see ***Box 1.5***).

Box 1.5: Key influences on the new right

Friedrick Hayek (1899-1992) was an economist but it was his philosophical work on liberty which was of greatest intellectual influence on new right thinking in both the US and UK. Hayek stood in the liberal tradition and contributed to the emergence of neo-liberalism. According to Desmond King his work 'represents the most complete and coherent statement of the liberal principles of individualism, a limited constitutionally specified role for the state and faith in the market' (1987, p 14; see also Tomlinson, 1995).

Milton Friedman (1912-2006) was also an economist, best known for his espousal of monetarism, which informed new right economic policy. Monetarism challenged Keynesian economics and in policy terms translated into cuts in public expenditure and the prioritisation of low inflation over maintaining employment. Friedman shared Hayek's belief in the market as the main source of economic freedom and the state as a coercive force (King, 1987).

It is important to emphasise that there is no single new right position, other than in the rejection of both the middle way and social democratic consensus that had dominated the post-war era in Britain. Broadly there are two strands of new right thinking, which came together in Thatcherism, which is how the application of new right thinking in Britain is popularly labelled. They are summed up by Andrew Gamble (1988) as 'the free economy and the strong state'.

The first, neo-liberal, strand is economic and is influenced in particular by Hayek and Friedman. It stems from classical liberalism with its emphasis on the market and on the individual and their rights (although not, as we shall see in Chapter Seven, social rights). The other, neo-conservative, strand is moral; it represents a social authoritarianism, emphasising social institutions such as the family and community and values such as responsibility. At times the two strands reinforced each other but sometimes they came into tension with each other, for instance when economic liberalism undermined communities and families through the destruction of paid work opportunities. By and large, it was the economic neo-liberal strand that was seen as pivotal to new right thinking and therefore that will be the main focus here, other than where the neo-conservative, moral strand was especially relevant to welfare debates.

New right thinking is distinguished by a very positive attitude towards the market and a very negative attitude towards the state, at least as a source of welfare. The market is seen as the fount of economic prosperity because it is the most efficient allocator of resources. But its significance for the new right goes much deeper than that, as expressed by David Marsland, a new right welfare theorist (see ***Box 1.6***).

Box 1.6: David Marsland on the significance of the market

The market is a precondition both of freedom and of human dignity. Only a market can guarantee people a real choice in relation to those most fundamental aspects of their lives which currently fall under the control of the Welfare State – education, health care, housing and protection against misfortune.... Moreover, by requiring – indeed constraining – individual choice, the market schools us to prudent consideration, careful judgement, autonomy and self-reliance. It is thus the seedbed of human dignity as much as it is the foundation of freedom. (Marsland, 1996, p xii)

The new right look to 'the strong state' of Gamble's epithet, in order to create the conditions necessary for the operation of the market and to maintain law and order. However, in the name of freedom it also emphasises the need to protect the individual from the state, which is regarded as coercive. And, as Marsland makes clear, in the area of welfare it promotes a minimalist approach to the state, which must be subordinated to the market. The welfare state and the taxes needed to fund it are criticised on the grounds that they are:

- Based on a philosophically incoherent position. In particular, it is argued, the welfare state embodies an ideal of social justice linked to economic equality which is false (see Chapter Eight) and involves the translation of needs into social rights, which are regarded as illegitimate (see Chapter Seven).
- Economically damaging. They reduce economic competitiveness and the welfare state is both economically inefficient and ineffective as a means of providing welfare.
- Politically damaging because they widen the role and scope of the state and create interest groups who fight for state resources.
- Socially damaging. The welfare state is paternalistic; undermines individual autonomy and personal and family responsibility; takes away freedom of choice thereby diminishing liberty; crowds out other forms of welfare provided by the family and community and the voluntary and private sectors; and creates moral hazard (see **Box 1.7**).

Box 1.7: Moral hazard

The idea of 'moral hazard' derives from insurance. *The Blackwell Dictionary of Social Policy* gives the example of car insurance: drivers might drive more recklessly in the knowledge that it covers any damage to their car, thereby increasing the costs of insurance companies. In the field of welfare, Madsen Pirie of the Adam Smith Institute explains: 'anything you do to relieve distress will instigate more of the behaviour which caused the distress' (quoted in Barry, 1999, p 63). Although the term is most widely used by the new right with reference to welfare, it has also been used by others with reference to government bailouts of the banks during the economic crash of 2008-09.

Question: think of a welfare state policy that, it might be argued, creates moral hazard.

Mrs Thatcher, in a foreword to Marsland's book, sums up the new right's perception of the social damage caused by the welfare state:

> It undermines the spirit of enterprising self-reliance without which the freedom we so much treasure in Britain cannot be assured.... I am glad to see that he emphasizes particularly the destructive effects on character and social behaviour of welfare dependency. The underclass life created by misconceived state welfare poses a grave threat to freedom and civility.... The majority of the population should be encouraged to provide for themselves, through market and mutual agencies, for the whole range of their welfare needs. (1996, p ix)

Although the ideological goal was to reduce the role of state as far as possible in welfare, in practice the new right government realised that there were limits to which the market could simply replace the state. It therefore increasingly looked to inject the philosophy of the market into the operation of the state through 'quasi-markets', defined as 'simulations of market conditions in public services through the separation of the purchasing from the provision of services and the introduction of competition, businesslike processes and consumer choice' (Alcock et al, 2002, p 200). The bureaucratic-professional ethos of the public sector made way for the target-setting, performance-centred, 'managerial state' in which managers held organisational power (Clarke and Newman, 1997; Clarke, 2008). At the same time, the third sector was regarded in instrumental terms: policy aimed 'to ensure that voluntary organisations became effective and efficient alternative providers of services to the state, working under the discipline of contract' (Lewis, 2005, p 121).

Underlying these shifts lay not just a negative view of the state but also a particular view of human nature and motivation, which coalesced for the new right in '**public choice theory**' (see *Box 1.8*).

Box 1.8: Public choice theory

Public choice theory involves 'the application of the methods of economics to the study of politics and, in particular... the assumption of self-interested behaviour'. Indeed, 'it is the assumption of self-interest which underpins public choice theory's hostility towards the state' (Hindmoor, 2006, pp 80, 82). Public choice theory denies the idea that there is something that can be called 'the public good', which involves individuals putting other people's interests above their own.

Public choice theory marked the arrival of the knaves both as providers and users of welfare. With regard to providers, public choice theory views public officials and professionals as motivated not by concern for the public good but by their own self-interest. This means, in particular, that bureaucrats act as a motor for welfare state expansion by maximising their budgets 'because increases in budget will be positively related to salary, power, patronage, public reputation' (Hindmoor, 2006, p 91). Users are no longer seen simply as passive pawns but as knaves responding to incentives and disincentives according to their own self-interest. As such they possess agency and therefore the potential to become queens through the injection of market mechanisms into the welfare state (Le Grand, 2003).

The underlying view of human nature/motivation as the self-interested, rational economic 'man' reflects the economic, neo-liberal strand in new right thinking typified in the work of Charles Murray on the 'underclass' (see Chapter Five). In contrast, the social authoritarian strand sees welfare state users, or at least poor welfare recipients, as either unable or unwilling to pursue their own economic interests and respond to incentives, so that they need to be compelled by the state to act in what the state sees as in their interests. Moral authoritarianism or neo-conservatism also decries the damaging effects on society of family breakdown, criticises the welfare state for undermining the traditional two-parent family and emphasises parental responsibility (Featherstone, 2004). It was this element of neo-conservatism, together with a belief in 'the nation', which was particularly influential on the new right in government. The British nation and culture were reasserted by the new right primarily as 'a form of defensive resistance to challenges to a sovereign, culturally homogeneous nation-state' (Williams,

2008, p 163). Harsher immigration controls and antipathy towards a strong European Union were among the consequences.

Overall, new right philosophy translated into a shift towards a more residual welfare state in which help is limited to the poorest. In social security this meant a downgrading of social insurance in favour of means-tested benefits for those on low incomes and private insurance for the better off. This was matched by increasing emphasis on the obligations of benefit recipients to seek and take paid work. There was a preference for cash over services as maximising individual choice. As noted already, market principles and a managerialist philosophy were introduced into service delivery. Income taxes for the better off and some benefits were cut and both poverty and inequality soared. Indeed, Alan Walker has described it as a deliberate 'strategy of inequality': 'rather than seeing inequality as potentially damaging to the social fabric, the Thatcher governments saw it as an engine of enterprise, providing incentives for those at the bottom as well as at the top' (1997, p 5).

The third way and beyond

The third way is the label used by its proponents to identify a significant shift in the nature of social democratic politics in the late 20th century. It is represented as the necessary modernisation of social democracy in response to global economic and social change. The third way is most commonly associated with Bill Clinton in the US and Tony Blair in Britain, although it has been taken up with varying degrees of enthusiasm by social democratic parties elsewhere too. It was born in the US, where the Democratic Party repositioned itself on the political centre ground in the late 20th century following a series of election defeats.

Repeated electoral defeat provided a similar spur for the British Labour Party. The creation of New Labour enabled it to distance itself from its former democratic socialist self, which was believed to be out of touch with voters. Influenced by the Clinton Democrats, once in power the third way offered Blair the shell of a political philosophy (although some question its credentials as a serious political philosophy). This could then be crafted to underline the distance between New and 'old' Labour as well as provide an alternative to the new right creed of Thatcherism, which had dominated the political landscape for the previous two decades. It was claimed that the third way is neither old left nor new right but instead transcends the old left–right divide. As Blair puts it, the third way 'moves decisively beyond an Old Left preoccupied by state control, high taxation and producer interests; and a New Right treating public investment, and often the very notions of "society" and collective endeavour as evils to be undone' (1998, p 1).

The third way's key thinker is the sociologist Anthony Giddens, once described as Tony Blair's 'guru'. Giddens has written extensively about the third way. His first book on the subject, *The Third Way* (1998), represents its most fully articulated intellectual exposition and has been translated into many languages. Giddens has participated in its political development both in Britain and on the international stage, as the ideas of the third way have been debated regularly at international political conferences. More recently this has been under the label of 'progressive governance', as that of the 'third way' has itself fallen out of favour.

It has been suggested that there are 'several variants' of the third way. These reflect: ambiguities within third way thinking; different national traditions; and the tensions between, on the one hand, political discourses and values and, on the other, practices and policies (Bonoli and Powell, 2004; White, 2001, 2004). What follows is a brief exposition of the third way as pursued by New Labour under Blair, together with some pointers to what lies beyond the third way in the post-Blair era, increasingly dominated by the Conservative leader David Cameron.

New Labour's third way

There are many interpretations of where the third way stands in relation to existing political ideologies. Some critics argue that, despite the 'neither old left nor new right' tag, New Labour's (and the US Democrats') third way is simply a continuation of the neo-liberal and social authoritarian philosophy of the new right: the wolf of neo-Thatcherism in social democratic sheep's clothing (see, for instance, Hall, 2003; Gray, 2007; Marquand, 2007). New Labour denies this. Blair dubs it the 'best label for the new politics which the progressive centre-left is forging in Britain and beyond' and argues that the third way offers traditional social democratic values 'in a changed world'. He asserts that 'it draws vitality from uniting the two great streams of left-of-centre thought – democratic socialism and liberalism – whose divorce this century did so much to weaken progressive politics across the West' (1998, p 1). Giddens subtitled his book 'the renewal of social democracy'. Driver and Martell, in their initial analysis of New Labour, suggest that it has to be understood as 'an exercise in post-Thatcherite politics', shaped by Thatcherism yet also representing a reaction against it (1998, p 1). In an updated analysis, they point to both continuity and change: 'a government taking politics and policy-making *beyond* Thatcherism' (2002, p 26, emphasis in original).

In fact, it is possible to trace a degree of continuity between the third way and each of the dominant ideological perspectives outlined already. In some respects, New Labour's third way most resembles the centre-ground political stance of the middle way. It shares the middle way's belief in 'neither an omnipotent state nor an all-embracing market' (Glennerster, 1999, p 29) and in the importance of partnership between the state and other providers of welfare. It is avowedly pragmatic, as summed up in the motto 'what matters is what works' (Blair, 1998, p 4), although, unlike the middle way, its pragmatism is couched in the language of modernisation. It places considerable emphasis on social cohesion and, as we shall see in Chapter Eight, equality of opportunity.

As explained already, proponents of the third way, such as Giddens, emphasise its social democratic credentials (although the 's' word in democratic socialism is rarely spoken). In particular, Giddens argues that 'third way politics should preserve a core concern with social justice' and should promote democracy (1998, p 65). The priority given by New Labour to combating child and pensioner poverty also attests to its social democratic roots. At the same time, those critics who dismiss New Labour as simply adopting the neo-liberal new right philosophy of the Thatcher governments can point in particular to: its pro-market stance in both economic and social policy; its aversion to traditional 'tax and spend' policies (even though public spending did rise after its first couple of years in power); its espousal of managerialism; its authoritarian law and order policies; and the preoccupation with welfare 'dependency'.

The third way is thus pro-market and ambivalent about the state. The contrast with the earlier social democratic attitude towards the market is underlined by Driver and Martell: 'pragmatic acceptance has turned under Tony Blair into positive celebration of the free market...in his hands the idea of social policy underpinning capitalist success goes beyond older Labour formulations of it providing a counterbalance or complement between the two' (1998, pp164-5). Embrace of the market is presented in part as a response to globalisation. Blair sees 'the embracing of globalisation as inevitable and also as desirable' (interview in *The Guardian*, 15 May 1998). Indeed, it has been suggested that globalisation represents 'the central idea through which [New Labour's] thinking is organized' (Rustin, 2008, p 274).

The ambivalence towards the state sets the third way apart from both the new right and democratic socialism: it shares neither the former's antipathy towards the state nor the latter's unequivocally pro-state stance. The third way still believes 'in the power of government to promote the common good' (Blair, 1998, p 15), but the nature of government must change. Blair warned soon after coming to power that 'the era of "big government means better government" is over. Leverage, not size, is what counts. What government does, and how well, not how much, is the key to its role in modern society' (1998, p 15). In place of the providing state, the third way promotes the enabling and the social investment state, in partnership with the private and voluntary sectors (see *Box 1.9*). The voluntary or third sector is accorded a much more significant role than under democratic socialism. In place of the contract culture of the new right, the relationship between the voluntary sector and the state is framed as one of partnership, epitomised in a national Compact (Lewis, 2005).

Box 1.9: The 'enabling state' and the 'social investment state'

In the *enabling state*, the emphasis in social security policy is on providing a 'trampoline' not a 'safety net'. In other words, the state is there to help people to help themselves and to exercise responsibility. The enabling state is an 'active' welfare state, which encourages 'independence, initiative and enterprise for all'; this is contrasted with the traditional 'passive' welfare state which, it is claimed, fosters 'dependency' (Blair, 1999, p 13).

The term '*social investment state*' was coined by Giddens. The guideline, he argues, 'is investment in *human capital* wherever possible, rather than direct provision of economic maintenance. In place of the welfare state we should put the *social investment state* (1998, p 117, emphasis in original). This means that the state should be prioritising education and training over social security. Although there is considerable emphasis on the need to integrate economic and social policy, it is on terms that do not challenge the traditional subordinate 'handmaiden' relationship of the social to the economic, criticised by Titmuss (1974, p 31; for a critique, see Lister, 2004b).

The use of the discourse of social investment also helps to distance third way politicians from traditional commitments to social spending. In their joint statement of the Third Way/Die Neue Mitte, Blair and the then German Chancellor, Gerhard Schröder, assert that 'public expenditure as a proportion of national income has more or less reached the limits of acceptability. Constraints on 'tax and spend' force radical modernisation of the public sector and reform of public services to achieve better value for money' (1999, p 29). Reform of public services has become a signal for the injection of market forces in the name of consumer choice. For all the talk of a pragmatic, what-works approach, the impression is given that the private sector is assumed to be superior to the public as a point of ideological faith.

Blair makes a distinction between 'pragmatic means' and 'fixed values' (1998, p 4). Followers of the third way talk a lot about values, although these are not always articulated in any depth. The four key values are outlined in **Box 1.10**.

Box 1.10: The third way's key values

* *Responsibility.* Giddens suggests 'no rights without responsibilities' as a 'prime motto for the new politics' (1998, p 65). This contractual expression of the relationship between rights and responsibilities was enthusiastically adopted by New Labour politicians particularly in the area of social rights (which will be discussed in more detail in Chapter Seven).
* *Inclusion.* Paid work and education are seen as the primary routes to inclusion (see also the discussion of social exclusion in Chapter Five).
* *Opportunity.* Opportunity is similarly interpreted primarily in terms of paid work and education.
* *Community.* Community is invoked as a unifying value in contrast to democratic socialism's concern with social class divisions on the one hand and the individualism of Thatcherism on the other. The emphasis placed on community reflects the influence of communitarianism (see *Box 1.1.*) on New Labour's third way thinking.

These values, as articulated by New Labour, reinforce each other. Thus, for instance, people are expected to exercise their responsibilities to improve their skills and enter the labour market in return for the new opportunities opened up for them. Opportunity and inclusion together replace the traditional social democratic concern with equality. According to Giddens, third way politics 'defines equality as inclusion and inequality as exclusion' (1998, p 102) and, as we shall see in Chapter Eight, 'equality of opportunity', bracketed with aspiration, has eclipsed the more traditional social democratic ideal of greater 'equality of outcome'. In a newspaper article to mark the launch of the Social Exclusion Unit, Blair explained that it 'will embody a core New Labour value:"community" or "one nation".... Our contract with the people was about opportunity and responsibility going together' (1997). Stuart White suggests that the vague concept of community can be understood as a derivative of the other values:

> If there is sufficient 'opportunity', then nobody suffers 'social exclusion', which seems necessary for 'community'. If people meet their responsibilities, then nobody will be free-riding unfairly on the efforts of others, and this, too, seems necessary

for 'community'. Thus 'community' refers to the quality of social life made possible by securing 'opportunity' and general respect for 'responsibility'. But 'community' is also something that helps to produce these goods … it is an asset that can help to secure opportunity and to nurture a stronger sense of civic responsibility. 'Community' is both an end that is realized through 'opportunity' and 'responsibility', and a crucial means to their realization. (2004, pp 29-30)

The emphasis on responsibility means a much greater emphasis on agency and a more judgemental view of human nature than in traditional social democratic thinking. Le Grand (2003) characterises the third way, alongside neo-liberalism, as treating welfare providers and users as primarily knaves and queens, rather than knights and pawns, in the name of user power and choice. In the Introduction we saw Labour MP Frank Field's rejection of the altruistic view of human nature held by Titmuss. Blair himself offers a more measured assessment: 'Human nature is cooperative as well as competitive, selfless as well as self-interested' (1998, p 4). He appeals to an enlightened view of self-interest, which links the individual to the wider community, more than the narrower individualistic view of the new right.

When enlightened self-interest provides insufficient motivation for certain groups such as welfare benefit recipients, the third way dictates that obligations have to be enforced. A central theme of New Labour social policy, particularly with respect to social security, is a clear attempt to change or 'remoralise' human behaviour in the name of responsibility and community. Social democratic critics question New Labour's reluctance to promote responsibility and community at the other end of the income scale through higher taxation on the wealthy. Taxation policy exemplifies a shift in practice from the social democratic appeal to altruism and solidarity to the appeasement of individualistic self-interest.

Appeals to community are sometimes couched in the language of 'one nation' and Britishness. In his treatise on the third way, Giddens argues that, in 'the global age', 'social democrats should seek a new role for the nation in a cosmopolitan world' (1998, p 129). He puts forward the ideal of the 'cosmopolitan nation' open to difference and 'multiple affiliation' (p 130), and linked to other nations through mechanisms of global governance such as the European Union and the United Nations. In power, national economic competitiveness in the global market has been a central driver of New Labour social policy, as exemplified in the idea of the 'social investment state'. Moreover, according to Norman Fairclough:

the representation of the global economy as a field of intensifying competition for survival between nation-states not only entails a focus on national unity rather than division, it also leads to elements of nationalist discourse in, for instance, the commitment to 'national renewal' and to Britain being 'the best', appeals to the 'British spirit' and to 'our destiny as one of the great nations of the world' (2000, p 35).

While New Labour is 'tolerant' of diversity, the ideal of the cohesive nation and a national 'we' must not be undermined by cultural divisions and, post-Iraq, the threat of terrorism; thus the ideal of multi-culturalism to which it initially subscribed has been replaced by an emphasis on integration and Britishness. Britishness has also been invoked in the wake of devolution. In this context, Margaret Wetherell suggests that 'for many politicians and policy-makers, fostering and re-defining inclusive national identities such as "Britishness" has seemed a positive strategy for developing integration and cohesion, and is one obvious response to the evidence of "identity deficit" experienced by many white English' (2008, p 311). Another response in the international context has been more exclusionary policies towards asylum-seekers and immigrants.

Williams points out how the link between nation and community extends to family, as New Labour 'strove to present an image of a "one nation" Britain based upon "strong families" and "strong communities"' (2008, p 163). *Box 1.11* reproduces her summing-up of New Labour's policy orientation towards 'the family'.

Box 1.11: Fiona Williams on the key characteristics of New Labour's policy towards 'the family'

A moral and economic imperative of the importance of paid work for fathers and mothers has brought together support for working parents, investment in children's opportunities especially in education, and parental responsibilities, in the fight against child poverty and social exclusion. In addition there has been greater acknowledgement of the diversity of partnership relationships [particularly with the introduction of civil partnerships for same-sex couples] that marks a waning influence of a morality 'from above'. (Williams, 2005, p 300, emphasis in original; see also Featherstone, 2004, Ch 4)

We can see in *Box 1.11* some of the key elements in the social policies that have emerged from New Labour's third way. Investment in education together with active labour market and training policies and the intensification of paid work obligations attached to social security benefits aim to equip people to compete in the global market. In addition, the modernisation of public services has entailed both the use of market mechanisms and the involvement of private and third sector partners. Income tax rates have been cut and redistribution through the tax and benefits system in the social democratic tradition has largely been by stealth.

And beyond

Gordon Brown, who had been joint architect of New Labour and replaced Blair as Prime Minister in 2007, never signed up to the idea of the third way and when Chancellor hinted at more social democratic leanings. Nevertheless, he subscribed to many of the third way's tenets and in particular its prioritisation of global economic competitiveness and its emphasis on responsibility and opportunity. It is Brown who has been most preoccupied with the idea of Britishness and, during his time as Prime Minister, he appeared increasingly to have embraced the Blairite agenda of marketisation in public services. Those who had been hoping for a return to a more traditional social democratic stance may look instead to Scotland, where the Scottish Nationalist Party is pursuing more of a social democratic social policy agenda (albeit within limits, as emphasised by Mooney et al, 2008).

In the same way that New Labour was created after successive electoral defeats, so David Cameron is attempting to forge a 'modern', 'liberal', 'compassionate' or 'progressive' Conservatism to distance the party from the legacy of Thatcherism. However, in what he calls 'Cameron's masterclass in shades of political ambiguity', Sunder Katwala observes that 'according to audience and mood, "progressive Conservatism" is presented as both corrective to and continuation of the Thatcher legacy' (2009, pp 7, 4). Talk of Cameron as the 'heir to Blair' may have been political spin, but, while he would not use the term, Cameron is in effect forging the Conservatives' own 'third way', as he trespasses on to political territory which once belonged to Labour. In a cheeky piece of political cross-dressing, which conveniently glosses over the Conservatives' role in the earlier increase in poverty and inequality, he claims that:

> it is the Conservative Party that is the champion of progressive ideals in Britain today…. If you care about poverty, if you care about inequality, if you care about the environment – forget about the Labour Party…. If you count yourself a progressive, a true progressive, only we can achieve real change (2008a).

Like New Labour, Cameron identifies social mobility (discussed in Chapter Eight) as an important goal in this context – indeed he has called it 'the most important progressive aim of all' (2009a). Yet, he remains committed to cutting inheritance tax.

According to Richard Reeves, 'Cameronism', as it is already being dubbed, 'emphasises the pragmatic over the theoretical; takes an essentially optimistic view of human nature; favours the devolution, rather than centralisation, of power; stresses social, rather than economic, progress, and places more faith in society than the state' (2008, p 64). Despite its modern tag, this is in many ways resonant of the middle way conservatism of Macmillan (Marquand, 2008). Indeed, Cameron has asserted that the Conservative Party should draw once again on the one nation tradition of the middle way, which, he said, 'is about society as well as the economy' (Grice, 2009). Cameron's prioritisation of the social is of particular interest from a social policy perspective. It is reflected in the concern 'to reverse Britain's social breakdown' (Cameron, 2008b) and use of the language of well-being and social justice (which, as we shall see in Chapter Eight, is deemed illegitimate by new right thinkers). Former Labour Cabinet Minister James Purnell suggests that 'the history of the past 30 years can be seen as Labour learning to accept efficiency and markets, and then the Tories accepting social justice' (2009, p 29).

Cameron projects himself as 'as radical a social reformer as Mrs Thatcher was an economic reformer' intent on mending 'Britain's broken society' (quoted in *The Guardian*, 18 August 2008). The core value is social responsibility, which Cameron has described as 'the essence of liberal conservatism' and as 'the big idea': 'the belief that we are all in this together and will only build the good society we all want to see if every participant – government, business, the voluntary sector, individuals and families – plays their part' (quoted in Finlayson, 2007, p 5). His 2009 conference speech referred to responsibility 21 times. In a subsequent lecture he described 'this emphasis on responsibility [as] absolutely vital' (Cameron, 2009b). Reeves, who heads the British think tank Demos, which has forged links with Cameron's Conservatives, believes that they are also 'determined to pick up where Tony Blair left off.... The new Conservative/old Blairite mission is to use consumer choice to produce better, fairer public services' (2009, p 41).

A key dividing line drawn by Cameron between the Conservatives and New Labour is in relation to the role of the state. This line has been drawn increasingly boldly as the Conservatives have used the economic crisis to argue for massive cutbacks in public expenditure as part of an ideological assault on the state or 'big government'. Cameron looks to society, and in particular the third and informal sectors, rather than 'the large, clunking mechanism of the state' (2006) as the main drivers of social progress. His 'alternative to big government is not no government' or even 'smarter government' but government that uses 'the state to remake society' (Cameron, 2009b). This stance has been described as 'a third way in relation to the state, combining hostility with a qualified recognition that it has a vital role to play' (Richards, 2009).

At the same time, while 'Cameronism' is pro-market, it does not share the new right's overriding faith in the unfettered market (Osborne, 2008). There is an acceptance of the reality of family diversity; but, simultaneously, a preoccupation with family breakdown and a desire to bolster marriage through the tax system speak to more traditional conservative concerns. Harsh policies to reduce 'welfare dependency' and to limit immigration follow in the footsteps of both the new right and New Labour; and new right eurosceptic hostility towards a strong European Union lives on.

'Cameronism' is still a work in progress. However, these early drafts suggest that, like the third way and the earlier conservative middle way, it will locate itself on the political centre ground, even if it sometimes tacks further to the new right (particularly with respect to public spending), just as sometimes New Labour has tacked further to the social democratic left.

Summary

This chapter has provided an introduction to the key political philosophies and ideological perspectives that have guided British governments since the Second World War. It has covered:

- The main Western political traditions on which these ideologies draw: *conservatism; socialism; liberalism; neo-liberalism; libertarianism;* and *communitarianism.*
- *The middle way* – a label used to describe the pragmatic stance towards the state and market adopted by post-war Conservatism but also associated with social liberals such as Beveridge and Keynes.
- *Social democracy/democratic socialism* – a more overtly ideological pro-state and anti-market philosophy with core values of equality, liberty and fellowship or solidarity.
- *The new right* – also an overtly ideological position which combines neo-liberalism and neo-conservatism. In the name of liberty, it embraces the market and rejects the welfare state, although it looks to a strong state to maintain law and order and enforce responsibility.
- *The third way* – a return to middle way pragmatism with regard to the state and policy tools combined with an emphasis on the values of responsibility, inclusion, opportunity and community. Although it is presented as a renewal of social

democracy, its espousal of the market is rooted in the neo-liberal new right. Beyond the third way lies 'Cameronism'. This represents the Conservatives' attempt to replace New Labour in the political centre ground, drawing on a number of earlier political ideologies.

Further reading

The Student's Companion to Social Policy **(Alcock et al, 2008)** offers a good starting point for all the perspectives discussed in this chapter. **George and Wilding (1994)** provide a comprehensive and accessible account of the ideological perspectives up until the mid-1990s and **George and Page (1995)** do the same through a focus on key thinkers. Two useful, critical accounts of the new right are **King (1987)** and **Gamble (1988)**. Key early texts on the third way and New Labour are **Giddens (1998)** and **Driver and Martell (1998)**. A more critical position can be found in **Finlayson (2003)** and more international perspectives in **White (2001)** and **Lewis and Surender (2004)**. **Deacon (2002)** and **Le Grand (2003)** are key texts on the changing political construction of human motivation and behaviour and **Cudworth et al (2007)** provide a helpful introduction to ideological perspectives on the state.

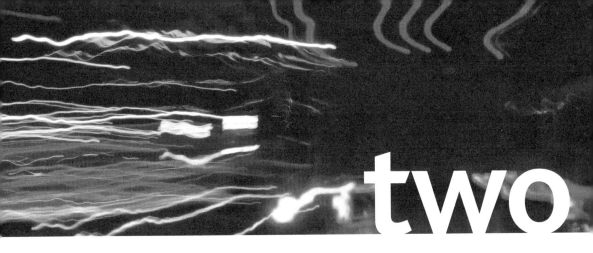

two

Critical perspectives: Marxism, feminism, anti-racism and environmentalism

This chapter gives an introduction to the main theoretical perspectives that have provided a political critique of dominant political ideologies as well as a critical analytical tool. It covers the main tenets of Marxist, feminist, anti-racist and green philosophies, which take social class, gender, 'race' and the environment respectively as their central analytical categories. It pays particular attention to what they say about the welfare state and their impact on social policy thinking.

Marxism

Marxism is one of the most important strands of socialism (summarised in **Box 1.1**). Its originators, Karl Marx and Friedrich Engels, wrote in the middle decades of the 19th century. Since then, it has evolved through the work of a range of theorists, developing a variety of Marxist interpretations and perspectives, to which it is not possible to do justice in this brief summary. It enjoyed something of a revival among radicals in the 1960s and 1970s and, although less prominent today, Marxism remains an important theoretical approach, which has also fed into post-Fordism (discussed in Chapter Three). Indeed, the global financial crisis of the late 2000s has prompted renewed interest in Marxist analysis among politicians and the media, with sales of his most famous work *Das Kapital* booming (including in cartoon form in Japan). Moreover, as a revolutionary politics, Marxism has contributed to the global social justice and anti-capitalist movement, which emerged at the turn of the 21st century. This section provides a brief introduction to some of the key tenets of Marxism before looking at what it has to say about the state – in particular the welfare state – and about agency. It concludes with the case made for Marxism's continued relevance to social policy.

A materialist theory: economic production and social class

Marxism is a *materialist* theory above all else, in other words it is grounded in the economic relations of production. This means that the starting point for any analysis of society is how economic production is organised or how a society produces the goods that meet its members' needs. Economic production is organised differently at different points in history. Marxism is, therefore, grounded in an empirical analysis of economic relations.

The mode of production forms the economic base of society. This base then influences other social institutions, which form the superstructure above it. In classical Marxism, the political system, the state, the legal system and social institutions such as the family, together with the social relations associated with them and dominant ideologies (ideas and beliefs) are all largely (although not totally) determined by the mode of production. It is thus described as a theory of economic determinism. However, this does not necessarily mean that everything is simply 'reduced to its "economic logic" – each sphere has its own processes and laws which must be understood and grasped in their own terms while being located in, and related to, the rest of the social world' (Ferguson et al, 2002, p 21).

The mode of production about which Marx and Engels wrote and which is still dominant throughout the world, although in a different form today, is capitalism. Key to the Marxist analysis of capitalism is a distinction between the 'use–value' and 'exchange value' of the products of human labour (see **Box 2.1**.)

Box 2.1: Commodification and the products of human labour

Use value refers to the intrinsic value of the products of human labour in meeting human need; *exchange* value derives from what these products are worth in exchange with other commodities. Take the example of vegetables grown on an allotment: the food you grow for your personal consumption has a use value, which is the nutrition and enjoyment you get from home grown vegetables; if you take some of the food to sell at a farmers' market, its exchange value is the money you get for it, which you can then spend on other goods. Contemporary Marxists use the concept of 'commodification' to describe how capitalism turns goods, services and also labour into commodities that have an exchange value, as they are bought and sold in the market.

The central Marxist criticism of capitalism is that it is built on the exploitation of the working-class majority by the minority bourgeoisie who own and/or control the means of production. Thus it is also a theory based on social class. It is a very particular conceptualisation of social class, which is different from the way in which the term is used in everyday talk where it tends to refer to a gradation of upper, middle and working classes. Marxist class analysis is based upon a dichotomy between two opposing classes, with any other groups accorded only marginal importance. On one side is the proletariat or working class (labour) who have to sell their labour power in order to subsist. As a result, they are alienated or estranged from their own labour in the sense that they control neither the processes of production nor the product of their labour (Ferguson et al, 2002). On the other side are the capitalist bourgeoisie (capital) who exploit that labour power by means of their ownership and/or control of the means of production, which gives them economic power. Exploitation takes place through capital's extraction of 'surplus value' from labour, with the surplus value becoming greater, the lower capital can keep labour's wages. This sets up a fundamental conflict of interests between the two classes, which also spurs the dynamics of change through working–class struggle. The Marxist theory of class struggle has thus also shaped Marxism as a revolutionary political ideology aimed at economic, political and social transformation. Marxism is not just a theory of change but also a commitment to effect radical change.

Contemporary Marxism recognises that changes in the capitalist mode of production since Marx wrote have resulted in alterations in the composition of both bourgeoisie and proletariat. Some contemporary Marxists are also willing to acknowledge the importance of other sources of social division such as those covered in this chapter; nevertheless social class remains more or less central to their analysis and is seen as the driving motor of change. In a social policy context, Ferguson et al argue 'against the grain of current critical welfare thinking' that the oppressions associated with such social divisions 'have their origins in the social and economic relations of capitalism'; and, as Marxists, they reassert 'the central role of the working class in bringing about social change' to end oppression (2002, pp 95, 107).

The state

There is no single Marxist theory of the state. What unites the theories is the belief in the state's link to 'the economic organization and structure of capitalist societies' (Lavalette, 1997, p 65). The state is regarded as 'a set of institutions and practices intimately connected with, but subordinate to' the dominant mode of production (Lavalette, 1997, p 63), although some strands of Marxism accord it a degree of autonomy. Broadly, the state is not a neutral body but exists to further the interests of the ruling class. Under capitalism, the state's 'primary activity is to maintain the conditions for the existence and expansion of capitalism as a socio-economic system' (Lavalette, 1997, p 63), for example by aiding capital accumulation and safeguarding private property. The action taken by capitalist states to shore up the banking system during the credit crunch of 2007-09 provides a good example of this. As President Bush put it, the money put into the banking system by the US government was 'not intended to take over the free market but to preserve it' (cited in *The Independent*, 15 October 2008).

According to a leading 20th century Marxist, Ralph Miliband: 'the intervention of the state is always and necessarily partisan: as a class state, it always intervenes for the purpose of maintaining the existing system of domination, even where it intervenes to mitigate the harshness of that system of domination' (1977, cited in George and Wilding, 1994, p 104). It is through the welfare state that the state 'intervenes to mitigate' the system's harshness. Marxism as a philosophy predates the welfare state and some contemporary Marxists reject the term 'welfare state' because it implies a separation from the capitalist system of which it is seen to be a part. Nevertheless, contemporary Marxists have contributed towards the theorisation of the development and operation of welfare states. How they do so varies according to the underlying theory of the state to which they subscribe, but broadly Marxists understand the development of the welfare state in three main ways, as:

- a response to the requirements of capital for the reproduction of labour power. In other words, capital needs workers and potential workers to be reasonably educated and sufficiently healthy to be able to work and reproduce themselves;
- a response to class conflict and the demands of the working class;
- pre-emptive action designed to undermine working-class radicalism.

While theorists vary as to which of these positions they emphasise, together these interpretations illustrate how Marxists regard the welfare state as a contradictory institution. Their attitude towards it is therefore ambivalent and more critical than that of democratic socialism. Insofar as the welfare state provides concessions to the working class and improves their lives, Marxists acknowledge that it merits a degree of support; yet at the same time, they attack it for promoting the interests of capital and for operating as an instrument of oppression and social control (see Chapter Four).

The contradictory nature of the welfare state has been explicitly theorised by contemporary neo-Marxists, most notably Claus Offe and James

O'Connor (see Dean, 1995; Gough, 1995). O'Connor argues that 'the capitalist state must try to fulfil two basic and often mutually contradictory functions – *accumulation* and *legitimation*' (1973, cited in George and Wilding, 1994, p 115, emphasis in original). In other words, the welfare state has to support capitalism and ensure its profitability (accumulation), partly by ensuring the availability of a fit workforce, while at the same time it has to make the capitalist system acceptable (legitimation).

In this way the welfare state is integral to capitalism. Offe explains the contradiction: 'while capitalism cannot coexist *with*, neither can it exist *without* the welfare state' (1982, p 11, emphasis in original). This means that, 'for Offe, the welfare state is central because it both sustains and threatens the existence of capitalism' (Dean, 1995, p 220). It threatens capitalism's existence, O'Connor (1973) argues, because in sustaining it through the function of legitimation, expenditure on welfare benefits and services can outstrip what the economy can afford leading to a 'fiscal crisis of the welfare state' (the title of his most influential work). This last argument about lack of affordability is similar to the position taken by the new right. However, unlike the new right, who stand at the opposite end of the political spectrum, Marxists do not use it to make the case for cuts in the welfare state.

Agency and structure

On the question of agency, Marxism's economic determinism would suggest that the emphasis is more on structure than on agency: humans (and their behaviour) are regarded primarily as the product of their environment and of structural forces rather than as individual rational agents. This is illustrated by Marxist explanations of poverty (see **Box 2.2**). Nevertheless, in a famous passage, cited in the Introduction to this volume, Marx made the point that individuals make their own history but they do not do so in conditions of their own choosing. In other words, Marxism does not completely deny agency. In particular, as already observed, it emphasises the collective agency of the working class as a historical force for change. Also, for Marx, productive and creative labour is at the heart of what it means to be human.

Box 2.2: Marxist explanations of poverty

Gerry Mooney describes Marxism as the 'best known of structural explanations' of poverty (2008, p 69). Marxist analysis locates the cause of poverty within the very nature of capitalism. In his 'historical sociology' of poverty, Tony Novak asserts that 'poverty is a product of capitalism. It both arose with the development of capitalism, and is continually created and recreated by it' (1988, p viii). 'Poverty serves ultimately as the motor of the capitalist labour market and its incentives to work. It is also this that makes poverty, and the continuing threat of poverty, a necessary and inescapable feature of capitalist society' (Jones and Novak, 1999, p 20). It is perpetuated by the state: the maintenance of poverty 'as the primary incentive to work has throughout history overshadowed all other considerations in the state's dealings with poverty' (Novak, 1988, pp viii-ix).

Drawing on Novak's work, Mooney explains that 'the entire thrust of the Marxist approach is to locate the discussion and analysis of poverty within the wider context of class relations and inequalities within capitalist society' rather than treat it as an isolated problem. 'For Marxists the production and accumulation of profit, of wealth, is also simultaneously the production and accumulation of poverty, want and misery' (Mooney, 2008, p 69).

Influence on social policy

Marxism's influence on Western social policies has been described as 'marginal' (Fitzpatrick, 2001, p 133), and probably few social policy analysts would describe themselves today as Marxist. Nevertheless, it has contributed to our understanding of the tensions facing welfare states in capitalist societies. George and Page argue that despite its 'failings, Marxism provides a better explanation of the development and function of the welfare state than most … other ideologies' (1995, p 200). Marxism is also contributing today to a social policy interest in political economy, which combines a focus on politics and economics (see *Box 2.3*).

Box 2.3: Marxism and a political economy approach to social policy

In a themed section of *Social Policy and Society* on 'Political Economy and Social Policy', Chris Holden makes the case for closer links between social policy and political economy. He argues that 'the growing importance of processes of 'globalisation' and 'the increasingly explicit linking of economic and social policies by government' (as exemplified by the earlier discussion of the 'social investment state', see Box 1.9) 'make this a particularly opportune time to apply the Political Economy approach to the concerns of Social Policy' (2005, p 173). He cites the Marxist contribution to what has been 'a strong tradition of Political Economy analysis of the welfare state' (Holden, 2005, p 177).

The case for the continued relevance of Marxism to social policy is made by Ferguson et al in their 'classical Marxist' analysis of social policy and defence of the welfare state:

> The ideas of Marx and those who have followed him … are of enormous relevance to understanding the nature of welfare and welfare provision within advanced capitalism. Marxist analyses of the dynamics of capitalism, class, the State, the family, as well as of alienation and oppression are … powerful explanatory tools that help make sense of a whole range of current welfare issues and debates. (2002, p 16)

Feminism(s)

There are a number of strands in feminism, including those which are rooted in the other critical perspectives discussed in this chapter: Marxist, black and anti-racist, and eco feminism. Commentators therefore sometimes talk about feminism*s*. The key groupings, most commonly reflected in social policy analysis, are summarised in **Box 2.4**. Such categorisations are, however, rather crude and over-simplified. This is one reason why, by and large, feminist social policy analysis is fairly eclectic and draws on various strands of feminist thinking to apply a gendered lens to social policy rather than being rooted in any one particular approach. The account here will therefore focus more on the commonalities of feminist social policy analysis than on the differences. Alison Jaggar's 'working definition', which 'identifies feminism with the various social movements dedicated to ending the subordination of women' (1994, cited in Bryson, 1999, p 5), underlines both these commonalities and feminism's status as a political movement (as well as a set of theoretical positions).

Box 2.4: Key strands of feminism reflected in social policy analysis

- *Liberal feminism* draws on the liberal political tradition (see *Box 1.1*), in particular its prioritisation of the individual, and on liberalism's language of individual rights. Liberal feminism is also sometimes known as equal rights feminism, as it presses the case for women's equal opportunity with men, particularly in education, employment and politics. 'The belief that society's treatment of women violates their rights to liberty, equality and justice, and in addition creates a waste of women's skills and abilities is the basis of liberal feminism' (Williams, 1989, p 44).

- *Socialist and Marxist feminism* share a structural analysis, which locates the exploitation of women primarily in capitalist economic relations. This exploitation extends to the household through women's unpaid labour. While they both emphasise class as well as gender relations, they differ in the relative priority they accord them. In line with the Marxist tradition, Marxist feminism tends to subordinate gender to class divisions and to highlight class divisions among women. Socialist and Marxist feminists also differ in the extent to which they engage in reformist politics, aimed at improving women's economic and social condition.
- *Radical feminism* is rooted in 'a theoretical analysis of male power which [is] focused on the concept of *patriarchy*' – 'a shorthand for a social system based on male domination and female subordination' (Bryson, 1999, p 27). Radical feminism has been in the forefront of feminist analysis of women's oppression within the private, familial, sphere, with a particular focus on male physical power as expressed in domestic violence and rape.
- *Black and anti-racist feminism* represents a reaction against feminism's marginalisation of black women, which was first vocalised in the 1970s and 1980s. It rejects accommodation through the mere 'add-on' of women of colour without decentring white women and thereby transforming feminism. Instead it has 'directed analyses of women's exploitation and oppression away from a notion of woman as a unitary and Western category, and towards analyses that were more inclusive of all women, while not resorting to tokenistic inclusion of non-white, non-Western women' (Bhavnani, 2001, p 4).
- *Postmodernist feminism*, like black feminism, challenges the notion of a unitary woman. But it does so at a more fundamental level, which rejects the very category 'woman' and the idea of fixed gender identities, together with sweeping theories of capitalism or patriarchy (see Chapter Three).

These last two strands of feminism have contributed to a more differentiated gender analysis, which at its best addresses how gender intersects with other social divisions, notably those associated with 'race' and ethnicity, class, sexuality, disability and age.

Question: Can you think of the kinds of social policies for which each of these strands of feminism is likely to argue?

The feminist critique of social policy emerged in the 1970s and 1980s. However, a number of its insights can be found in the writings of early and mid-20th century feminist campaigners, such as Eleanor Rathbone who campaigned for the introduction of family allowances. The late 20th century critique was initially based on two key points. The first was the importance of welfare issues to women's lives and the importance of women to welfare. In the words of a pioneering feminist social policy text: 'Only an analysis of the welfare state that bases itself on a correct understanding of the position of women in modern society can reveal the full meaning of modern welfarism' (Wilson, 1977, p 59). The second point was that, despite women's centrality, they were completely marginalised in post-war social policy writing, which failed to grasp the significance of gender for understanding welfare.

The feminist critique, which has unfolded subsequently, has developed a gendered analysis of the institutions, relations and discourses which constitute social policy. This has led to a more normative attempt to 're-gender' those institutions, relations and discourses so that they better reflect the varied perspectives and needs of women. It is acknowledged that this critique has 'enormously enriched the study of social policy' (George and Wilding, 1994, p 157). Indeed, it has posed a fundamental challenge to the discipline, causing it to rethink both its focus and some of its most basic concepts. In the rest of this section we explore in turn feminism's contribution to social policy understanding of the family, state and labour market and then how a gendered analysis has thrown a new light on a number of key concepts in the study of social policy.

Family

Feminist analysis has drawn attention to the *family* as a key site of welfare. This, together with its consistently gendered analysis, marks out feminism's contribution to social policy. It has illuminated the ways in which the family interacts with the other key institutional bases of social policy analysis: the state, labour market, and voluntary/private sectors, with often different effects on women and men. This reflects the broader feminist re-conceptualisation of the relationship between the domestic private sphere (traditionally associated with women) and the public sphere of the state and labour market (associated with men) (Lister, 2003a). This questioning of the traditional **public–private divide** has had three main implications for social policy (spelt out in *Box 2.5*)

Box 2.5: The implications for social policy of the questioning of the public-private divide

- It has translated a number of issues deemed 'private' into legitimate concerns of public policy. Domestic violence is a prime example.
- It has turned the spotlight on the impact of public policies and practices on relations within the family. For instance, a range of public policies, including

childcare and social security, affect mothers' access to an independent income, which in turn shapes their relations with partners and children.

- It has demonstrated the ways in which gender relations in the private sphere – for example the amount of time that each parent spends on child care and housework – differentially shape the access of men and women to the public sphere of the labour market and politics.

Question: Think of other examples to illustrate each of these points.

Feminist analysis has also illuminated how the family operates both as a material site of production, reproduction, distribution and consumption and as an ideological force. As a material site, feminist analysis has opened up what was the closed box of the family. It has explored the extent to which families remain the main source of care of children and older people and, in particular, highlighted how much of this care is provided by women. It has revealed the importance of looking at how material resources – wages, social security benefits, goods and services and time – are distributed within families between men, women and children, with implications for the incidence of poverty and hardship. In each case, it has also evaluated the impact of public policies, providing evidence for campaigners.

At the level of ideology or discourse (a concept explained in Chapter Three), feminism has exposed the ways in which the traditional family of a married heterosexual couple and children has been privileged over and devalued other ways of living such as lone parent and gay and lesbian families. The common use of the more neutral term 'families' instead of 'the family' represents a deliberate move to disassociate the family as an institutional base of welfare from 'the family' as an ideological model. Another example of the ideological significance of language for feminist scholars is provided by Brid Featherstone. She cautions against

the use of ungendered terms such as 'parent' and 'parental responsibility'... [which] can obscure the multiple and differing investments men and women continue to make in mothering and fathering, and the complexities that may be arising as a result of a range of changes in how mothering and fathering may be being carried out. (2004, p 10)

Featherstone's warning also serves as a reminder that feminist analysis focuses not just on women's position in the family but also on that of men (see also Featherstone, 2009); and by extension changes in mothering and fathering have implications too for children. She explains why feminism is therefore so important to understanding families and to the development of family policies (see ***Box 2.6***).

> ## Box 2.6: The importance of feminism to understanding families and family policies
>
> First, feminist investigations 'help illuminate *why* there have been changes in adult men and women's relationships which have led to differing family forms and differing practices in family life becoming more prevalent. Second, feminist analyses can offer important and neglected insights into the consequences for all concerned – men, women and children – crucially through demonstrating why gender continues to matter. Finally, they offer important pointers for those concerned to locate family support practices within a policy framework which can actively support the building of more democratic families' (Featherstone, 2004, p 41, emphasis in original).
>
> *Question:* What do you think Featherstone means by 'more democratic families' and how can social policies encourage such families?

State

It has been argued that 'women's lives are more dependent on and determined by state policies than men's' (Hernes, 1987, p 37). There is no single feminist theory of the state (see ***Box 2.7*** for a summary of the positions adopted by different strands of feminism). Moreover, feminists vary in the extent to which they are willing to engage with the state, 'which is seen, at one and the same time, as enabling and constraining, as a potential ally and as an oppressive force' (Charles, 2000, p 5). This ambivalence, Nickie Charles explains, reflects the contradictory nature of the state itself as much as differences within feminism. It is also indicative of how women's relationship to the state is mediated by other social divisions such as social class, 'race', sexuality, age and disability. Nevertheless, however great the ambivalence, from a social policy perspective it is difficult not to engage with the state. As Charles argues, engagement with the state is essential 'because the state regulates access to the resources that women need in order to be able to change gendered relations of power' (2000, p 209). While she acknowledges that 'engaging with the state courts the danger that feminist interests will be lost sight of and issues redefined in non-feminist terms', she also maintains that 'it holds out the promise that feminist demands will be met and feminist interests represented within and by the state' (2000, p 28).

Box 2.7: Feminist conceptualisations of the state

- *Liberal feminism*: the neutral state, which acts as a benign and 'neutral arbiter between different interest groups' (Kantola, 2006, p 119) and to which feminists can appeal to improve women's position.
- *Radical feminism*: the patriarchal state, which serves men's interests and reinforces gender inequalities. The notion of the patriarchal state has also been adopted more widely in feminist analysis of the state.
- *Marxist feminism*: the capitalist state, which sustains capitalism. *Socialist feminism* combines Marxist feminists' analysis of the capitalist state with radical feminism's identification of the state's patriarchal nature.
- *Black and anti-racist feminism*: the racist state, which reinforces racial as well as gender inequalities.
- *Postmodernist feminism*: the post-structuralist or postmodernist state, which does not represent a single set of interests or operate as an undifferentiated unity but which nevertheless has gendered effects (see also Chapter Three).

Source: Kantola (2006)

Question: Which of these conceptualisations do you think best captures the state in your country?

Johanna Kantola concludes that, despite the disagreements between its different strands, feminism's main contribution to understanding the state:

> has been to expose the gendered and patriarchal character of state institutions, practices and policies … Feminists show that the state impacts on women in gender-specific ways and helps to construct gender relations, but at the same time, the activities of different women and women's movements impact on the state. (2006, pp 118–9)

This contribution has been of especial value in understanding the welfare state. Feminist scholarship has exposed 'the discriminatory character of welfare programs and their function to reinforce sexist arrangements in domestic and public life' in the face of a dominant literature, which simply did 'not use gender as a category of analysis' (Gordon, 1990, pp 18, 10). The state's ambiguous nature is particularly apparent in the field of welfare, as the same institutions can simultaneously support and oppress women. Take for example the social security system: this can provide women with the independent income necessary to leave a relationship, yet in many countries it also serves to perpetuate their economic dependence within that relationship by basing entitlement on the couple rather than the individual.

Comparative welfare state analysis shows also how not all states are the same. In particular, some Nordic feminists have argued that the Nordic welfare states of Sweden, Norway, Finland, Iceland and Denmark have the potential to be 'women-friendly' welfare states (see ***Box 2.8***). In its initial stages, comparative welfare state analysis focused very much on the relationship between 'state and economy, and in particular between work and welfare' (Lewis, 2000, p 37). The feminist critique of this gender-ignorant approach has added in the 'unpaid work that is done primarily by women in providing welfare' mainly in the family but also in the voluntary sector (Lewis, 2000, p 37).

Box 2.8: The women-friendly welfare state

The term 'women-friendly state' was first coined by the Norwegian feminist scholar, Helga Hernes. She defines it as a state which 'would not force harder choices on women than on men, or permit unjust treatment on the basis of sex' and in which women as well as men 'can be both autonomous individuals and parents' (1987, pp 15, 29). A women-friendly state is also, she argues, one in which 'injustice on the basis of gender is largely eliminated without an increase in other forms of inequality, such as among groups of women' (1987, p 15; see also Lister, 2009a).

Question: What social policies would you propose in order to create a women-friendly welfare state?

Drawing on Hernes (1987), Christine Hallett (1996) analyses women's relationship to the welfare state as service users, providers and participants in the political process, able to shape the nature of welfare provisions. This analysis supplies a helpful frame for demonstrating women's central role as *providers* of welfare in the statutory, voluntary and private sectors and the family through their paid and unpaid labour and as *users* of welfare on behalf of themselves and their families. In contrast, while women have had some influence on the shape of welfare through provision of services and campaigning, they are still less likely than men to have formal power as welfare state *shapers*.

Whether the state is regarded as patriarchal or women-friendly, what the various feminist analyses share is an understanding of the welfare state as a profoundly gendered institution. As such it interacts with families and helps to regulate the relationship between them and the labour market in ways that help to shape gender relations.

Labour market

One starting point for feminist analysis of the labour market is thus to situate the position of women and men within it in relation to their position within the family, as mediated by the state. This is a further example of the need for social policy analysis to highlight how the public–private divide moulds women's and men's options. A long-standing debate in feminism has been between those who prioritise women's equality in the public sphere of the labour market and those who prioritise adequate recognition and support for women's responsibilities for the care of children and others in the private domestic sphere. This is one key element in what has been dubbed the 'equality vs. difference' dilemma: should women's demands be framed in terms of equality with or difference from men (Lister, 2003a)? This dilemma can be identified in the differing feminist positions taken in response to the current emphasis in most welfare states on treating lone mothers as paid workers whose caring responsibilities should be subordinated to their paid work obligations.

The other starting point for feminist analysis of the labour market is an exploration of the ways in which the labour market itself operates as a gendered institution. While feminist scholars differ in the relative weight they attach to these two perspectives, few would dispute that women's access to the labour market is shaped in part by the extent and nature of their family responsibilities. The more time that women spend on caring for children and older relatives and on doing housework, the less time they have available for paid work. By the same token, men who have women to undertake their domestic work for them are freed up to spend longer hours on paid work. Paid work offers the potential of economic rewards, independence and power in a way that unpaid work does not. This explains why many feminists argue that shifting the domestic gendered division of labour is critical to improving women's economic position, together with state policies which help both women and men combine paid work and family responsibilities.

> *Question:* Which state policies do you think are most important in helping women and men combine paid work and family responsibilities?

Furthermore, the paid work that women do in the labour market often mirrors the unpaid work they do in the home, which helps to explain why it tends to be low paid. At the same time, if men are able to earn higher wages than women, it makes economic sense for a couple to pursue a traditional gendered division of labour, thereby setting up a vicious circle.

The continued gendered pay gap, which operates to a greater or lesser extent world-wide, is one example of how the labour market operates as a gendered institution. It reflects, in part, continued occupational segregation, which means that women and men are often doing different kinds of work. Also, men still find it easier than women to climb occupational hierarchies: women both hit glass ceilings and get held back on sticky floors. Despite their increased participation in the labour market world-wide, they also often find themselves part of workplaces that are imbued with a masculinist, exclusionary ethos. In its more extreme forms, this ethos involves sexual harassment.

Concepts

The gendered lens provided by feminist analysis has shone a new light on a number of important concepts in social policy. Key examples are listed in *Box 2.9*.

Box 2.9: Feminist rethinking of important concepts in social policy

- *Work*: instead of equating work with paid work, as often still happens, feminist analysis has broadened our understanding of work to include caring, housework and also voluntary work (Irving, 2008).
- *Care*: it was something of a breakthrough to reveal that care *is* work and often very demanding work. Feminist research has demonstrated the importance of this work in both its paid and unpaid forms. It has explored the gendered processes of care and the relations involved in caring and being cared for, together with the values associated with caring (Leira and Saraceno, 2000).
- *Dependence*: in contrast to the dominant preoccupation with dependence on welfare in the public sphere, feminist analysis has explored the implications of women's economic dependence on men in the private sphere and how that has been underpinned by welfare policies. It has also revealed the unequal relationship of interdependence of which it is a part, in which men are often dependent on women for care and servicing (Lister, 2003a; see also Chapter Five).
- *Citizenship*: feminist scholarship has exposed women's traditional exclusion from full citizenship to be not accidental but a product of the gendered assumptions upon which mainstream notions of citizenship have been constructed (Hobson and Lister, 2002; Lister, 2007c; see also Chapter Seven).

- *Nation and community*: feminist theorists have highlighted how women's relationship and men's relationship to nation and community are constructed differently. Women are often treated as cultural symbols of the nation and as responsible for maintaining community cohesion. What they wear and how they behave, in both public and private spheres, are judged through the prism of nation and community (in particular ethnic community – see **Box 2.14**). An example is the enormous significance attached to Muslim women's wearing of the headscarf or veil in a number of European countries (Lister et al, 2007).
- *Time*: feminist analysis treats time as a gendered 'scarce resource alongside and interacting with status, money and power' (Bryson, 2007, p 173). It is a resource essential for undertaking different forms of work and for active citizenship. Moreover, as Valerie Bryson shows, 'the ways in which time is used, valued and understood in contemporary capitalist societies are central to the maintenance of gender inequalities in public and private life' (2008, p 185).

Anti-racism

Black and anti-racist feminists emphasise how we are all shaped by our 'race' and ethnicity as well as our gender. This means that feminist and anti-racist approaches to social policy need to be considered together. As in the case of feminism, the label 'anti-racism' represents shorthand for a variety of theoretical and political approaches. Nevertheless, they are united by their belief in racial and ethnic equality. If gender and the perspectives of women were for a long time marginalised in social policy, 'race' and the perspectives of black and minority ethnic groups were even more so. Moreover, they continue to be marginalised. Gary Craig spells this out:

> It is important to acknowledge that neglect of the issue of 'race' is not confined to social policy as *political practice*; it is shared by the *academic discipline* of social policy. It is still not uncommon for mainstream social policy texts to treat debates on 'race' and racism as marginal. This is striking considering that the social policy discipline is concerned centrally with issues of citizenship rights, welfare, equality, poverty alleviation and social engineering. This lacuna extends to the practice of social research ... [and] to social policy teaching and to the high-profile social policy journals. (2007b, pp 610-11, emphasis in the original)

Social policy (as opposed to the race relations literature dealing with social policy issues) only really started taking the issue of 'race' on board in the late 1980s and, as Craig's criticism suggests, it has done so only imperfectly. Yet the issue of 'race' is crucial to understanding the development of the welfare state and the social relations of welfare, both historically and today. Before exploring further how anti-racist perspectives illuminate our understanding of social policy and the welfare state, we need to clarify a number of key terms: 'race', racialisation, racism, multi-culturalism and ethnicity (see *Boxes 2.10–2.14*).

Key concepts used in anti-racism

Anti-racist critiques take as their starting point that 'race' and ethnicity are central categories in social policy and that they have to be deployed in order to provide an accurate and comprehensive analysis of welfare institutions. However, behind that seemingly straightforward statement is considerable disagreement about key concepts and how they should be applied, which can only be touched on here. We start with the central concept of '**race**' in *Box 2.10*.

Box 2.10: The concept of 'race'

'"Race" entails distinguishing people on the basis of physical markers, such as skin pigmentation, hair texture and facial features, and placing people into distinct categories' (Pilkington, 2003, p 2). Typically these categories are placed in a hierarchy, with white regarded as superior to black. You may have noticed that I always put the word 'race' in inverted commas. This is quite common in the literature, although less so in the US (see Ratcliffe, 2004). It is a way of saying that the notion of 'race' has no scientific basis as a classification of peoples: in other words that people cannot be divided into separate groups on the basis of genetic or physiological characteristics because there is greater genetic diversity *within* groups classified as 'races' than *between* them. Nevertheless,

> despite being void of scientific validity, the concept of 'race' retains a central position in the contemporary mind. It is still assumed by large swathes of the world's population to represent real, empirically identifiable differences between groups of its peoples ... It is a way of ordering groups hierarchically and deterministically, that is the inferiorization of certain groups is deemed to apply in all places and for all time. (Ratcliffe, 2004, p 27)

Social scientists take the position that 'race' is therefore a social construction (see Chapter Five) rather than an empirical fact. As such, it can be understood as 'the construction of a category of belonging on the basis of physical variations found among human bodies' (Lewis, 1998d, p 99).

Some social scientists argue that the critique of the concept of 'race' means that we should not use the term, because it simply gives credence to the idea that racial differences are real. However, in practice most still do use it. As Anthias and Yuval-Davis point out, 'from a sociological point of view, "race" denotes a particular way in which communal differences come to be constructed and therefore it cannot be erased from the analytical map' (1993, p 2). In a social policy context, Penketh and Ali elaborate on the point: 'the notion of "race" and racial difference has come to be an entrenched part of our culture. It may be socially constructed, but social constructions have consequences that affect real people' (1997, p 103). Thus, it is possible to use such concepts strategically, while remaining critical of them (Law, 1996).

As well as putting the word 'race' in inverted commas, social scientists use the notion of **racialisation** as a way of flagging up its socially constructed nature (see ***Box. 2.11***). The term racialisation is particularly helpful in social policy where it is used to analyse the ways in which certain social issues and problems become linked to 'race'.

Box 2.11: The concept of racialisation

The term *racialisation* can be used in a variety of ways but at its heart is the use of racial categories to differentiate or to describe. So, for example, Wright and Magasela write that in South Africa 'during the apartheid era poverty lines were racialised', with a lower poverty line for black people than white people (2007, p 12). The 2008 presidential election in the US was highly racialised. Barack Obama's candidacy and prospects were continually analysed with reference to his 'race'; and the widespread joy at his victory was in large part a reflection of the 'racial' symbolism and significance of an African-American family entering the White House, built by slaves, four decades on from the final outlawing of segregation in the US. Subsequent political debate in the US around Obama's presidency has also been clearly racialised.

Given its connections to racism (see ***Box 2.12***), racialisation cannot be a neutral process of categorisation. Williams defines it as a process by which 'a social group becomes constructed as "other" on the basis of a supposed race/ethnic/cultural difference' (1995, p 139). This 'other' is typically regarded in negative terms. This can be seen in the ways in which policy discourses are racialised. For example, in the US, debates about poverty and welfare are described as racialised, reflecting the greater risk of poverty and need for welfare among the African-American population. Because of the underlying racism, this racialisation of welfare is used simultaneously to malign African-Americans (as welfare recipients) and welfare recipients (as a racialised group). Barbara Ehrenreich writes that 'the stereotype of the welfare recipient – lazy, overweight, and endlessly fecund – had been a coded way of talking about African Americans at least since George Wallace's 1968 presidential campaign' (2002, p vii). (Note too how sexism is intermingled with this racialised stereotype, as lone mothers are the main recipients of welfare in the US.) While racialised discourse is more overt in the US than in the UK, it nevertheless exists in the latter. For instance, the problem of a lack of adequate stocks of social housing in some areas has been racialised by the identification of immigrants as the source of the problem by some white working-class residents (Garner, 2009).This has been encouraged by the racist British National Party.

Question: Can you think of other examples of the racialisation of social policy debates?

As *Box 2.11* underlines, the process of racialisation is problematic because of its association with **racism**.

Box 2.12: The concept of racism

Racism has been described as 'a messy concept, as it encompasses attitudes, behaviour and outcomes and has been conceptualized in a variety of ways' (Ahmad and Craig, 2003, p 91). Popularly it tends to be understood in terms of individual prejudice and discriminatory acts motivated by it. This view has been influential on much policy thinking but is criticised as incomplete in much of the literature. For example, Penketh and Ali maintain that 'any analysis of racism needs to go beyond the individual and cultural prejudice usually associated with the term, to recognize the structural and institutional nature of racism' (1997, p 104). This is acknowledged in the Macpherson Report on the Stephen Lawrence Inquiry into the British police investigation of the racist killing of the black teenager. The report uses the term 'institutional racism' to mean:

> The collective failure of an organisation to provide an appropriate and professional service to people because of their colour, culture or ethnic origin. It can be seen or detected in processes, attitudes and behaviour which amounts to discrimination through unwitting prejudice, ignorance, thoughtlessness and racist stereotyping which disadvantages minority ethnic people. (Macpherson,1999, para 6.34)

This definition of institutional racism is helpful in pointing to structural factors and to how 'practices may be racist in terms of their effects' (Anthias and Yuval-Davis, 1993, p 13), even if these practices are not motivated by racist prejudices. This is also sometimes referred to as indirect discrimination (Pilkington, 2003).

However, some critics argue that the notion of institutional racism should not discount the continued existence of deliberate direct discrimination.

Question: In Paris a judge ruled that it was not racist for an extreme rightwing group, which distributed food to homeless people, to provide soupe au cochon (pork soup), a traditional French dish, and to stipulate that recipients had to eat the pork soup in order to receive any other assistance. This was challenged on the grounds that it discriminated against Jews and Muslims who do not eat pork on religious grounds (cited in *The Guardian*, 3 January 2007). The judge argued that since the group had not refused to serve Jews and Muslims it could not be accused of discriminating against them. Do you agree with the judge's ruling that this was not racist?

Note how what is at stake here is a matter of religion and culture and how the Macpherson definition of institutional racism refers to culture and ethnic origin as well as colour. Tariq Modood has argued that 'colour-racism is the foundation of racism rather than the whole edifice'. Cultural-racism 'uses cultural differences to vilify or marginalise or demand cultural assimilation' (Modood, 1998, pp 171-2). It is targeted at those perceived as not trying to fit in, with Muslims the main example that Modood gives. This form of racism, expressed through prejudice and hostile treatment, has become more prevalent in recent years, particularly following the terrorist attacks of 11 September 2001 and, in Britain, 7 July 2005.

The increased prominence of cultural racism has coincided with a growing political challenge to the notion of **multi-culturalism** in a number of countries (Craig, 2008). Multi-culturalism has increasingly been regarded as a threat to social cohesion.

Box 2.13: The concept of multi-culturalism

Most societies today are multi-cultural in the sense that they are culturally diverse. Multi-cultural*ism* refers to 'a normative response to that fact' (Parekh, 2006, p 6). It is a response that cherishes this diversity, makes it central to a society's image of itself and recognises the cultural demands of minority groups. In contrast, a monoculturalist response seeks to assimilate minority cultures into the mainstream culture (Parekh, 2006). Amartya Sen makes a further distinction between genuine multi-culturalism, in which cultures mingle and are affected by each other and 'plural monoculturalism', in which they coexist 'side by side, without the twain meeting' (2006, p 157).

Culture is typically taken as the key marker of **ethnicity** (Mason, 2000).

Box 2.14: The concept of ethnicity

'Ethnicity at its most general level involves belonging to a particular group and sharing its conditions of existence' (Anthias and Yuval-Davis, 1993, p 8). In addition to culture, the key components shaping this belonging are: common language, social customs, religion, history and geographical or national origin.

The term ethnicity is often used interchangeably with 'race', including in policy documents (Culley and Demaine, 2006). However, even though processes of racialisation and racism create close links between them and in practice there can be some overlap, they are distinct concepts. Pilkington describes them as 'both categories which involve drawing boundaries between people' (2003, p 11). He represents the distinction as between boundaries drawn on the basis of physical markers ('race') and cultural markers (ethnicity). Moreover, he maintains that ethnicity involves a shared identity while 'race' does not necessarily do so. This does not mean, though, that ethnicity necessarily denotes either a dominant or a unitary identity. David Mason, for instance, points out that:

it is possible to be simultaneously English, British, and European, stressing these identities more or less strongly in different aspects of daily life. Similarly, the same person might identify as Gujerati, Indian, Hindu, East African Asian, or British depending on the situation, immediate objectives, and the responses and behaviour of others (2000, p 13).

Although social scientists generally accord the concept of ethnicity a legitimacy that 'race' lacks, there are other problems to be aware of. First, how many times have you seen the term 'ethnic group' used to describe a majority as opposed to minority ethnic group? Not very often I suspect. Moreover, it is common to refer to members of minority ethnic groups as 'ethnics'. This tendency to conflate 'ethnic' and 'minority ethnic' betrays an assumption among the majority population that only minorities have an ethnicity. It is important therefore to remember that we all – members of both majority and minority groups – have an ethnicity. This is the case even though research indicates that ethnicity is more important to the identity of minority than majority ethnic groups (Stone and Muir, 2007).

> *Question:* To which ethnic group(s) do you feel that you belong? (The quotation from Mason above might be helpful here.) How important is ethnicity to your sense of identity?

Second, the notion of ethnicity is often treated as a fixed cultural essence:

> Minority ethnic groups can be attributed a very static identity in which it is assumed that all members of the group will speak a certain language, have certain dietary habits, religious practices and marriage and family customs, for example. Some forms of multi-culturalist social policy and practice make these assumptions of uniformity about minority ethnic groups and so may fail to provide services which meet genuine needs. (Penketh and Ali, 1997, p 105)

However, ethnicity does not have to be understood that way. Critical anti-racist theorists suggest that, instead of seeing it as a rigid straitjacket, ethnicity can be used by people to construct belonging in an active way, while still drawing strength from their ethnic roots. This is an example of a strand in contemporary anti-racist theorising, influenced by postmodernism (see Chapter Three), which rejects essentialising, homogeneous constructions of 'race' and ethnicity. Instead, it argues that the way people experience ethnicity and racism is not uniform but is mediated by other elements shaping belonging such as gender and class. In particular, there is a considerable body of black feminist scholarship, which analyses the intersections between gender and 'race'/ethnicity (together with other social divisions).

Just as popular notions of 'race' and ethnicity have been problematised so have the terms '**black**' and '**white**'. A socially constructed understanding of 'race' points to how blackness and whiteness do not represent 'categories of essence but [are] defined by historical and political struggles over their meaning' (Bulmer and Solomos, 1999, p 8). With reference to the label 'black', some black activists argue that it provides a powerful political category since its claiming as a positive identity in defiance of its stigmatisation; others object to diverse non-white groups being classified under a single label. In particular some people of mixed-'race' reject a classification that denies their dual heritage. The term 'Asian' too is a label imposed on diverse ethnic groups (Sardar, 2008). In the US, shifting categorisations of the Latino-Hispanic population illustrate how black and white are not fixed distinctions (see *Box 2.15*).

> **Box 2.15: An example of how the line between 'black' and 'white' can shift: the Latino/Hispanic population in the US**
>
> In an article entitled 'Redefining "race" in North America', Philip Kretsedemas observes that 'even though anti-immigration groups have portrayed Latinos (and Mexican immigrants in particular) as a threat to white, American culture, changes in the US census have made it much easier for Latinos to identify as white' (2008, p 835). These changes mean that Latinos can now, if they so wish, identify themselves as white and Latino/Hispanic or black and Latino/Hispanic. In the 2000 Census, 48% of Latinos identified as white and only 2% as black. Kretsedemas argues that such developments mean that 'it is important to appreciate the constantly changing and contested nature' of racial categories of 'black and 'white' (2008, p 838).

In contrast to 'black', 'Whiteness remains a relatively underdiscussed and underresearched "racial" identity' (Bonnett, 1997, p 173). One consequence is that, in the same way that members of majority ethnic groups do not think of themselves as such, so white people in white-dominated societies tend to see white as 'natural' and as disconnected from processes of racialisation. However, in Britain there has been a naming of whiteness recently, which connects it to class, in two different ways. One has been in the face of what is seen as the threat to a white working class marginalised both economically and, with reference to multi-culturalism, culturally. This was epitomised in a BBC season in 2008 entitled *White*. This prompted a number of newspaper articles with titles such as 'How Britain turned its back on the white working class' (*The Observer*, 2 March 2008) and 'White, working class – and threatened with extinction' (*The Independent on Sunday*, 9 March 2008). Racist groups such as the British National Party exploit this sense of marginalisation.

The other way in which whiteness and class have been linked has been through a form of racialisation of the white working class, which locates them 'on the periphery of whiteness because of their class position' (Preston, 2007, p 14). Terms such as 'white trash' in the US and 'chav' in the UK are used to denote an inferior form of whiteness. The derogatory deployment of the word 'chav' has been described as 'middle class hatred of the white working class, pure and simple' (Hampson, 2008, p 19). Thus the label 'white' can be used to highlight *class* divisions, but in a way that identifies cultural difference rather than structural inequality as the source of these divisions (Bottero, 2009). As Kjartan Páll Sveinsson argues, in the introduction to a collection on the white working class:

> feigning white working class disadvantage as an ethnic disadvantage rather than as class disadvantage is exactly what rhetorically places this group in direct competition with minority ethnic groups. As such it does little to address the real and legitimate grievances poor white people in Britain have ... The white working classes are discriminated against on a range of different fronts, including their accent, their style ... the postcode of their homes ... But they are not discriminated against because they are white. (2009, p 6)

At the same time, the label obscures the ways in which certain white *ethnic* groups, such as Jews and the Irish in Britain, can also be negatively racialised and subjected to discrimination and stereotyping. 'Anti-Travellerism' has been identified in Ireland and England (Clark, C., 2008; McVeigh, 2008); and there is growing concern about the demonisation and persecution of Romas and other Gypsies in Europe more generally, in particular in Italy and Eastern Europe. In turn, Eastern European immigrants to Britain can be subjected to prejudice.

Having pointed to some of the complexities involved in the concepts used in anti-racist theories, we turn now to consider the contribution made by these theories to our understanding of the welfare state.

Anti-racist analyses of the welfare state

Anti-racist theorists argue that a 'racial' lens is critical to interpreting the development and nature of what are racially structured welfare states:

> A crucial element in most modern welfare states is that they have developed to a large extent in response to changing understandings and interpretations of 'race' and that they have in turn helped to shape and reshape the ways in which racial divisions are understood in the societies in which they are part. The Western European welfare states were created in part as a means of defining the continued status of their residents and citizens, in sharp contrast to the outsiders for whom access was to be limited. (Cochrane, 1993, p 11)

Ian Law identifies the legacy of imperialism and longstanding links with immigration legislation as key in the racial structuring of the British welfare state:

Regulation to exclude 'aliens', denizens (permanent settlers without British nationality) and particular racialised categories of British citizens from access to welfare benefits is evident in immigration legislation and wider social policy reforms from the Victorian period onwards ... The racialisation of the British welfare state drew on eugenic notions of the quality of the race and the nation in order to maintain imperialism ... Postwar welfare reforms and immigration legislation have continued to institutionalise racially exclusionary rules that determine eligibility for welfare benefits. (2009, p 76)

More specifically, historical analysis of the British welfare state shows:

- Residence qualifications for welfare pre-date the modern welfare state.
- Notions of nation and welfare citizenship were linked in the first half of the 20th century, with nationality written into entitlement to the benefits introduced at the beginning of that century.
- The conjoinment of welfare entitlement to immigration controls goes back to control of Jewish immigration early in the 20th century.
- The post-Second World War Beveridge Plan emphasised 'race' and nation in the context of what proved to be the sunset of the British Empire. A much-quoted observation is that 'housewives as mothers have vital work to do in ensuring the adequate continuance of the British race and British ideals in the world' (Beveridge, 1942, para 117).
- Immigration from the Caribbean was officially encouraged in the 1950s and 1960s in order to fill low paid jobs in the welfare state, especially the National Health Service in the face of labour shortages. Yet no real consideration was given to the welfare needs of these workers and their families.

In the contemporary welfare state, Shafquat Nasir argues, drawing on Williams (1989), that:

- 'Entitlement and access to provision have been, and continue to be, heavily affected by 'race' and nationality.
- Black people experience welfare agencies differently from the White/indigenous population.
- Universalism within theories underpinning welfare often results in services being inappropriate to Black people' (Nasir, 1996, p 17).

Nasir is referring to the effects of racialisation and racism and to the failure of welfare services to accommodate ethnic differences, so that the multi-cultural society of the UK is not served by genuinely multi-culturalist services. Similar criticisms are made by Craig two decades later (see ***Box 2.16***).

> ## Box 2.16: 'Race' and the contemporary British welfare state
>
> With regard to racism in the welfare state, Craig writes:
>
> > Despite the range of liberal 'community relations' initiatives and a series of race relations legislative interventions, it is clear from the range of research reported above and much besides that racism persists in all welfare sectors. The position of minorities within the health services remains that they are in general trapped in the lowest levels of the employment structure despite their large numbers; they are more likely to be criminalised by a criminal justice system which they view, with good reason, as hostile to them; they have – with some exceptions – poor outcomes in housing, education, in the mental health system and the labour market, not because of some inherent genetic inability, but because of structural barriers to their improvement and a plethora of individual acts of racism. (2007b, p 620)
>
> Craig cites a number of examples of the failure to provide genuinely multi-cultural, ethnically sensitive services:
>
> > BME [black and minority ethnic] pupils are disadvantaged systematically by the education system because of its inability to respond flexibly to different cultural contexts ...Minorities also have greatest difficulty in accessing appropriate health provision, often because of the failure of health services to respond to specific cultural needs such as for interpretation, to ethnically linked ailments such as sickle cell disorder, or by ethnically or culturally matched provision. (2008, pp 241-2)
>
> Another example is mental health care. Minority ethnic patients are disproportionately likely to be admitted to mental hospitals in England and Wales (*The Guardian*, 7 December 2005). Once there, a survey undertaken by the official Mental Health Act Commission found that 'mental health services are providing an "appalling" level of care to black and mixed race inpatients' (*Community Care*, 16-22 November 2006).
>
> Craig suggests that 'the inability of state welfare to respond to the needs of minority groups is a reflection of its failure to offer them opportunities to participate adequately in important decision-making mechanisms and shape the way in which

services are delivered' (2008, p 242). So, like women, members of minority ethnic groups are under-represented among the 'shapers' of welfare.

Lucinda Platt is another social policy analyst who has thrown light on the experiences of minority ethnic groups in the British welfare state. On the one hand she emphasises the growing diversity between minority ethnic groups, which 'can be as great as differences between minorities in aggregate and the majority' (2008, p 376; see also Pilkington, 2003). On the other hand she has documented the continued disadvantage in the labour market and above average risk of poverty experienced by minorities in aggregate compared with the majority and the discriminatory treatment they can experience in the social security system (Platt, 2007). Law concludes that 'the racialisation of migration and welfare has led to poor welfare outcomes for migrants and minority ethnic groups in the UK' (2009, p 87).

Environmentalism

Environmentalist or green philosophy (I use the terms interchangeably) differs from the other critical perspectives discussed in this chapter in that its central analytical category does not derive from divisions between people (class, gender and 'race'/ethnicity). Instead, its focus is the environment and all of humankind's relationship to it. What it shares with the other critical perspectives is its dual status as both a theoretical position and a mobilising ideology for a political movement. There is also a degree of synergy between environmentalism and the other critical perspectives (see *Box 2.17*).

Box 2.17: Links between environmentalism and the other critical perspectives

- *Eco-Marxists* (and socialists) add the destruction of the environment to their critique of capitalism and the market system (Fitzpatrick, 2001; Cahill, 2007). It is possible to identify an increasingly strong red/green perspective on the left.
- *Eco-feminists* make connections between the patriarchal subordination of women and 'man's' exploitation of nature. Some argue that 'women have a stronger physical, emotional, and spiritual connection to nature' (McHugh, 2007, p 33); others that the qualities associated with women's role as carers give them a more holistic understanding of the environment and human beings' place within it (Cahill, 2007).
- Although there is not a theoretical position explicitly identified as eco-anti-racism, some anti-racists do make links between racism and environmental

degradation, particularly in the US (Lekhi and Newell, 2006). In the British context, Maria Adebowale borrows the notion of '*environmental racism*' from the US to point to the 'links between "race" and environmental inequality' (2008, p 264).

Environmentalism emerged on the political scene during the 1970s and 1980s as an expression of growing concern about the environmental impact of economic growth and an intensified consumerism in industrialised societies. The acceleration of global warming means that it is now being taken more seriously by politicians, although environmentalists would argue still not nearly seriously enough.

From a social policy perspective, environmentalism potentially represents a direct challenge to the post-war welfare state and to dominant approaches to social policy, which have been explicitly premised on economic growth as the main means of meeting the cost of improvements in welfare. Moreover, since it has implications for all aspects of social policy, environmentalists such as Michael Cahill and Tony Fitzpatrick (2001) stress that the environment is not simply a topic that can be added on. Cahill and Fitzpatrick have, together and separately, played an important role in injecting an environmental perspective into the study of social policy in Britain and this section draws heavily on their work. It is their view that 'sustainability issues are now being seriously addressed' in the subject (Cahill and Fitzpatrick, 2001, p 470). Nevertheless, Fitzpatrick's earlier observation that 'ecologism has not achieved the kind of systematic and comprehensive influence upon the academic study of social policy which has been accomplished by feminism' (1998, p 6) still holds true: mainstream social policy thinking has not yet really risen to the challenge posed by environmentalism.

In this section, we will begin by introducing the key tenets of green thinking. We will then look at what green theory says about the state and in particular the welfare state. This leads us into green social policy, which can also be linked to the emergent concept of environmental justice.

Green thinking

Green thinking is primarily normative or value driven. It offers an ideal world different from the present one. It comes in many different guises, often dubbed weak vs. strong, light vs. dark or shallow vs. deep. John Ferris (1991) makes a distinction between 'technocentrism' (the equivalent of weak/light/shallow approaches) and 'ecocentrism' (the equivalent of strong/dark/deep). (See ***Box 2.18***.)

Box 2.18: A classification of green thinking drawing on Ferris (1991)

'*Technocentrism*' is typified by a belief that environmental problems can be sorted out by technocratic means, for example taxes that make polluters pay. It is a reformist position, which does not represent a challenge to the dominant economic or political order. It can therefore be incorporated easily within capitalism. One label given more recently to such approaches is 'environmental modernisation'. Michael Jacobs, who has promoted the notion of environmental modernisation, suggests that it could be seen as 'an application of the Third Way into the environmental field' (1999, p 29). Cahill identifies environmental or ecological modernisation as 'an increasingly influential theme' in environmental politics and one which 'represents the stance of the Labour government. Proponents of this viewpoint believe that ... the tools of industrial management can be utilized to achieve more environmentally benign economic behaviour' (Cahill, 2007, p 580). Examples include recycling, green taxes and proposals for emissions trading schemes.

'*Ecocentrism*' represents, in contrast, a fundamental challenge to the economic order premised on economic growth and consumption. It therefore rejects both capitalism and socialism.

The green critique originates in 'the idea that we live in a world where we are obliged to acknowledge that we face biophysical and social constraints. Central to the Green critique of industrialism is the idea of limits' (Ferris, 1991, p 25). Ecocentrism shares with Marxism a rejection of capitalism but for very different reasons. The main foci of this critique are:

• the capitalist urge to growth, which is the source of environmental crisis;
• use of large-scale technology, which encourages over-consumption of resources and is environmentally damaging;
• capitalism's acquisitive, consumerist, individualistic ethos, which encourages over-consumption through the creation of needs and exploitation within and between societies and of other species;
• anthropocentrism, which means that the non-human world is seen purely in terms of its instrumental use to humans rather than of being of value in its own right.

In place of the industrial, capitalist ethos, environmentalists propose the notion of '*sustainable development*'. Like most other elements of greenism, this comes in stronger and weaker forms. The most widely accepted definition is that coined by the Brundtland Commission, which popularised it: 'development which meets the needs of the present without compromising the ability of future generations to meet their own needs' (cited in Cahill, 2007, p 576). This implies:

- extreme care in use of the earth's physical resources so as to avoid their depletion;
- a stronger focus on meeting the needs that really matter (explored further in Chapter Six).

Green critiques of the welfare state

Before turning to the green critique of the welfare state, we need first to identify how green theory treats the state more generally. Despite its 'general neglect ... in much green theory and practice', Paterson et al. nevertheless identify four key elements in the 'highly critical stance' adopted by a range of green critiques of the state (2006, p 136). These are outlined in **_Box 2.19_**.

Box 2.19: Greenism and the state

According to Paterson et al. (2006), green theory identifies the following problems with the state:

- the 'spatial disjuncture' between the jurisdiction of states and the global scale of ecological problems (p 136);
- its bureaucratic and instrumental nature, in which means become ends and state institutions 'evolve to become their own ends' (p 140);
- the ways in which 'historically existing states have engendered environmental degradation as part of their normal operations and internal logic' so that the state represents an instrument of 'domination, violence and accumulation' (p 140);
- the 'thin' and disempowering model of citizenship offered by the democratic state, which reduces the citizen to the 'bearer of formal legal rights' (p 143; see also Chapter Seven).

Paterson et al. counsel against total rejection of the state on the one hand and naïve assumptions that 'the state can unproblematically realize green goals' on the other. Instead they call for a strategic green orientation in which 'green states are made by green citizens ... forcing states to change' (2006, pp 152-3). Environmentally aware social democrats, in contrast, would argue that only the state has the power and authority to impose the changes necessary to combat global-warming; such changes cannot be left to the market or to the actions of individuals, however

---

important the latter are. An example of a green intervention, which acknowledges the necessary role of the state, is the Green New Deal proposed by a group of 'new economists' (Green New Deal Group, 2008).

The more specific green critique of the welfare state applies the more general theory of the state and also has echoes of other critical perspectives (Fitzpatrick, 1998). Its main propositions are:

- The welfare state deals with the symptoms rather than causes of social problems, which lie in the very nature of industrial society.
- It is too environmentally costly in terms of its drain on resources and reliance on economic growth.
- Professionals 'disable' clients through taking over responsibility and undermining their competence and independence. They are part of a nexus of surveillance and social control functions (see also Chapter Four).
- Some services, such as medicine, are over-reliant on high levels of technology.
- Welfare is distributed and administered through large, bureaucratic organisations.
- The national welfare state represents a national rather than global response to the problem of reconciling social welfare with economic growth, thereby displacing problems onto poorer countries in the global South.

Ecological concerns about the inadequacy of the welfare state to meet contemporary needs also underpin the notion of the 'risk society', associated in particular with the work of Ulrich Beck. The implications of Beck's theory of the risk society for the welfare state are spelled out by O'Brien and Penna (see *Box 2.20*).

Box 2.20: The risk society and the welfare state

A welfare system operating within a compensatory framework, in which the central struggles revolve around shares of the cake (who gets how much) and grounds of entitlement to portions of it (why do they get it), makes sense only if the 'cake' is itself a desirable good, that is, if the acquisition of shares does indeed enhance individual and collective welfare. What happens, however, if the cake is intrinsically poisonous, if its production is the cause of individual and collective sickness and illness and if possession of its portions is life-threatening rather than life-enhancing? What if the socio-economic system, which ostensibly 'guarantees' welfare, is a system for the production and distribution of hazards and risks, rather than a system for the production

> and distribution of wealth and welfare? ... Contemporary society is a 'risk society' to the extent that the production, displacement and mediation of ecological hazard increasingly drives technological innovation, market development, political regulation and capital investment as well as cultural perception and social organisation. (O'Brien and Penna, 1998, pp 174-5)

Fitzpatrick (1998, p 11) argues that the 'principles and institutions of welfare', which constitute the welfare state, represent a 'productivist model' based on three interrelated elements:

- economic growth;
- an employment ethic which values wage labour over all other forms of human activity;
- an 'accumulative impulse' which measures welfare in narrow materialist terms.

In contrast, greenism offers an 'ecological model' of welfare (Fitzpatrick, 1998, pp 16-22), based on:

- Sustainable growth.
- Ecologically oriented indicators of development and welfare. Such indicators widen understanding of economic progress to embrace quality of life, which 'concerns the relationship between the individual, society and the environment' (Cahill, 1999, p 99). For instance, the new economics foundation has developed an Index of Sustainable Economic Welfare, which measures well-being, in place of Gross Domestic Product.
- A work ethic, which does not confuse work with employment. Instead, it values, through social policies, forms of human activity other than waged work, most notably caring, community and voluntary work. A key policy demand of Green political parties is a basic or citizen's income, which provides each individual with an unconditional income so that they can choose which kinds of activities they pursue rather than be required to undertake or seek paid work.
- An approach that is less reliant on a centralised state to administer welfare in a top-down manner. Instead, within a regulatory framework provided by the state, greens favour decentralised, localised forms of welfare, which are undertaken as far as possible on a self-help or mutual aid basis. They promote a 'social economy' through alternative forms of welfare such as:
  – LETS (local exchange trading systems), which are 'a non-profit making form of systematic barter, where goods and services are traded without the need for money' (Fitzpatrick, 1999, p 158);

- time banks, in which time represents the currency exchanged and everyone's time is worth the same amount (see nef, 2008);
- credit unions, which encourage savings and provide loans, particularly among people on low incomes.

According to Fitzpatrick, green social policies such as these look to 'the emergence of a newly empowered "welfare citizen"' (2003, p 322). Indeed, environmentalism has given rise to the more general notion of 'ecological citizenship (discussed in Chapter Seven). More fundamentally still, the ecological model requires 'self-actualization …: the necessity of changes in lifestyle expectations, values, and for some, consciousness itself', as part of 'a post-materialist insistence upon divorcing our sense of personal worth from our standard of living' (Fitzpatrick, 1998, p 21).

Fitzpatrick himself, while sympathetic to this stance, also brings to it the eye of critical social policy (1998, 2003). In particular, he argues that post-materialism cannot be divorced from a more materialist concern with social justice (see Chapter Eight), if it is not to reinforce existing socioeconomic inequalities. He argues that 'divisions between rich and poor (both nations and individuals) make it clear that environmental crises are more the product of a socioeconomic system biased towards inequalities rather than the product of humanity per se' (2003, p 322). This points to the emergent concept of 'environmental justice' (outlined in ***Box 2.21***).

Box 2.21: The concept of environmental justice

The notion of 'environmental justice' is more strongly developed in the US, than Britain, in response to evidence 'that a majority of environmentally polluting plants are close to deprived neighbourhoods' (Cahill, 2007, p 592). The racialised distribution of deprivation in the US resulted in the identification of 'environmental racism', which in turn prompted an environmental justice movement with roots in the earlier civil rights movement (Lekhi and Newell, 2006).

In Britain, the idea of environmental justice marries environmental concerns with the concept of social justice (see Chapter Eight). In a volume on social justice, published by the left-of-centre think tank, the Institute for Public Policy Research, Foley et al argue that:

> The connection between environmental protection and distributive justice should underpin our modern day understanding of sustainable development. It has become more widely recognised that the poor tend to suffer disproportionately from environmental degradation and indeed

that social inequalities are among the very causes of environmental harm (2005, p 178; see also Adebowale, 2008).

Foley et al identify the global dimension of environmental injustice. Poorer nations pay the environmental price for richer nations' massive carbon footprints (see also **Box 8.10**). While they acknowledge that, in practice, environmental and pro-poor social justice priorities can sometimes be in conflict, their 'core argument is that environmental sustainability is compatible with social justice; indeed, in many instances it is a necessary condition to achieve wider social justice objectives' (Foley et al, 2005, p 179). This is for two main reasons:

- Over the longer term, social justice requires conservation by the present generation in order for there to be sufficient resources available to ensure social justice for future generations.
- In the shorter term, social justice requires the fair distribution of environmental as well as material goods.

This leads to the enunciation of three principles of environmental justice:

1 'The precondition principle' – the protection or renewal of any natural resource 'which is a precondition for human life and wellbeing';
2 'The distributive principle' – the distribution of environmental 'goods' and 'bads' according to 'principles of social justice';
3 'The just impact principle' – environmental policies should, insofar as is possible, be progressive in their impact, which means, in particular, that they should not harm low income groups (Foley et al, 2005, pp 180-1).

Some other articulations of environmental justice place greater emphasis on rights (which are also an element of ecological citizenship). So, for instance, Adebowale identifies, as a main component of environmental justice, 'the right of all to a fair environment' (2008, p 256) and Brenda Boardman argues that another principle of environmental justice is that 'communities and individuals should have a right to know and the ability to respond to distributed environmental hazards' (1999, p 4).

The new economics foundation has introduced the term 'sustainable social justice'. It argues that this will require a transformation of the welfare system and 'a new social settlement that depends less on the market economy and instead values and nurtures two other economies – the resources of people and the planet' (Coote and Franklin, 2009, p 1). This new social settlement will, among other things, 'promote well-being for all, putting equality at the heart of social policy' (2009, p 1, see also Chapters Six and Eight).

Question: Can you think of some specific examples of environmental injustice?

Fitzpatrick (1998) concludes that social policies are likely to have to draw on both the 'productivist' and 'ecological' models, which he identifies, for the foreseeable future. In Britain (and more widely) the productivist model continues to dominate. Nevertheless, Cahill suggests that 'the commitment to sustainable development at both local and central government level means that the debate is now beginning to concern itself with the "how" rather than the "why" of sustainability' (2007, p 594). He also observes that 'the discourse around "quality of life" does have the potential to link environmental issues and social policy' (2007, p 594). This discourse, often couched in the language of well-being (see Chapter Six), is increasingly prominent in political debate.

> **Question:** Can you list some examples of green social policies
> – either existing or proposed?

Summary

This chapter has discussed four critical perspectives, which combine analytical and political critique of dominant political ideologies. These are:

- *Marxism* – key analytical categories are class and the economic relations of production. Marxists regard the welfare state as a contradictory institution: promoting capitalism but also protecting the working class from the full force of capitalism's harsh impact.
- *Feminism* – the key analytical category for the various strands of feminism is gender. Feminist social policy provides a critical gendered lens for understanding the family, state and labour market and for re-thinking a number of important concepts in social policy.
- *Anti-racism* – key concepts used in anti-racist social policy analysis are 'race', 'racialisation', 'racism', 'multi-culturalism' and 'ethnicity'. Anti-racist analyses demonstrate the ways in which the development and current operation of the welfare state are shaped by processes of racialisation.
- *Environmentalism* – the key analytical category is the environment. Green thinking comes in various guises, some of which represent a fundamental challenge to traditional social policy. Green approaches tend to share a critical approach to the centralised welfare state and to favour more local, mutual forms of welfare, which acknowledge the value of forms of work other than just paid employment.

The notions of 'environmental justice' and well-being represent potential links between environmentalism and social policy.

Further reading

Williams (1989) still provides the best introduction to critical perspectives, grounded in analyses of class, gender and 'race', even though some of the details are now dated. The most comprehensive Marxist account of social policy can be found in **Ferguson et al (2002)**. **Gough (2000)** reflects on various issues of importance to social policy from a Marxist perspective. The section on feminism(s) draws on **Lister (2000)**. **Pascall (1997)** and **Charles (2000)** are good (albeit rather dated) examples of feminist social policy analysis. **Hobson et al (2002)** explore a number of key concepts from a feminist perspective. **Bryson (1999)** links feminist theories with policy debates. Three texts, which combine anti-racist theory and policy analysis, are **Law (1996)**, **Pilkington (2003)** and **Ratcliffe (2004)**. More up-to-date are two shorter contributions by **Craig (2007b, 2008)**. As already mentioned, **Cahill and Fitzpatrick** together **(2001)** and separately **(Cahill, 2001, 2007, 2008; Fitzpatrick, 1998, 2003, 2011)** provide useful introductions to green social policy. **Huby (1998)** is described as 'essential reading' by **Cahill (2008)**. **Coote and Franklin (2009)** offer a new approach, which they dub 'green well fair'.

Part Two

Theoretical perspectives as an analytical tool

Post-Fordism and postmodernism

The theoretical perspectives explored in this and the following two chapters are essentially analytical frameworks, which social policy has drawn upon in order to make sense of society and of policy interventions. Unlike those discussed in the previous two chapters, these perspectives are not deployed in the political arena by governments or social movements, even if their analyses may, in some instances, be influenced by or reflect them. Returning to the distinction made by O'Brien and Penna (1998), outlined in the Introduction, they represent 'social' rather than 'normative' theories, that is they are explanatory and analytical rather than prescriptive.

The common prefix of 'post' reflects the ways in which the two theoretical perspectives of post-Fordism and postmodernism work with a shared analysis of societal change. Their respective foci complement each other: post-Fordism offers a theory of change that focuses on the economy and the state in late-capitalism; postmodernism is more concerned with cultural and social change. They share an interest in differentiation and diversity as opposed to uniformity.

However, a key difference between them derives from post-Fordism's roots in contemporary Marxism: like Marxism it represents a materialist approach, grounded in the economic relations of production and focusing almost exclusively on class divisions. Post-Fordism draws in part on neo-Marxist theories of the state. Also, like Marxism, it purports to provide a comprehensive account of economic and social change. In contrast, postmodernism can be understood as the very opposite: a shift in focus from material things to the way in which we talk about and construct these things, that is words and discourses. It also, as we will see, rejects the kind of overarching explanations offered by post-Fordism (and Marxism). Nevertheless, much of post-Fordism's analysis of the political economy chimes with postmodernist concerns and it is therefore not surprising that social policy analysis often brackets them together. In some ways, post-Fordism can be understood as a bridge between Marxism (discussed in Chapter Two) and postmodernism. It is a bridge crossed by some theorists who draw on both Marxist and postmodernist thinking, despite the fundamental differences between the two (see **Box 3.7**).

Post-Fordism

Post-Fordist theory developed in the last two decades of the 20th century as an attempt to make sense of changes in advanced capitalist societies: what some on the political left called 'New Times' (Hall and Jacques, 1989). There are a number of different approaches that bear the label of post-Fordism (see Amin, 1994). Bob Jessop's work has been particularly influential among welfare state theorists and it is his account of the basic tenets of post-Fordism and its implications for the welfare state that I outline here. The two key economic trends driving post-Fordism are changes in the labour production process and economic globalisation.

Changes in the labour production process are what give post-Fordism its name. The argument is that we have seen a shift from a Fordist mode of production (which takes its name from the motorcar manufacturer Henry Ford and which was at its height in the mid-20th century), to a post-Fordist mode. The key elements of each are summed up in **Box 3.1**.

Box 3.1: The shift from Fordist to post-Fordist modes of production

The Fordist mode of production was characterised by:

- the centrality of manufacturing industry;
- assembly line production of standardised products for mass consumption;
- centralised organisation;
- a homogeneous manual work force.

It has been largely replaced by a post-Fordist mode characterised by:

- the increased significance of the service sector and a decline of manufacturing industry;
- the flexible production of customised products – niche marketing for segmented consumption;
- decentralised organisation;
- a two-tier labour force in which the skilled 'core' enjoys decent pay and working conditions together with a degree of security and the unskilled or semi-skilled periphery suffer low pay, few employment rights and insecurity.

Economic globalisation provides the wider economic context for these changes. The globalisation of capital markets and of trading relations together with the rise of new technologies mean that nation states have less power to regulate their own economies. This, Jessop (1994a, pp 264–6) argues, is leading to the 'hollowing out' of states as they lose much of their former power in both the economic and social spheres, although the extent of this diminution of power is disputed.

A shift towards a post-Fordist welfare state

The transition from the Fordist to post-Fordist economy is mirrored in an ongoing shift in the form taken by the welfare state (which, as in Marxism, is understood as functional to the needs of capital): typically from what Jessop (1994a, 1994b, 2000) terms the Keynesian welfare national state (KWNS) to an incipient Schumpeterian workfare post-national regime (SWPR).[1]

The KWNS was marked by a commitment to full employment promoted by demand-side economic policies, which aimed at ensuring sufficient jobs, within relatively closed economies. It was associated with strong trade unions and top-down corporatist modes of government, which incorporated trade union and business leaders into the economic policy-making process. The commitment to full employment was complemented by redistributive social policies, which were aimed at providing security against risks such as unemployment and at minimising poverty and inequality.

In the SWPR, social policy is subordinated to economic competitiveness and the requirements of the international market in a more open global economy. Rather than promising security (however imperfect), as a bulwark against the market, social policy is increasingly oriented towards reinforcing the disciplines of the market. In particular, social security policies are geared more towards moving people into paid work than guaranteeing security – hence the 'workfare' in the SWPR. 'Activation' of unemployed and workless people is a watchword of policy. Labour market flexibility is promoted through supply-side economic policies, which are designed to improve the supply of labour, rather than expand demand, and therefore the number of jobs, in the economy. Education and training policies, aimed at improving skills, play a key role.

The KWNS and SWPR represent ideal types, in which the contrasts between the two are deliberately emphasised; in many cases, as Jessop (1994b, p 35) acknowledges, 'the contrast will be less marked' in practice. (Indeed, the same is true of the shift from the Fordist to post-Fordist economy – just take a look at local high streets, which increasingly look the same, where small local shops and cafés have been replaced by larger chain outfits.) Moreover, there is no single route to post-Fordist welfare, and just as the KWNS took different forms in different countries, so does the SWPR. The most dominant of these forms is the neo-liberal (Fitzpatrick, 2001).

Some commentators have also warned that the labour market polarisation between core and periphery, associated with a neo-liberal post-Fordist economy, could accelerate a transition to a two tier welfare state:

> At worst it may lead to a wholesale residualisation of state welfare, as the securely employed middle classes and the skilled 'core' of the working class defect from public welfare, leaving the state to provide residual welfare services for an excluded minority at the least possible cost to a majority who are now sponsors but not users of these public services. (Pierson, 1994, p 101)

Peter Taylor-Gooby, in a critical account of post-Fordism, sums up this 'new welfare settlement' as follows:

> Since full employment, redistribution and expensive universal services are no longer seen as feasible, the new welfare can only justify social spending as investment in human capital and as the enhancement of individual opportunities. Welfare states are all driven in the same direction by the imperatives of international competition. (1997, p 171)

> ***Question:*** Make a list of current social policies, in the welfare state in which you live, that could be said to illustrate the characteristics of the SWPR outlined here.

The social policy literature highlights a number of weaknesses in post-Fordism as a theory of welfare state change. With its explanatory emphasis on structural change in the economy and on technological change, post-Fordism has been criticised for its 'economically and technologically deterministic' account of the welfare state (Rodger, 2000, p 26). As such, it pays little regard to individual and collective agency. Colin Hay describes it as 'a rather agentless process without a subject' (2004, p 44). Whereas Marxist accounts of the welfare state have at least worked with a theory of class struggle, post-Fordist analysis tends to downplay the role of struggle (including those of social movements) in shaping contemporary welfare states (Carter and Rayner, 1996; Loader, 1998). A related criticism refers to its failure to account for 'the significance of social relations other than class

… [which] is particularly serious for any study of the welfare state … for it is in this area that the social relations not only of class, but of gender and "race" – not to mention age, disability and sexuality – are most apparent' (Williams, 1994, p 50).

New forms of welfare state delivery

The account of the shift to the SWPR focuses on the goals of the welfare state and its relationship to the economy and the labour market. Another strand of post–Fordist welfare state theory is more concerned with *how* welfare is organised and delivered. Williams (1994, p. 53) dubs this the 'radical technological approach'. From this perspective, the key characteristics of the application of the Fordist model to the welfare state were: standardisation in the name of universality; centralisation and top-down bureaucracy; hierarchy; and 'the remoteness of services to users' (Williams, 1994, p 54). In the education field, for example, Stephen J. Ball suggests that 'the provision of schooling in the UK has begun to resemble a post–Fordist economy of education in so far as educational institutions are moving away from mass production and mass markets (comprehensivism) to niche marketing and "flexible specialisation" (selection, specialisation and privatisation)' (1998, p 200). Again, however, the contrast can be overstated. For instance, how far the KWNS was Fordist *in form* is disputed. Clarke and Newman, for instance, 'are not persuaded that the delivery of *universalist* welfare services can be constructed as an equivalent to *mass* consumption. Such services involved the elaborate construction of complex forms of differentiation and categorisation of users, needs and "treatments"' (1997, p 24, emphasis in original).

In a discussion of the positive potential of post–Fordism for the welfare state, Williams cites the work of Robin Murray who:

> suggests that a socially valued, decentralised and equitable, democratic, and user-led public service could be possible through the development of some of the elements of post–Fordist methods of management and production – an open system of organisation, a skilled and cohesive labour force, decentralised autonomous working groups, accessible methods of information gathering, processing and reporting. (Williams, 1994, p 54)

Williams also draws here on Paul Hoggett's work. Subsequently, with Simon Thompson, Hoggett has sketched 'a radical vision of a welfare society'. They argue that 'if a system of governance is to respond effectively to the diversity of human requirements, individuals and groups must have real power to articulate and define their needs and determine the manner in which they will be met' (Hoggett and Thompson, 1998, p 237).

These formulations could be said to represent an idealised version of how post-Fordism welfare *might* look. The reality in Britain is rather different, reflecting post-Fordism's neo-liberal inflection, even though government ministers use a similar language to describe it. 'Diversity', 'empowerment' and 'personalisation' are among the buzz words that pepper New Labour ministerial speeches and documents about the welfare state. Some examples are set out in *Box 3.2*.

> ## Box 3.2: Examples of the use of a post-Fordist discourse by the New Labour government
>
> A fundamental shift from a 20th century welfare state with services largely collective, uniform and passive ... to a 21st century opportunity society with services which are personal, diverse and active. (Blair, 2004)
>
> Personalisation is crucial to the effectiveness of public services and tackling social exclusion, particularly among the most disadvantaged. People rightly expect services to be tailored to their own needs and circumstances. (Written answers, *House of Commons Hansard*, 31 January 2007, col 382W)
>
> This chapter sets out our intention to devolve power in welfare to allow us to draw on the expertise of the providers of employment support, on local communities and individuals ... This White Paper confirms our intention to ... develop a single employment programme which meets the needs of job seekers and others with a more personalised support path ... This White Paper also confirms our intention to devolve power to individuals, to allow them to design services that fit their needs, not the needs of the system ... This new focus on an empowering welfare state will mean that we can deliver the support that people need more effectively and efficiently ... And giving control to individuals will help them to move quickly on the path to independence and, where this is right for them, work. (Department for Work and Pensions, 2008, p 45)
>
> Some groups in the Jobseeker's Allowance regime need more personalised support: increased flexibility to some groups on Jobseeker's Allowance would target those most at risk and move more people back into work more quickly, cutting benefit dependency at its root. (Department for Work and Pensions, 2008, p 72)

Question: What are the specific ways in which these quotations exemplify a post-Fordist approach to the welfare state?

Post-Fordism is not a label that is used in political debate but it nevertheless helps us to make sense of both the kind of rhetoric quoted in **Box 3.2** and actual policy developments. The quotations from the welfare reform White Paper in **Box 3.2** refer to two key areas of policy where developments can be interpreted in a post-Fordist framework: labour market activation and support for disabled people.

Individualised case management through the use of personal advisers has been central to New Labour's New Deal welfare-to-work programmes. Mark Considine has analysed this approach in the Australian context with reference to post-Fordism. Case management provides 'increased scope for entrepreneurial behaviours by officials, and greater discretion in the treatment of clients' (Considine, 1999, p 186). In response, clients are expected to share responsibility: they are 'called upon to help produce their own programme effects, rather than being consumers of pre-existing, or "finished" services' (Considine, 1999, p 187). Considine's research into the Australian employment assistance programme appears to confirm 'a number of important aspects of the post-Fordist era'. In particular, 'all officials record higher levels of discretion in relation to clients than expected from traditional universal systems of registration and referral' (1999, p 199).

The idea of personalisation has been promoted most explicitly with regard to social care and the support of disabled people. It has taken its most concrete form in individual budgets: 'the allocation of a sum of money to eligible individuals for them to decide to spend as they wish on a "package of support"' (Beresford, 2008, p 9). Peter Beresford spells out contrasting perspectives on personalisation, which could be said to represent post-Fordist welfare in its idealist and neo-liberal forms (see **Box 3.3**).

Box 3.3: Peter Beresford on personalisation in social care

On the optimistic side, there are those who believe that, given the freedom to spend their individual budgets as they wish, service users will gain a new freedom, selecting their support from an ever-widening menu of possibilities. Skilled independent brokers will be available to help service users to plan and organise the package of support that they want in order to live their lives to the full. We may even enter a new era of social care where the consumer becomes king, able to pull down a much broader and more imaginative menu of support ... with state aid. (Beresford, 2008, p 11)

> In contrast, 'those with less faith in the rhetoric of personalisation fear that there may merely be a process of rebadging where the language of consumerism and control does little more than overlay arrangements that remain essentially the same' (Beresford, 2008, p 12). 'One of the ironies of personalisation is that, while its mantra has been "involving service users" and increasing service user "choice and control", service users and their organisations generally feel they have had little say in shaping or development' (2008, p 10).

In other words, the neo-liberal post-Fordist rhetoric of individual control, choice and empowerment does not necessarily translate into genuine power for service users. Nor does it resolve the tensions that continue to exist between diversity and standardisation and top-down control and decentralisation (Needham, 2008, p 191). Catherine Needham sees personalisation as an expression of the 'choice agenda' in the welfare state (2008, p 191). While she concludes that it is 'premature to draw conclusions about the impact of choice as a policy mechanism ... more conclusive is the triumph of choice as an idea. There is currently no major political party leader that does not call for services to be more responsive to individual users' (Needham, 2008, p 192).

The emphasis on personalisation and choice in welfare is often justified with reference to changing consumption patterns and expectations. As *Box 3.1* suggests, Post-Fordism is applied to the analysis of consumption as well as of production. Indeed, consumption takes centre stage over production, with implications for those without the money to participate fully in the post-Fordist consumer economy and society (Rodger, 2000; see *Box 3.4.*).

Box 3.4: Zygmunt Bauman on poverty in the consumer society

> In a consumer society, a 'normal life' is the life of consumers, preoccupied with making their choices among the panoply of publicly displayed opportunities for pleasurable sensations and lively experiences. A 'happy life' is defined by catching many opportunities ... As in all other kinds of society, the poor of a consumer society are people with no access to a normal life, let alone to a happy one. In a consumer society however, having no access to a happy or merely a normal life means to be consumers *manquées*, or flawed consumers. And so the poor of a consumer society are socially defined, and self-defined, first and foremost as blemished, defective, faulty and deficient – in other words, inadequate – consumers. (Bauman, 2005, p 38)

The Fordist approach to consumption was epitomised in Henry Ford's famous dictum that 'you can have any colour car that you want, so long as it is black'. Today, consumers expect to be able to choose from a wide range of colours and accessories. Alan Warde makes the link with the welfare state: the post-Fordist scenario 'presupposes a type of consumer who cannot possibly derive satisfaction from universally provided, collectively financed and state-allocated services' (1994, p 223). This is where 'the demanding, sceptical, citizen-consumer' (Department for Social Security, 1998, p 16), mentioned in the Introduction, comes in. The shift to new cultures of consumption also provides one of the links made in the literature between post-Fordism and postmodernism, to which we will now turn.

Postmodernism

Perhaps the best starting point for trying to understand postmodernism is to consider what is meant by modernity and modernism. Modernity refers to a historical period and modernism to a way of thinking, which originated in the 18th century Enlightenment. It is a way of thinking that is characterised by a belief in: reason, rationality, order, science, progress, and the ability to achieve gradual improvement in human welfare as well as human emancipation from, for instance, poverty and ignorance, through the harnessing of production and technology. In other words, a belief that human beings can consciously change their conditions for the better is at the core of the modernist philosophy. Modernism developed during an age of grand theories such as Marxism, and political struggles were typically directed at economic inequalities of class in an attempt to achieve the redistribution of economic resources and power.

Postmodernity and postmodernism represent a paradigm shift in which postmodernity represents the condition or state of the world and postmodernism a way of thinking about and understanding it. As a condition, postmodernity is typically characterised as one of flux, diversity, fragmentation and lack of certainty. It is associated with the post-Fordist economy and the rise of non-class forms of politics based on identity. (It should be noted, however, that some theorists, such as Anthony Giddens, prefer the term 'late modernity'.)

As a way of thinking, it is not possible to identify a single postmodernist position. Like the condition it describes, it is characterised by a diversity of positions and thinkers. Of these, Michel Foucault[2] is probably the most influential in social policy (and we will discuss his work in greater depth in Chapter Four). We will first consider a number of key features of postmodernism, before explaining how it treats the state. We will end by drawing attention to some of the debates that postmodernism has generated within social policy.

Key features of postmodernism

Discourse

As explained in the introduction to this chapter, postmodernism represents a break with the materialist analysis of Marxism and post-Fordism. It shifts the analytical focus from 'things' to 'words' (Barrett, 1992, p 201). In other words, instead of analysing facts in the material world such as sex discrimination or poverty, it is more interested in how such facts are represented and constituted in language and discourse, which creates frameworks of meaning. 'At its most fundamental, postmodernism asks questions about the way we see the world and denies that something called reality actually exists in a form that can be directly and simply observed' (Carter, 1998b, p 7). This does not mean denial of the existence of the material world. Instead, postmodernism argues that the material world does not have meaning outside the system of rules and conventions or 'discourse' which gives it meaning. So, for example, if you take a cricket bat, outside the discourse of cricket it is simply a shaped piece of wood with a handle.

The significance of discourse lies also in its link to power. Certain discourses have more power than others in shaping how we see the world. So, for example, the dominant discourse of 'welfare dependency' constructs social security claimants as passive and lazy. Such a discourse is likely to create unsympathetic attitudes among the wider population and set up resistance to raising benefit levels. This is reinforced by a parallel discourse of 'hard working families', which implies only those in paid work are worthy of support. The example underlines how discourses are bound up with material practices, so that a postmodernist discourse approach does not necessarily have to be divorced from material needs. One of postmodernism's tasks is to deconstruct discourses in order to lay bare their assumptions and internal contradictions. This can also mean revealing how the discourses of excluded groups have been marginalised or effaced. So, to pursue the example of welfare dependency: some feminists and disability activists would inject a counter-discourse of inter-dependence in order to challenge the construction of lone mothers and disabled people as passive dependants. (See also Chapter Five.) Similarly the discourse of 'hard work', which ignores unpaid care and voluntary/community work (see the discussion of feminism in Chapter Two), reinforces the construction of benefit claimants as passive dependants.

Question: Can you think of other dominant social policy discourses that are likely to have an adverse impact on the material conditions of particular marginalised groups?

From the universal to the particular

Another critical distinguishing feature of postmodernism is its rejection of all 'meta-narratives' (grand theories or big stories) and claims to truth. In other words, postmodernism rejects any theory or account of change that attempts to explain everything within one totalising framework or to establish universal causes across societies and historical periods. Examples of such 'meta-narratives' are Marxism or traditional strands of feminism, which identify capitalism or patriarchy as fundamental causes of exploitation and oppression. This means what is often referred to as 'the death of history' – the idea of linear progress over time. At the same time, postmodernism does not believe that experts can shape 'progress' through the kind of social engineering typified by the gradualist strand of democratic socialism associated with Fabianism in the UK (see Chapter One). All attempts at building 'the good society' (something that many in the field of social policy would like to think that their work contributes to) are thus dismissed as doomed to failure.

Instead of grand universalising theories and assumptions about ubiquitous social progress, postmodernism focuses on the need to understand social phenomena in the context of specific times and places. Thus, it also rejects the universalism of modernity in favour of the particular and contingent, which is another way of saying that nothing exists separate from its particular context. So, for example, postmodernism does not believe that it is possible to appeal to universal ideals such as equality, based on the idea that we should all be treated the same as human beings. This is because we are different kinds of human beings, differentiated by, for instance, gender, ethnicity and age and also shaped by particular cultural settings.

This preoccupation with what divides us rather than with what unites us is another of the hallmarks of postmodernist analysis. Like post-Fordism, it emphasises diversity, differentiation and fragmentation. In doing so, it also renounces dualist binary thinking. Such thinking typically divides the world into either/ors with one side of the binary divide disconnected from and superior to the other – for example, mind/body, male/female. Instead postmodernism recognises the multiplicity of differences that crosscut and construct each other. Difference is thus seen as plural, fluid and relational rather than oppositional and fixed. One side of the binary divide takes its meaning from the other, rather like the yin–yang symbol in Eastern thought. So, at its simplest, black has no meaning without white.

Identities and subjectivities

This way of thinking has implications too for understanding identity and the nature of the welfare subject, as mentioned in the Introduction. Gail Lewis makes the link in a social policy context:

> Conceptualizing welfare through the lens of difference makes it clear that it is equally important to dismantle the notion of a universal subject who stands above the particularities of social differences and instead conceive the population of welfare users as *all* equally constituted through particularity and difference. In this way, even the middle-class, white, English, Protestant, nuclear family that is currently positioned as the model welfare subject is incorporated as one kind of particularity reflecting difference of social condition. Instead of those defined through difference being hierarchically positioned in relation to an apparently transcendent (and normative) universal, social policy's project will be reconceived as one of how to promote social justice for a highly fragmented population of users and recipients. In this approach difference itself becomes the universal condition. (Lewis, 2003, p 106, emphasis in original)

For some feminists, postmodernism represents 'a natural ally' and 'provides a basis for avoiding the tendency to construct theory that generalizes from the experiences of Western, white, middle-class women' (Nicholson, 1990, p 5). 'Postmodernist feminist theory encourages a political practice, which recognizes that the diversity of women's needs and experiences means that no single solution, on issues like child care, social security, and housing, can be adequate for all' (Fraser and Nicholson, 1990, p 35). Yet there are also fears that postmodernism risks erasing the categories of 'women' and 'gender' altogether, thereby undermining feminist struggles.

Postmodernism does not simply emphasise the differences between people. It also questions the very notion of a universal, essential subject with a single, fixed identity. Instead, the individual is made up of multiple identities, the relative dominance of which shift according to context. 'The postmodern self is multi-faceted and collaged from a person's multiple locations and attributes ... chosen by the wearer rather than imposed by the sociologist or policy planner' (Carter, 1998b, p 8).

In its strongest form, postmodernism would argue that our idea of ourselves as autonomous individuals with a sense of our own identities is nothing more than an illusion. There is no innate self; everything is socially produced or constructed (see Chapter Five). There is no individual agent even. This can be problematic from the point of view of political movements, if there is no individual agent to take political action in consort with others with whom they identify. However, as we shall see, postmodernism comes in weaker as well as stronger forms. Thus, Fawcett and Featherstone argue that 'the notion of a core self does not have to be rejected, merely reformulated. Accordingly, we can be seen as having a shifting core that continually changes in relation to others' (1998, pp 77–8). This is illustrated by the examples in **Box 3.5**, which also throw light on how identities can be imposed as well as chosen.

Box 3.5: Multiple identities

In a 'Manhattan Muslim's tale', written shortly after 9/11, Anika Rahman, a lawyer, explains:

> I am so used to thinking about myself as a New Yorker that it took me a few days to begin to see myself as a stranger might: a Muslim woman, an outsider, perhaps an enemy of the city. Before last week, I had thought of myself as a lawyer, a feminist, a wife, a sister, a friend, a woman on the street. Now I begin to see myself as a brown woman who bears a vague resemblance to the images of terrorists we see on television and in the newspapers ... As I become identified as someone outside the New York community, I feel myself losing the power to define myself and losing that wonderful sense of belonging to this city. (*The Guardian*, 20 September 2001).

In his autobiography, Barack Obama writes 'My identity might begin with the fact of my race, but it didn't, couldn't, end there' (2007, p 111).

In a letter to *The Guardian*, Dr Frances Bell questioned the use of the label 'pensioners'. She asked: 'What defines the moment when a person changes into a pensioner? Currently I think of myself as a person. An aunt, a scientist, a writer, a voluntary worker, a participant in cultural events and so on. Yes, I'm retired and receiving a pension, but I prefer any other label to the P-word.' (7 April 2006).

Question: What identities describe how you think about yourself? Are some more dominant in some contexts than others? Are there any identities that you feel others impose upon you?

The examples in ***Box 3.5*** also serve as a reminder that it is not just postmodernists who talk about multiple identities. The Nobel Prize-winning economist, Amartya Sen, for instance, has written a book called *Identity and Violence* (2006). In it he criticises the tendency to pigeon-hole people according to a single identity because, he argues, such labels can, in extreme cases, promote violence and bitter division. In Rwanda, for instance, the identification of people as either Hutus or Tutsis denied all the other aspects of their identities in the pursuit of bitter and violent conflict. Noorjehan Barmania, writing in *The Guardian*, cites Sen in support of her own resistance to such pigeon-holing. She describes herself as 'a South African, a Londoner, an Asian, a quantity surveyor, a writer, a feminist and Muslim. Not one of these identities is all-consuming. And there are a great many Muslims like me' (14 December 2007). Nevertheless, increasingly, in the West, the politicisation of Muslim identity means that those who follow Islam are seen as nothing but Muslims regardless of how they see themselves. As the journalist Gary Younge observes in a collection on Muslim identities in Britain, 'It is up to Muslims how much prominence they wish to give to this identity. They do not choose how much prominence others wish to assign it' (2005, p 32). This can be particularly problematic for women struggling against oppression justified in the name of cultural difference, when they are expected to subordinate their identities as women to their cultural or religious identities (Gupta, 2003b).

Identity has been one area in which it is possible to discern the influence of postmodernist thinking on social policy. ***Box 3.6*** contains two examples, both of which engage with postmodernism in a critical way.

Box 3.6: Examples of postmodernism's influence on thinking about identity in social policy

The aim of the argument here has been to show that aspects of postmodern theory can be utilised in the analysis of social policy without necessarily abandoning a commitment to understanding structural inequalities. The 'regulation of the poorest groups' is not only material but also involves a discursive regulation which is inscribed with categories of identity. This is particularly relevant when analysing appeals to difference and 'identity politics' found in 'new social welfare movements'. On what basis do such movements appeal to identity and how are these identities expressed as 'interests'? How can identities become the basis of political agency? (Taylor, 1998, p 348) (See also Chapter Nine.)

[This article] aims to show how a social relations approach to identity and welfare subjectivities ... has been integral to opening up the discipline of

> social policy ... The principal concern for analysis has been to deconstruct subordinated identities in order to redress an imbalance in the focus on welfare users as problematic by virtue of their 'abnormal' identities and to explain the occurrence and impact of 'bottom-up' challenges to policy. (Hunter, 2003, p 324)

Power and the state

The reference in Box 3.6 to 'the regulation of the poorest groups' reflects postmodernism's focus on the micro-politics of power. This refers to the ways in which power is diffused through society and in which welfare institutions, in particular, discipline and regulate welfare subjects. This will be the subject of the next chapter but it is relevant also to how postmodernism treats the state.

Hillyard and Watson contrast postmodernist thinking on the state with traditional formulations such as those found in Marxism or feminism where 'the state was postulated as having an objective existence as a set of institutions or structures. It was thought to play a key role in organising relations of power and it was thought to operate as a unity, albeit a contradictory or complex one' (1996, p 337). Postmodernism questions the very idea of the state as an entity representing a set of interests, be it capitalist or male. Instead, it 'interprets the state not as a "thing" but as a practice or ensemble of practices' (Finlayson and Martin, 2006, p 155).

This means, as Pringle and Watson argue, that 'the state is now regarded as too diverse, divided and contradictory to evoke as an entity ... Work on the welfare state has recognised the need to shift our analyses to particular institutions and their specific histories, rather than assuming any unity or integration of its parts' (1992, p 63). So the state should be seen as 'erratic and disconnected rather than contradictory' (Pringle and Watson, 1992, p 63). Pringle and Watson argue not for abandoning the state as a category, 'but for a recognition that, far from being a unified structure, it is a by-product of political struggles' (1992, p 67). In social policy, this encourages us to analyse how different parts of the state approach a particular issue. For example, in the UK, the Department for International Development has endorsed a human rights approach to poverty, which is completely lacking in domestic departments such as the Department for Work and Pensions.

A 'great leap backwards' or 'a small step forwards' for social policy?

Writing in 1998, John Carter observes that 'postmodern ideas have been practically invisible in the pages of the central social policy journals – as research tools, theoretical frameworks or even the subject of negative critique … Relatively speaking then, welfare's postmodern period – if it happens at all – is much later and less wholehearted than that seen' in other disciplinary areas (1998c, pp 18-19). While it is probably true to say that social policy never did wholeheartedly take a postmodern turn, it is nevertheless possible to identify postmodernist influences (also explored further in Chapter Four). Moreover, Carter's own edited collection (1998a) contributed to a spirited debate about the value of postmodernism for social policy, much of it played out in the pages of the *Journal of Social Policy* and *Critical Social Policy*.

The main protagonist against – Peter Taylor-Gooby – describes postmodernism as 'a great leap backwards' (1994, p 385). In essence his argument is that its preoccupation with diversity and identity 'functions as an ideological smokescreen, preventing us from recognising some of the most important trends in modern social policy' (1994, p 385). In particular, it diverts attention from the continued impact globally of market liberalism, rooted in modernity, and the growing socioeconomic inequalities that it creates.

Those more sympathetic to postmodernism have countered that its attention to diversity, disciplinary processes and contested discourses is highly relevant to contemporary social policy analysis. Penna and O'Brien dubbed their response to Taylor-Gooby 'Postmodernism and social policy: a small step forwards?' (1996, p 39). They contend that postmodernism and related approaches 'address equally urgent questions about the political and cultural regulation of private and public life' as those raised by Taylor-Gooby (Penna and O'Brien, 1996, p 59). Moreover, 'the theoretical tools developed in the "post" debates point in new ways to redistributive issues in the relationships between economic exploitation and minority group oppression and encourage the development of more inclusive political and policy agendas' (1996, p 60). For Kirk Mann, 'the key point is that the scepticism of postmodernist accounts ensures a critical view of social policy' as providing a one-way progressive path to 'the good society' (1998, p 82).

Certainly, as Norman Ginsburg observes, postmodernism 'calls into question every element of modern social policy' (1998, p 268), which has been above all a 'modernist' subject concerned with material needs and collective means of meeting them. Both he and Hillyard and Watson pose the question as to whether a postmodern social policy is 'a contradiction in terms' (Hillyard and Watson, 1996, p 321). While acknowledging 'the contradiction arising from postmodernism's critique of meta-theory and mainstream social policy's commitment to universalism', the latter nevertheless conclude 'that the answer does not lie in the universal rejection of postmodernism but in the use of the ideas and insights to move the discipline in new directions' (1996, p 321).

It is useful therefore to distinguish between stronger and weaker forms of postmodernism. While it is difficult to reconcile stronger forms with the traditional concerns and approaches of social policy, it is possible to point to numerous examples in the social policy literature of how its weaker forms have been deployed to enrich a critical social policy, as advocated by Hillyard and Watson (see ***Boxes 3.6 and 3.7***).

Box 3.7: Some examples of the application of postmodernist ideas to critical social policy analysis

In an influential essay, Williams suggests 'three paths for social policy analysis which can draw on some of the most important insights of postmodernist thinking, but also retain and assert some less fashionable themes which are central to social policy thinking' (1992, p 210). These are:

- The development of 'the "bottom up" approach to diversity and difference in relation to needs for welfare provision and outcomes of existing policy and practice', with particular regard to 'more sensitised approaches ... around issues of gender, race, disability, age and sexuality, and their relations to class' (1992, p 210).
- Examination of 'the differential impact and implications for welfare of the changes (identified by some as post- or late modernity) taking place at the social, economic, political and cultural level' (1992, p 210).
- Exploration of how to reconcile 'needs for universal welfare provisions' and 'the need to meet diversity and difference' at the levels of policy planning, collective action and 'individual and collective empowerment to articulate needs'. (See also Chapter Six.)

Peter Leonard's book on *Postmodern Welfare* is subtitled 'Reconstructing an emancipatory project'. From 'a political and intellectual history rooted in Marxism', Leonard adopts 'a perspective which engages with postmodernism alongside feminism and anti-racism, and demands the acknowledgement and celebration of diversity in cultures, sexualities, abilities, ages and other human characteristics which, within an unreconstructed modernity were excluded, suppressed or discriminated against' (1997, p xiii). Leonard sketches a 'new, emancipatory project of welfare' (p 162), which combines universalist ideals such as justice and equality with attention to diversity and cultural specificity, through a politics of solidarity combined with a politics of difference. Its 'objectives are to meet both common and particular, culturally specific human needs as the preconditions necessary to the exercise of moral agency' (1997, p xiv).

The examples in ***Box 3.7*** refer to an explicit attempt to apply postmodernism to social policy. However, as the discussion on identities illustrated, it is possible to draw on postmodernist ideas to inform social policy analysis without subscribing wholesale to postmodernism. Indeed, according to Mann, there would appear to be 'a prima facie case for suggesting that there is some measure of agreement between some analysts of postmodernity, some critical social policy accounts and an increasingly critical "orthodox" approach to social policy' (1998, p 97).

Summary

- Post-Fordism and postmodernism share an analysis of social change, focusing respectively on the economic and the social/cultural.
- According to Post-Fordism, a transition from a mass Fordist to a flexible post-Fordist mode of economic production is mirrored in a shift in the form taken by the welfare state: from what Jessop terms the Keynesian welfare national state (KWNS) to an incipient Schumpeterian workfare post-national regime (SWPR). In the SWPR social policy is subordinated to global economic competitiveness.
- The post-Fordist welfare state also promises more decentralised, diverse and personalised forms of welfare; service users are regarded as consumers with choice.
- Postmodernism represents a break with the materialist approach of Marxism and post-Fordism. It is preoccupied with discourses and the power associated with them.
- Postmodernism rejects 'meta-narratives', universal claims and binary thinking in favour of the particular and diverse.
- Its construction of the individual as holder of multiple identities has influenced thinking more widely.
- Postmodernism questions the idea of the state as a unified entity representing a single set of interests.
- There has been a lively debate in social policy about the value of postmodernism for the subject. In its strongest forms, postmodernism is incompatible with the traditional concerns and approaches of social policy but in weaker forms, it arguably has brought new insights.

Further reading

Amin's reader **(1994)** provides a useful general introduction to post-Fordism. **Fitzpatrick (2001, pp159-63)** provides a good summary from a social policy perspective. The edited collection by **Burrows and Loader (1994)** is an essential source for debates around post-Fordism's application to the welfare state.

Carter's edited collection **(1998a)** provides a good starting point for exploring how social policy has engaged with postmodernism. Key contributions to the debate about the value of postmodernism to social policy have been **Taylor-Gooby (1994)**; **Hillyard and Watson (1996)**; **Penna and O'Brien (1996)**; and **Mann (1998)**. As illustrated in the text, examples of how social policy and welfare theorists have applied postmodernism can be found in **Williams (1992)**; **Leonard (1997)**; **Taylor (1998)** and **Hunter (2003)**. In addition, **Rodger (2000)** offers an analysis of the changing nature of the welfare state and society, drawing on both post-Fordism and postmodernism.

Notes

[1] The term 'Schumpeterian' here refers to the early 20th century economist Joseph Schumpeter's emphasis on the importance of promoting innovation and flexibility in the name of economic competitiveness within open economies.

[2] Foucault is often described as a post-structuralist rather than a postmodernist and this is indicative of how the two terms are often used interchangeably even though their meanings differ. Postmodernism derives from post-structuralism but the relationship between the two is not that clear-cut. One, over-simplified, way of seeing it is to think of post-structuralism as a philosophical approach and postmodernism as its application in particular spheres – artistic as well as social theory. For the sake of simplification of two complex approaches, this chapter conflates the two under the label of postmodernism, because their implications for social policy are effectively the same.

Social control, regulation and resistance

In this chapter, we explore various theoretical perspectives that interpret the welfare state as an agent of social control, discipline and regulation. It is perhaps inevitable that the reaction of some radical theorists to the earlier dominant characterisation of the welfare state as a benevolent force went to the opposite extreme of focusing purely on its controlling and punitive side. Yet, to suggest that social policies are purely about control is as simplistic as believing that they are purely about welfare. It conveys a view of social policy as one big conspiracy theory. Likewise, as the radical criminologist, Stanley Cohen (1985, p 2), has warned, there is a danger that social control can become something of a 'Mickey Mouse' concept, explaining everything and therefore nothing and used in so many different ways as to become almost meaningless.

That said, theories of social control and regulation have provided useful correctives to more starry-eyed interpretations of the development of the welfare state, as well as criminal justice institutions, as a one-way journey from punitive measures and cruelty to humanitarianism and enlightenment. Rather than viewing social policy as a matter of *either* welfare *or* control, we need to examine specific institutions and policies in order to determine the particular mixtures of welfare/control that they represent, as well as who is controlling/regulating whom and where. Newman and Yeates (2008a, p 13) point to the 'many examples of entanglement' between social welfare and crime control policies. The entanglement is even thicker when control is understood in its broader sense, embracing but extending beyond crime control.

We begin with a brief overview of 'modernist' approaches to social control. The bulk of the chapter, however, will build on the discussion of postmodernism in Chapter Three and explore the influence of Michel Foucault. Here the language typically changes to that of 'discipline' and 'regulation' rather than social control. The chapter uses the examples of criminal justice, the family and social security policy to illustrate how Foucauldian perspectives have been applied in social policy. It concludes by drawing attention to the possibilities of resistance both in everyday life and in more organised collective forms.

'Modernist' approaches

In a critical essay on social control theories of social policy, Joan Higgins observes that 'the concept of social control is crucial in explaining both the growth of social policies and their effects. It raises important questions about the legitimacy of state intervention, the maintenance of order and the protection of individual freedom' (1980, p 1). As this statement implies, the state is very much the focus of modernist accounts of social control.

The use of the term 'social control' tends to be associated with radical theorists, particularly those influenced by Marxism, who emphasise its coercive and repressive side (see, for instance, Cohen, 1985). However, in classical sociology it is associated more with theorists, such as Emile Durkheim and Talcot Parsons, concerned with how societies can achieve social order without excessive coercion. In other words, the emphasis is on cooperation and harmonious cohesion. Such theorists subscribe to a 'functionalist' model of society in which society is understood as a social organism whose maintenance depends on each individual part fulfilling its function.

While this can be seen as an essentially conservative (with a small 'c') doctrine, radicals cannot simply dismiss a concern with social order out of hand as oppressive. Social order can also be important, for instance, as a means of safeguarding the rights of minority groups and protecting the safety of disadvantaged groups and communities. As Blakemore and Griggs point out, 'the difference between an ordered and disordered society can mean the difference between being free to walk alone at night without fear of intimidation or violence, or not' (2007, p 114) – a difference of particular importance for women and visible minority groups.

> **Question:** Can you think of examples of current policy where social control policies to promote social order are justified by policy makers with reference to the interests and needs of disadvantaged or minority groups?

Marxist-influenced approaches are, in their own way, functionalist also, in that they too regard welfare institutions of social control as performing a function. In this case, though, the function is that of maintaining capitalism and the ruling class and is the subject of critical analysis (see Chapter Two). While, as explained in Chapter Two, it is a materialist theory, some Marxists do also pay attention to the role of ideology in legitimating mechanisms of social control. Lee and Raban present social control as a continuum:

> with soft elements (compliance, persuasion and ideological invocation) at one end, and hard control (force and repression) at the other – the iron fist and the velvet glove. The term becomes attractive [to Marxists] for linking these two, and opening up the possibility of 'revealing' hidden agendas or rationales lurking behind seemingly innocuous and caring social policies. (1988, p 106)

As well as Marxism, Higgins (1980) identifies radical literatures on the 'urban crisis' and on social work (which criticises social workers for acting as social tranquillisers) as key examples of the application of social control to social policy. Since her article, the development of what is often termed 'critical social policy' has provided many more examples of the use of notions of social control. Nevertheless, her categorisation of the main forms and mechanisms of social control, which goes beyond Lee and Raban's hard/soft division, is still useful (see **Box 4.1**).

Box 4.1: Joan Higgins' categorisation (1980) of forms of social control (abridged)

- *Repression* – for instance, the use of welfare policies to deter urban disorder or to force people into work;
- *Co-optation* – for instance, encouraging involvement in urban projects to dampen criticism and opposition or participation in community development as 'a soft approach to securing the consent of the governed' (Brent, 2009, p 258);
- *Integration* – this may be achieved through, for instance, social insurance policies, which encourage investment in society and one's own future;
- *Paternalism* – for instance through the provision of assistance in kind rather than cash so as to ensure that the assistance is used in what is deemed to be the recipient's best interests;
- *Conformity* – for instance, social workers exerting control over clients to get them to conform to prevailing norms and values.

Question: Can you think of examples of specific social policies today, which illustrate these forms of social control?

Higgins is critical of the rather sloppy way in which the concept of social control has often been used, frequently with little or no reference to actual empirical evidence. Nevertheless, she concludes that 'social control theories of social policy hold out exciting possibilities for the development of critical and insightful theory' (1980, p 23). Arguably, Foucauldian approaches have subsequently contributed to the development of just such a theory.

Foucauldian approaches

The term 'Foucauldian' refers to theoretical frameworks influenced by the writings of the French philosopher, Michel Foucault (see **Box 4.2**).

Box 4.2: Michel Foucault (1926-1984)

Foucault was both an enormously influential intellectual and an activist. He was a philosopher who also studied psychology. His writings were based on practical as well as intellectual work. For instance, he worked at one stage as a researcher in a hospital. His works include studies of the treatment of mental illness, prisons and sexuality. He is generally described as a post-structuralist or postmodernist (although he himself rarely used the latter term). His activism embraced gay rights and the prison system and he was arrested when he participated in the student rebellions of May 1969 in Paris. One dictionary entry states that 'his intellectual presence is felt throughout the social sciences' (Cohen, 2006, p 214).

Foucauldian approaches mark a shift away from the kind of functionalist thinking that marked earlier theories of social control. In line with postmodernist theorisation of the state, discussed in Chapter Three, the focus of analysis is not the state as such. Instead, broader notions of 'governmentality' (the mentality, techniques and practices involved in the exercise of political power at all levels) and 'governance' (the processes through which political power is exercised through a range of government and non-government bodies) are used to convey the wide range of mechanisms and institutions through which the behaviour of populations is moulded or governed. There is a particular emphasis on the ways in which individuals are encouraged to govern their own behaviour. Governmentality has been described as the 'how' of governing (McKee, 2009, p 466). Its meaning is illustrated from a criminological perspective by Pat O'Malley:

> 'the state' becomes merely one site – or rather a complex of sites – in which government is located. Governmentality work has examined how government of crime is practised, not simply

by police and the criminal justice 'system', but also by the insurance industry, communities, potential victims, shopping centre managers and so on (O'Malley, 2001, p 134).

Insofar as it is the state that is exercising control, the focus shifts from the aims of the state to specific techniques and mechanisms of regulation and discipline in specific locations and institutions at the interface with the population. Thus, for instance, a study of social security policy would be more interested in the power relations involved in how it is administered at 'street level' than in the policies developed by national government.

> *Question:* Can you think of other examples of the power relations involved in one-to-one encounters within the welfare state? What understanding do you gain of your own experiences of such encounters from this perspective?

Power

At the heart of this approach is the theory of power developed by Foucault. As mentioned in Chapter Three, the focus of interest is the micro rather than the macro politics of power: 'nothing in society will be changed if the mechanisms of power that function outside, below and alongside the state ... on a much more minute and everyday level, are not also changed' (Foucault, 1980, p 60). O'Brien and Penna point out that:

> In many ways, the systems of power described by Foucault are instituted not by openly coercive or repressive state agencies but by a very wide miscellany of civil institutions. They are systems of power (or 'micro power') that are inculcated into the behaviours, habits and practices of an entire society of people with the consequences that the rules, codes and procedures of regulation and control are experienced as 'normal' features of institutional and everyday life. (1998, p 120)

Foucault's theory of power distinguishes between 'sovereign power' and a bi-polar model of 'bio-power' and 'disciplinary power' (see *Box 4.3*). At one level this distinction reflects a historical shift in the nature of power, but at another it also identifies the operation of different kinds of power today. Foucault was interested primarily in bio- and disciplinary power, which are interrelated.

Box 4.3: Sovereign and disciplinary power

Sovereign power refers historically to centralised power exercised by an individual sovereign over his or her subjects. It was a negative power to take life, in other words the right to torture or execute subjects. Translated into modern terms, it represents what Foucault calls a 'juridico-discursive model of power' (1978, p 82) in which:

- power is possessed (in particular by the state or the ruling class);
- the flow of power is from top to bottom (mainly through the institutions of the state and the law);
- power is primarily repressive (in other words, it is used to stop people doing things and is backed up by sanctions).

Disciplinary power involves a range of techniques deployed to produce 'a docile body that may be subjected, used, transformed and improved' (Foucault, 1977, p 198). In other words, it is about achieving compliance. It is 'exercised directly over individuals in institutions such as prisons, schools and factories' (Harris, 1999, p 31).

Bio-power is concerned with life and death and the health and productivity of bodies. It is about power *over* life rather than the power *to take* life. Bio-power developed with the rise of the medical, psychiatric and welfare professions. The collection of information on reproduction, mortality, health and life expectancy provided the mechanisms for new means of control over bodies (Foucault, 1978).

It is possible to identify a number of key elements of Foucault's notion of power, which stand in contrast to sovereign power. At the heart of his formulation of disciplinary and bio-power is the idea that power is intimately bound up with knowledge and that it operates through the construction of particular forms of knowledge. Knowledge implies power and power implies knowledge. We can see this most clearly in relation to professions such as the medical profession, whose specialist knowledge can give medical professionals power over their patients. Foucault saw the idea of the 'confession' as central to the power-knowledge nexus. Sophie Watson explains the significance for social policy:

> Surveys, questionnaires and interviews all investigate and intrude upon the most intimate aspects of personal and social life. In order to qualify for assistance or benefits the notion of privacy is stripped away. The homeless person, the criminal, the social security claimant are constantly monitored and surveyed and

called upon to give information which may be prejudicial to them. (2000, p 69)

A good example is provided in an Australian study of the use of case management in the governance of employment services. Using a Foucauldian theoretical framework, McDonald and Marston comment on:

> the power of confession in case management as a key interpersonal technology in transforming and 'freeing' the self. Case management practices often involve forms of disclosure, a process described by one case manager as 'an onion, peeling back the various layers until you get to the core'. People 'spill their souls'. (2005, p 385)

McDonald and Marston's study also demonstrates another important aspect of the Foucauldian understanding of power: 'the micro relations of power and authority that are invoked in the everyday politics of welfare reform' (McDonald and Marston, 2005, p 374). As indicated previously, power is analysed from the bottom up rather than the top down in line with the idea that power is dispersed throughout society and that what is interesting and important is the 'micro-physics' of power (Foucault, 1977, p 26; Watson, 2000, p 68). Thus, McDonald and Marston use this approach to 'argue that it is necessary to understand street-level implementation as a form of policy making, rather than an afterthought of political decision making' (2005, p 376).

For Foucault, power is exercised rather than possessed. It is relational and inherent in relationships. It can shift so that it is not a question of total unchanging domination or of total submission of one party to another. Take, for instance, the university lecturer. She has power over the grade that a student gets for a module she teaches. But the student can also exercise power through, for instance, how she behaves in seminars or through the feedback that she provides, either individually or collectively. Another example is provided by a gay teacher, who explains, in a letter to *The Independent*, why he has always refused to answer students' questions about his sexuality: 'because I am afraid of the power my students may wield over me consequently' (7 November 2009). Foucault's theory of power has been controversial among feminists (see *Box 4.4*).

Box 4.4: Feminist critiques of Foucault's relational conceptualisation of power

Feminists disagree about the value of Foucault's relational understanding of power. Some see its emphasis on the exercise of power within particular situations and relationships as helpful. Others contend that it fails 'to provide a theory of power for women' because his theory of power makes 'it very difficult to locate domination, including domination in gender relations' (Hartsock, 1990, pp 158, 169). In an exploration of tensions between Foucault and feminism, Caroline Ramazanoglu argues that 'by seeing power as everywhere and, at some level, as available to all, it can encourage us to overlook women's systematic subordination of other women, as well as systematic domination by men' (1993, p 10). The ubiquity of power makes it difficult to distinguish between its 'malign' and benign' forms and to identify 'the different kinds of power relations that cut across women's lives' (Ramazanoglu, 1993, pp 13, 15). While Foucault 'did acknowledge men's exercise of power over women, [he] denied that men can hold power' and that this represents 'a form of domination' (Ramazanoglu, 1993, pp 17, 22).

Linked to the relational conceptualisation of power, is the idea that power is productive as well as repressive. Power enables things to happen and people to act. Instead of relying on negative forms of coercion, which directly stop people doing certain things, it represents a more indirect form of control, which shapes the parameters in which people feel able to act. Thus they effectively regulate themselves within these parameters. Repression is only necessary when the more subtle exercise of power is unsuccessful. This brings us to the regulatory techniques through which disciplinary and bio power are exercised.

Regulatory techniques

Foucault was interested in the various techniques deployed to regulate and discipline in place of the earlier exercise of coercive sovereign power. These techniques operated not only in prisons and asylums but also, for instance, in factories, schools and workhouses. This is spelt out very clearly by O'Brien and Penna (*Box 4.5*).

Box 4.5: The techniques through which disciplinary power is exercised

O'Brien and Penna summarise the approach taken by Foucault in his key work on the topic: *Discipline and Punish*. Penal, welfare and educational institutions, together with factories:

> are characterised by 'regimes of [disciplinary] power' which subject their charges to surveillance, training, subordination and normalisation ... It is the continuity and multiple applicability of these techniques that mark out 'discipline' as a unique type of power ... the techniques for training and normalising inmates, with some variation according to context, took hold across the entire spectrum of public and private institutions. In clinics, hospitals, schools, factories, asylums, orphanages and workhouses, the principles of isolation, routinisation, ranking, recording and visibility served both to define the nature of deviance, need, personal or educational development, sickness and recovery and at the same time to instil a range of behaviours, compliances, regulations and moral-political codes into the institution's structures and practices ... The power to judge, to police, to diagnose and treat, to educate and assess and supervise *constitute* the disciplinary society ... As the powers of judgement, assessment, supervision, and so on become more entrenched in the maintenance of social order, so more and more people are drawn into the micro technologies. Powers to judge, assess or supervise are diffuse and decentred: no single central authority regulates or bestows them. Instead they are decentred and distributed throughout the social and institutional networks of the modern political order. (O'Brien and Penna, 1998, pp 115-17, emphasis in original)

O'Brien and Penna's account brings out the pervasiveness and ordinariness of the disciplinary techniques. They are interconnected but can be differentiated for purposes of analysis. The key ones, which we shall look at in turn, are classification, normalisation and surveillance.

Classification as a regulatory technique concerns the application of science to everyday life through, in particular, the procedures of medicine and the social sciences. In the 19th Century, social reformers, philanthropists and the criminal justice system all began to collect information, and in particular statistics, about the 'lower classes' in the name of moral improvement and containment rather than coercive punishment. Peter Squires explains how they developed the disciplinary technique of classification in order to contain problems of criminality and pauperism: 'It was classification in the penal system which gradually enabled the authorities to separate the "vicious and degraded" from the "reclaimable", and classification which, within the Poor Law, might help distinguish the "feckless and idle" or the fraudulent "clever pauper" from the "genuinely needy"' (1990, p 51). Within the contemporary welfare state, Nancy Fraser characterises classificatory regulation as post-Fordist in nature: 'Working largely through population profiling, [postfordist regulation] separates and tracks individuals for the sake of efficiency and risk prevention. Sorting the capable-and-competitive wheat from the incapable-and-noncompetitive chaff, postfordist welfare policy constructs different life courses for each' (2008, p 128). Professionals such as social workers, psychiatrists and statisticians exercise disciplinary and bio-power through a range of classification techniques. They use statistics to measure the deviance of both the individual and social body from the 'norm'. They are thus part of the wider technique of normalisation.

Normalisation is the process 'whereby all individuals are compared and differentiated according to a desired norm so producing homogeneity. It establishes the measure by which all are judged and deemed to conform or not' (Carabine, 1998, p 125). Foucault writes:

> The judges of normality are present everywhere. We are in the society of the teacher-judge, the doctor-judge, the educator-judge, the 'social worker'-judge; it is on them that the universal reign of the normative is based; and each individual, wherever he [sic] may find himself, subjects to it his body, his gestures, his behaviour, his aptitudes, his achievements. (1977, reproduced 2003, p 421)

Foucault observes how 'the disciplinary networks' outside the penal system – 'medicine, psychology, education, public assistance, "social work"' – 'assume an ever greater share of the powers of supervision and assessment' and represent 'mechanisms of normalization' (1977, reproduced 2003, p 422). They deploy their power to assess and diagnose according to professional or official norms. An example, which also illustrates how the regulatory mechanisms operate together, is provided later in *Box 4.7*.

What makes normalisation such a perfect mechanism of social control is that it often exercises pressure on people to conform through self-control and self-regulation in accordance with the desired norms, without the need for coercion. This, Foucault points out, is the most efficient and cost-effective form of control. An illustration is provided in a discussion paper, *Personal Responsibility and Changing Behaviour*, produced by the British Prime Minister's Strategy Unit. It discusses 'the potential for seeking behavioural change not only through a focus on individual persuasion' but also by 'changing the behaviour of significant figures around the individual – such as parents and peers – to make gradual changes to wider social norms' (Halpern and Bates, 2004, p 4). In other words the technique of normalisation is applied both directly and indirectly in order to modify the behaviour of individuals.

Foucault was particularly interested in the ways in which normalisation produces 'docile bodies'. This can be seen most strikingly in the area of health policy. A key message of an official review of the National Health Service was that 'a sustainable NHS that maximises life expectancy and health status will require citizens to be fully engaged in maintaining their own health' (Jameson, 2008, p 6). A prime example (echoed in health debates in the US) is the increased emphasis on diet and exercise in response to growing concerns about the effects of obesity. In his first interview in post as the then Health Secretary, Andy Burnham identified as a personal priority 'to embed in the NHS culture the promotion of physical activity' as 'a long-term insurance policy' (*The Guardian*, 8 June 2009). The point has been made that, in order to tackle obesity, governments are more willing to regulate individuals than they are the corporate sector, notably supermarkets.

> *Question:* Can you think of other examples of policies that represent normalising disciplinary techniques?

Foucault underlines the close link between normalisation and **surveillance** (as well as classification) in his reference to 'a normalising gaze, a surveillance that makes it possible to qualify, to classify and to punish. It establishes over individuals a visibility through which one differentiates them and judges them' (1977, p 184). Similarly, David Lyon, a leading contemporary theorist of 'the surveillance society', emphasises how classification and surveillance are interconnected: 'keeping track requires more and more sophisticated means of classification and categorization, that both feeds on surveillance data and stimulates the organizational appetite for them' (Lyon, 2007a, p 138). A report on primary education in the UK refers to the 'Stalinist overtones of a "state theory of learning" enforced by the machinery of surveillance and accountability" – league tables [and] testing targets' (*The Independent*, 16 October 2009).

Lyon defines surveillance as 'any collection and processing of personal data, whether identifiable or not, for the purposes of influencing or managing those whose data have been garnered' (2001, p 2). Most surveillance is routine; it is part of our everyday lives regardless of whether or not we have done anything wrong. Lyon portrays it as having 'two faces': 'the same process, surveillance – watching over – both enables and constrains, involves care and control' (2001, p 3).

For Foucault, Jeremy Bentham's idea of the 'panopticon' symbolised the all-seeing surveillance techniques and represented the 'perfect disciplinary mechanism' (Foucault 1977, reproduced, 2003, p 74). The panopticon was a penal institution in which cells were distributed like the spokes of a wheel. This meant that the inmates could be seen by the authorities from its hub at any time, but they could not know when they were being watched so they had to regulate themselves (as with the normalisation technique) under the all-seeing gaze. In Foucault's words, 'hence the major effect of the Panopticon: to induce in the inmate a state of conscious and permanent visibility that assures the automatic functioning of power' (1977, reproduced 2003, p 70). This represents 'the perfection' and 'efficiency of power': 'He [sic] who is subjected to a field of visibility, and who knows it, assumes responsibility for the constraints of power; he makes them play spontaneously upon himself; he inscribes in himself the power relation in which he simultaneously plays both roles; he becomes the principle of his own subjection' (1977, reproduced 2003, p 71).

Zygmunt Bauman refers to the 'panoptical drill' in his analysis of the disciplinary techniques involved in the inculcation of the work ethic in the 19th century. Paid work emerged as a pivotal form of classification. The workplace was, he explains,

> the setting in which the essential habits of obedience to norms and of disciplined behaviour were expected to be trained and absorbed ... Factories turned out many and varied commodities, but all of them, in addition, produced the compliant and conforming subjects of the modern state ... Whatever explicit reasons were given to justify the concern, invalidity, weakness of the body and mental impairment were seen as a threat and were feared because they cast their victims outside the reach of the panoptical drill on which the maintenance of social order relied; people out of employment were also masterless people, people out of control – not surveilled, not monitored, not subjected to any regular, sanctions-fortified routine. (Bauman, 2005, p 18)

Leonard applies the idea of the panoptic gaze to the welfare state:

> The history of the welfare state in Western societies might be seen as the refining of this gaze, its technological development, its proliferation through specialization and professional expertise, its justification as necessary for the promotion of the subject's well-being ... 'the gaze' is both a literal description of social practices [of professionals observing welfare subjects] and a

> metaphor for the monitoring and surveillance of subjects
> undertaken by the state apparatus. (1997, p 43)

Technological advance has enhanced the state's capacity for surveillance both in terms of the capacity to collect and store information on computers and directly to observe citizens in public spaces and a variety of penal and also welfare institutions. According to Graham and Wood, 'digitization facilitates a step change in the power, intensity and scope of surveillance' (2003, p 228). The use of surveillance has been stepped up following 9/11. This has had the effect of 'broadening and tightening the net of social control' to the extent that, Lyon concludes, 'the pendulum has swung so wildly from "care" to "control" that … some instances of early twenty-first-century surveillance are downright unacceptable, as they directly impugn social justice and human personhood' (2007b, p 368). In the UK, this has led to a growing chorus of warnings, including from the Information Commissioner, the Council of Europe's Commissioner for Human Rights and committees of both Houses of Parliament, that the country is turning into a 'surveillance society'.

While no one escapes the panopticon's all-seeing gaze, more marginalised groups tend to be subjected to more intensive forms of surveillance. Henman and Marston (2008) illustrate this with an analysis of 'the social division of welfare surveillance' (see ***Box 4.6***). It is also portrayed graphically in John Gilliom's study of low-income American mothers:

> who live every day with the advanced surveillance capacity of the modern welfare state. In their pursuit of food, health care, and shelter for their families, they are watched, analyzed, assessed, monitored, checked and reevaluated in an ongoing process involving supercomputers, caseworkers, fraud control agents, grocers and neighbors. They *know* surveillance. (2001, pp xii–xiii)

Moreover, the 'social sorting' involved in surveillance, for instance of those deemed to be potential terrorists, 'has exclusionary consequences' (Lyon, 2007b, p 371). This is one reason why, as observed earlier, Lyon argues that surveillance damages social justice (a concept discussed in Chapter Eight). An example is the controversial Preventing Violent Extremism programme in the UK, under which a range of agencies in areas with significant Muslim populations are being pressurised to gather intelligence about the young people with whom they work, regardless of whether or not they are suspected of any involvement in terrorism. As one critic observes, surveillance of this kind can undermine trust and discourage young Muslims from using services (Kundnani, 2009).

> ## Box 4.6: The social division of welfare surveillance
>
> Henman and Marston analyse 'the unequal distribution of surveillance practices and burdens' in the welfare context (2008, p 189). Using the case study of Australia, they demonstrate
>
>> the variations in welfare surveillance between the social, fiscal and occupational welfare domains. Just as different moral valuations – such as that between 'deserving' and 'undeserving' – significantly contributed to differences in welfare surveillance between welfare domains, the same moral valuations operated in a more graduated way to support differential levels of surveillance within the one welfare domain. For example, within the social welfare system, social insurance benefits often involve less intrusive surveillance than social assistance ... Those groups calculated by complex statistical methods to pose greater risk (of fraud, or long-term unemployment and so on) face greater surveillance. (2008, p 200)
>
> Henman and Marston draw the lesson that:
>
>> the social policy discipline needs to take more seriously the new developments in welfare surveillance and its consequent distribution of burdens ... With its concern with human wellbeing, the social policy discipline would clearly benefit from a greater engagement with differential (welfare) surveillance and practices of exclusion. (2008, pp 201-2)

The differential and exclusionary impact of surveillance is also a characteristic of its operation in the private sector. The financial services sector is often used as an example. 'Nowhere is the power of the "panoptic sort" more evident than in the financial services sector, where detailed personal histories and complex credit-scoring techniques are regularly used in order to differentiate and segment the customer base' (Dornan and Hudson, 2003, p 474). The effect, according to Dornan and Hudson, is to create '*differential* access, the "panoptic sort" segmenting and grading the market, providing increasingly competitive services for the better-off and increasingly expensive services for the less well-off' (2003, p 475, emphasis in original).

The private sector also deploys surveillance techniques differentially as an employer, targeting less skilled workers in particular. Through electronic means, such as tagging as well as cameras, a worker's every movement can be observed and recorded in the name of improving productivity. In her account of the time she spent in low-wage jobs, the American journalist Barbara Ehrenreich speculates that 'the indignities imposed on so many low-wage workers – the drug tests, the constant surveillance ... – are part of what keeps wages low' through making workers feel unworthy (2001, p 211).

Box 4.7: An example of the processes of normalisation, classification and surveillance: special education

Angela Morgan, author of a study of the operation of disciplinary power within the British special education system, observes that 'the creation of special education and the accompanying practice of segregation results in normalizing children's abilities and stigmatizing those who deviate from the norm. Special education also functions to objectify its subject (the child) through the processes of classification and division that are inherently involved in systems of governmentality' (Morgan, 2005, p 326). Morgan describes how children are allocated into 'technical categories of disabilities' by 'a large body of specialists, teachers, psychologists, doctors, and so forth' (2005, p 332).

She also analyses special education as 'a panoptic system. The mechanism of surveillance is captured within the assessment and statementing process, which instils disciplinary techniques within children, their parents and education administrators' (Morgan, 2005, p 332). Morgan identifies the ways in which children and/or parents together with administrators are held within the gaze of the panopticon.

> First, during the process of statementing a child is under constant surveillance from 'expert' decision-makers, so children and/or their parents are positioned within the periphery of the panopticon, with education administrators situated within the central watchtower. Vital to the special education system's panoptic function is that those in the periphery are aware of constant surveillance. Hence the continuous and constant reassessment of the child in the form of annual reviews in which further documentation is generated and archived. Teachers, educational psychologists and SEN [special educational needs] coordinators watch over and monitor the child on a daily basis...Second, it can also be seen that special education administrators may also be positioned within the periphery of the panopticon, as they too are under surveillance by higher authorities, as data they collect and decisions they make are under constant review. (Morgan, 2005, pp 332-3)

Question: Can you think of any other social policy examples where the processes of normalisation, classification and surveillance operate to discipline welfare subjects?

Sites of discipline and control

The previous section has provided an introduction to the key elements of Foucauldian approaches to regulation, focusing in particular on disciplinary techniques. The examples illustrated how these techniques are applied in the welfare context. In this section, we build on those examples to demonstrate how two important areas of social policy have been analysed from this theoretical perspective: the family and social security. We start, however, with a very brief account of the areas that particularly interested Foucault himself: criminal justice and mental health.

Criminal justice and mental health

Foucault's interpretation of the history of the penal system exemplifies his approach. Penal history involved a shift from the public infliction of physical pain or even death as the main form of punishment to the use of imprisonment in which inmates are separated from the outside world and subjected to a range of disciplinary techniques. With prison reform, these techniques were refined. Nevertheless, while on the face of it prison regimes became more humane, they are still essentially disciplinary in their everyday practices.

Contemporary criminologists have shifted the focus to the ways in which community-based forms of punishment represent the incorporation of a range of non-penal agencies into the net of the criminal justice system. 'From social workers via probation officers and the police to community groups and charity organisations, the criminal justice net has absorbed more and more non-penal agencies into its administrative and disciplinary remit' (O'Brien and Penna, 1998, p 128). In the process, the distinction between penal and welfare agencies becomes more blurred. In an analysis of the politics of antisocial behaviour, Squires illustrates how this net–widening process incorporates family members as well as community agencies, with, according to Nixon and Hunter (2009), gendered effects (see **Box 4.8**).

Box 4.8: The widening of the criminal justice net

The management of anti-social behaviour 'is devolved and disseminated to a range of new agencies acting under the umbrella of CDRPs [Crime and Disorder Reduction Partnerships] ... Such arrangements are only part of the story, however, for, as Foucault argued, the perfection of discipline should render its operation invisible and the burdens of discipline borne by its subjects. Thus the operation of ASBOs [Anti-Social Behaviour Orders] in the housing field and the enforcement of ABCs [Acceptable Behaviour Contracts] are left initially to other family members on threat of eviction. Likewise, the tough breach conditions attaching to the ASBO imply a sharp jump up the sentencing tariff and an important overlapping of civil and criminal legality. This broader responsibilization of social networks is reminiscent of the "micro-physics" of power described by Foucault or disciplinary relations at the capillary level' (Squires, 2006, p 153).

A collection of papers in *Social Policy and Society* (2009) explores the ways in which discourses and interventions around anti-social behaviour are deployed to 'discipline difference' (Nixon and Prior, 2009, p 73). An example they cite is an earlier essay on women and anti-social behaviour, where Nixon and Hunter point to 'the hidden but nonetheless compelling ways in which technologies to control conduct disproportionately affect women', as they are made responsible for the behaviour of male family members (2009, p 135).

Loïc Wacquant provides a critical account of the widening of the criminal justice net in the US, as penal sanctions and welfare supervision are forged 'into a single apparatus for the ... behavioural control of marginal populations' (2009, p xix).

Feeley and Simon point to the 'growth of community corrections in the shadow of imprisonment': 'Rather than instruments of reintegrating offenders into the community, [community-based sanctions] function as mechanisms to maintain control' (Feeley and Simon, 2003, p 439). These mechanisms deploy normalisation and surveillance techniques. Normalisation techniques include public shaming – the equivalent of the mediaeval stocks (see **Box 4.9**). Surveillance techniques have been facilitated by technological developments such as electronic tagging and now satellite tagging through the implantation of machine-readable microchips.

> ### Box 4.9: Examples of public shaming as a normalisation technique in the criminal justice system
>
> In the US, 'shame laws' have been introduced in some states, notably Tennessee. Shame punishment might include drunk drivers doing community service while wearing an orange jumpsuit branded with messages such as 'I am a drunk driver' or shoplifters standing outside Wal-Mart wearing a sign that says 'I am a thief put here by order of Judge McKenzie' (Shteir, 2006). Wacquant describes as 'law-and-order-pornography ... the accelerating inflection and inflation of penal activity conceived, represented, and implemented for the primary purpose of being displayed in ritualized form by the authorities – the paradigm for which is the half-aborted reintroduction of chain gangs in striped uniforms' (2009, p 297).
>
> In the UK, convicted criminals undertaking community service are now being required to wear 'vests of shame' – bright orange vests bearing the words 'Community Payback' in bold (*The Guardian*, 2 December 2008). A full page Home Office advertisement in my local paper invites the public to 'Have your say on how criminals pay back'. It explains that under the Community Payback scheme 'offenders have to wear bright orange jackets marked Community Payback, so you'll see them paying back for their crimes' (*Nottingham Evening Post*, 2 April 2009). According to Frances Crook, director of the Howard League of Penal Reform, 'the idea of flak jackets and community payback is more about bringing the ethos of the prison out into the community. It's about belittling, demeaning and punishing' (quoted in Robins, 2009, p 37).

Foucault (1965) traces the treatment of mental illness over the centuries. At the time of the Renaissance 'the mad' were set afloat in a 'ship of fools' (McNay, 1994). In the 19th century, they were locked away in asylums. The 20th century saw the development of psychiatry and then more subtle forms of regulation and discipline of people with mental health problems through psychotherapy, usually voluntarily sought. The techniques of classification and normalisation are clearly discernable in the treatment of people with mental health problems today. Mick Carpenter traces developments in UK policy, culminating in the 2007 Mental Health Act. This, he argues, combines '"tough" risk surveillance and coercion with a "soft" partnership approach with professionals and user organisations to foster internalised compliance by more "responsible" users with prescribed drug and treatment regimes' (2009a, p 223). As Sue White observes:

> the new psychological sciences have created yardsticks or norms, of supposedly universal validity, against which the behaviour

of subjects can be measured … Individuals increasingly self-monitor, assessing and passing judgement upon their own psychological health and social adjustment against the norms of appropriate behaviour, thoughts and emotions propagated by professions. (1996, p 70)

White is particularly interested in the ways in which 'decisions about who falls into which diagnostic categories are influenced by dominant and powerfully gendered assumptions underpinning psychiatric (and to an extent, lay) discourse about women and madness' (1996, p 72). She extends her analysis to social work, which 'has become imbued with notions of dangerousness and the implicit assumption that it is possible to categorize, and therefore to exert statutory control over, the potentially abusive dimensions of family life' (1996, p 73).

The family

The family has emerged as a key site for the analysis of the exercise of regulatory techniques. Bauman, for example, draws on Foucault's work to demonstrate how the family reinforced the factory in the development of the work ethic in the 19th century (***Box 4.10***).

> ## Box 4.10: Zygmunt Bauman on disciplinary techniques within the family
>
> Inside the family, husbands/fathers were prompted to perform the same surveilling/disciplining role towards womenfolk and children as factory foremen … performed in relation to them on the factory floor … Modern disciplining power, as Foucault insisted, was dispersed and distributed after the pattern of capillary vessels which conduct the blood pumped by the heart to the most distant tissues and cells of a living organism. The husband/father's authority inside the family conducted the disciplining pressures of the order-producing and order-servicing network to the parts of the population which the panoptical institutions would not otherwise be able to reach. (Bauman, 2005, p 18)

Jacques Donzelot's *The Policing of Families* (1980) has been particularly influential in the application of Foucault's ideas to the family. The family is subject to the processes of normalisation, surveillance and regulation by a range of professionals including the 'psy' professions, as he calls them.

In addition childhood is regulated by the 'tutelary complex' of educators, social workers, juvenile courts and so forth.

As the quotations from Bauman and White indicate, these processes are deeply gendered. This is brought out in a study of health visitors, cited by John Rodger in order to illustrate the regulatory aspects of the professional caring role: 'without coercion, and most often with the consent of mothers, they [the health visitors] monitor and construct conceptions of "good" and "bad" mothering habits' (1996, p 20). Both throughout the 20th century and today, it is poorer, working class mothers who are particularly subject to normalising and disciplinary techniques in an attempt to make them 'good' mothers. This is illustrated in Val Gillies' study of working class mothers (**Box 4.11**).

Box 4.11: The regulation of working class mothers

Val Gillies points to the ways in which middle class norms of child development and mothering are 'universalised and essentialised as a prior category against which normative evaluations of mothering rest' (2007, pp 146-7). She explores the implications for working class mothers who are raising children in a very different context. In a discussion of the simultaneous development of parenting classes and ASBOs, she points to 'the thin line dividing government efforts to "support" and enable, from a more authoritarian instinct towards coercion and regulation' (2007, pp 147-8).

Question: Can you think of examples of family policies that combine support and regulation?

In the contemporary welfare state, the mother is the key point of intervention, as it is usually through her that the professionals operate to ensure the good health and socialisation of children. Their surveillance of mothers also involves the self-surveillance of women trying to be 'good mothers'. Feminist theorist Carol Smart applies a Foucauldian analysis in a discussion of 'normalizing motherhood'. She suggests that 'as ideals of good motherhood became fixed into policies (say, for example, in relation to the feeding of infants) then it became feasible to apply these standards widely through teams of health visitors, doctors, social workers or NSPCC [National Society for the Prevention of Cruelty to Children] officers' (1996, p 46, emphasis in original). These 'calibrations of good motherhood', which applied initially to physical care, have been extended to 'include the immense realm of the psychological care and nurture of the child. Thus the good mother was no longer simply the one who fed and cleansed properly, she would be inadequate if she failed to love *properly* and to express this love in the *correct* fashion' (1996, p 46). Smart notes that 'the significance for Foucault of normalizing discourses is the way in which degrees of adherence to the rules are secured by the stigmas and impositions placed upon those who disregard them. Thus we can think in terms of "tests" that were and are imposed routinely to discover whether mothers meet or fail the standards of motherhood' (1996, p 47). While middle and upper class mothers are no longer exempt, 'the public focus remains largely where it has always been, namely with working–class mothers' (1996, p 47).

Social security and welfare

The social security system has been analysed as a system of social control in a number of texts, often combining modernist and Foucauldian perspectives. Some of this work places the contemporary social security system in historical context (see, for example, *Box 4.12*).

Box 4.12: A Foucauldian analysis of the development of social security

Hartley Dean identifies three interconnecting historical processes involved in the development of modern social security systems. They represent the replacement of:

- indiscriminate alms-giving by the 'complex panoply of the welfare state which scrutinises and documents each individual "client" or "case"';
- corporal punishments such as whipping by 'more discreet and less violent forms of coercion based on benefit penalties and disqualifications';
- 'crude processes of classification and surveillance associated with the workhouse and the Poor Laws' by 'administrative systems based on legal definitions and regulations to which citizens must submit in order to exercise their "rights"' (Dean, 1996, pp 78-9).

Dean analyses this last practice as 'a technique of disciplinary partitioning'. Whereas in the past this was a physical process of separation, in the modern social security system it is achieved through 'the multiplication of social security rules and procedures and a correlative division of the claimant population in accordance with the constitutive criteria of status and entitlement' (Dean, 1988/9, p 76). He sums up the overall process 'not as a story of progress towards the development of universal social rights, but as a story of developing state power and increasingly sophisticated methods of social control' (1996, p 79).

In his work on 'the emergence of a disciplinary "welfare state"' Peter Squires (1990, p 1) analyses the development of poor relief and social security during the 19th and 20th centuries in terms of the refinement of disciplinary techniques, associated primarily with the needs of capital for a supply of labour power. He analyses how the disciplinary role of the modern social security system is reflected in the perennial preoccupation with work incentives and with the construction of the 'genuine' as opposed to the fraudulent or 'workshy' claimant (see also **Box 4.13**). In similar vein, Jones and Novak point out that 'the "tough" messages of the social security system have always been seen as having a far wider applicability', acting as a deterrent to the wider working population (1999, p 194). They, along with Squires, Dean and others, also argue that such disciplinary techniques have become more overt in the social security system over recent decades.

Box 4.13: Surveillance and control in the social security/welfare system

In their study of welfare surveillance in Australia, Henman and Marston observe that

> The social assistance system has a long history of highly intrusive, detailed and ongoing surveillance of claimants and recipients to minimise fraud and ensure eligibility. A deep suspicion pervades the system ... Once eligibility to benefit is obtained, ongoing suspicion and surveillance are maintained through an elaborate web of intergovernmental data-matching, frequent reviews and regular reporting. Moreover, the level of surveillance within social assistance is graduated according to perceived level of risk and moral worth (2008, p 194).

Information technology has played an important role in the development of regulatory techniques in the social security system. Henman and Adler adopt a Foucauldian governmentality approach in their cross-national study of the impact of information technology on the governance of social security. Differences between countries notwithstanding, they conclude that 'it is clear that computerization has led to an increase in control over staff and claimants and that it has not empowered them' (2003, p 156). In the UK, the latest technological step is the introduction of lie detector tests in order to combat social security fraud (*The Observer*, 2 September 2007).

In the US, Wacquant draws attention to the practices of private firms involved in the administration of welfare:

> For a fee, these companies take over the supervision of new-style welfare recipients who, much like (ex-)convicts, find themselves the object of extensive record-keeping, constant testing, and close-up surveillance, allowing for the multiplication of points of restraint and sanction. In so doing, they ... enlarge governmental capacity to 'train' the urban poor for their appointed place in the new economic and civic division of labor. (2009, p 106)

Squires also analyses the means test as a disciplinary technique: 'The means test introduced a particularly intrusive and individualised form of disciplinary relationship between the state and the applicant' (Squires, 1990, p 138). Others have drawn attention to the disciplinary nature of the claiming experience in the modern social security system both in terms of the considerable power which officials have over claimants and more broadly: 'The stigma of being a claimant is an essential ingredient in a system designed to discipline claimants and to promote the values of insurance and individual and family self-help' (Ginsburg, 1979, p 104). The values of insurance and self help are inculcated in particular through social insurance systems (which link entitlement to social security to contributions paid while in paid employment). Patricia Harris analyses social insurance as part of what Foucault terms 'insurantial technologies', 'encouraging or compelling citizens to act on their own behalf' – a form of 'self-discipline' (1999, pp 38-9).

Resistance

So far we have explored different approaches to understanding mechanisms of social control and regulation. There is a danger that, from this perspective, we lose sight of the agency of the people whose behaviour is regulated by such techniques. Yet, the discussion of agency in the Introduction reminds us that we are more than the 'docile bodies' identified by Foucault (1977, p 198). Thus, some Foucauldian analysts also emphasise the importance of resistance. According to McDonald and Marston, for instance, 'resistant practices are the sorts of cracks and fissures that governmentality alerts us to look for' (2005, p 394). Those who resist 'can exercise some power as well as those who seek to govern them' (McKee, 2009, p 471).

Some critics contend that Foucault himself does not allow space for resistance. However, Lois McNay explains how, in fact, the conceptualisation of power in his later work implies resistance. Unlike violence, which allows for no opposition and which crushes any resistance, 'a power relation ... only occurs where there is the potentiality for resistance, that is to say it only arises between two individuals each of whom has the potential to influence the actions of the other and to present resistance to this influence' (McNay, 1994, p 127). Moreover, his own activism involved resistance (see ***Box 4.2***).

Leonard distinguishes between two kinds or levels of resistance: 'the micro-resistance of everyday life' and 'organized collective political resistance' (1997, pp 95, 139). In the welfare context, 'the micro-resistance of everyday life' takes us back to the 'micro-physics of power' as played out through the interactions between individual users and providers of welfare state services. In these interactions providers, as well as users, sometimes exercise resistance. This is one of the themes of a collection of essays on 'subversive' citizenship, which clarifies the significance for policy outcomes:

> Workers and users retain the capacity to act in ways that counter the dominant power of official policy and practice and that subvert the intended service outcomes. The counter-agency of workers and users in revising, resisting or refusing policy imperatives is thus critical to an understanding of why policy sometimes fails at the point of front-line or street-level delivery. (Prior, 2009, p 32)

Resistance is also expressed through the survival strategies deployed by low income users in particular. It may be overt or covert and its significance will vary according to context. Some examples of micro-resistance are provided in ***Box 4.14***.

Box 4.14: Examples of 'the micro-resistance of everyday life'

Graham and Wood point to the 'everyday practices of the targeted' as an example of the many forms of resistance against surveillance: 'In British towns young black men have been shown to develop elaborate practices to exploit CCTV system "blindspots"' (2003, p 244). John Flint explains how some young people have resisted 'mosquito' devices (which emit a high-pitched tone audible only to young people), deployed to drive them out of public spaces so as to combat anti-social behaviour: 'In a "subversive display of teenage ingenuity" children have appropriated the mosquito buzz as a mobile phone ring tone, enabling the covert use of text-message alerts in school classrooms!' (Flint, 2009, p 91).

In a welfare context, the case managers and clients, interviewed by McDonald and Marston in their study of employment services in Australia, provide a number of examples of 'resistance and refusal' (2005, p 393):

Some unemployed people, for example, are reported as being consciously anti-authoritarian in the face of coercive power ... Such clients, despite the empathetic efforts of the case managers 'going the extra hundred miles' will 'at the end of the day, still hate you'. In this respect, some participants refuse to be gracious about the identities they are asked to adopt. Other clients refuse to engage with the individualized dimensions of case management ... Others exercised agency by using the administrative rules and the liberal principle of choice: 'I said, "I think I'd like to exit from your agency. I'm not happy with the way you're handling this", and he said "That's not possible". I just found out that it *was* possible, and I exited on my own' [emphasis in original]. This example highlights that the technologies of power associated with a neo-liberal rationality, such as choice, can be exercised by those who are traditionally thought of as powerless. (McDonald and Marston, 2005, pp 393-4)

Most of the case managers in McDonald and Marston's study also gave examples of their own resistance. For instance, 'they collude with their clients to evade the disciplinary aspects of the income support system' (2005, p 395).

Gilliom's study of low income American mothers provides a number of examples of resistant survival strategies associated with 'engaging in a widespread cash economy and hustling whatever money and help they can' (2001, p 95):

As the Department of Human Services uses its surveillance system in an attempt to deter or punish behaviour which their clients define as both necessary and moral, an ongoing pattern of domination and resistance ensues. As the mothers resist, ... they not only resist the specific commands of the state welfare policy, but the related demands that the books of their lives be open to total surveillance ... And as mechanisms of surveillance push the issues of visibility and verification to the forefront of long-standing struggles between citizens and institutions, practices of deception, camouflage, and secrecy are the necessary politics of our times. Everyday tactics of evasion, subterfuge, and concealment, then, may very well become a defining form of politics in the surveillance society. (2001, pp 95-6, 101)

Question: Can you think of any examples of where you have shown resistance in your dealings with the welfare state – for instance in response to a teacher, lecturer or doctor?

Leonard describes 'the exercise of individual resistance, embedded in the micro-processes of everyday interaction with the welfare system' as 'necessary but insufficient' (1997, p 170). More organised, collective forms of resistance are therefore necessary in order to achieve change. There are a growing number of examples of organised collective resistance directed against surveillance in particular (see **Box 4.15**).

> ## Box 4.15: Examples of 'organised collective political resistance' against surveillance
>
> Lyon provides a number of examples of resistance to the increase in surveillance since 9/ll from around the world. He singles out Japan, in particular, where the Japanese Network Against Surveillance Technology was formed and where 'major protests and uncharacteristic civil disobedience followed the introduction of the national computerized registry of citizens in 2002' (2007b, p 374). Lyon observes how dissenters are themselves able to use 'the same kinds of technology that enable remote networked surveillance' to communicate with each other (2007b, p 374). A prominent example in the UK is the No2ID campaign, which spread through the internet. This is a national grassroots campaign established to fight the introduction of identity cards. Growing numbers of protesters are also using digital cameras and camera phones against the police and other agents of surveillance in what has been called the 'Synopticon' or 'sousveillance' (watching from beneath) (*The Guardian*, 9 and 11 April 2009). Sousveillance is becoming increasingly coordinated in response to the surveillance of demonstrations (Coatman, 2009). In the UK, for instance, Fit Watch has developed in resistance to police forward intelligence teams (Fits), which monitor activists at demonstrations and meetings. Fit Watch activists film the police and upload the evidence to the web and they attempt to block the police cameras with banners and placards (*The Guardian*, 22 June 2009).

Leonard focuses in particular on forms of collective resistance 'manifested in some of the new social movements organized primarily on the basis of social identity and having the potential to be active at every level in the social structure' (1997, pp 169-70). We will return to the role of new social movements in Chapter Nine. It is worth noting here that their struggles are in part struggles over discourses and meaning, in which dominant discourses about their members and their needs are resisted. We will explore further in the next two chapters how dominant discourses and interpretations of needs are resisted and contested.

Summary

- This chapter has discussed two sets of theoretical perspectives that interpret the welfare state as an agent of social control, discipline and regulation.
- *Modernist* approaches typically focus on the ways in which the state uses social policies as a mechanism of social control and on the functions of social policies for social order.
- *Foucauldian* approaches widen the focus beyond the state. Insofar as they engage with the state it is primarily at the level of everyday interactions.
- Key elements of Foucauldian analysis are, first, Foucault's conceptualisation of power as disciplinary and bio power and, second, the disciplinary techniques of classification, normalisation and surveillance.
- The chapter illustrates how these disciplinary mechanisms operate in the areas of criminal justice and mental health, the family and social security. It provides examples of the use of Foucauldian analysis in social policy research.
- Foucauldian approaches also provide insights into forms of resistance to discipline and control at the level of both individual everyday resistance and collective political resistance.

Further reading

Higgins (1980) and **Cohen (1985)** still offer good introductions to theories of social control. A number of social policy texts provide a general account of Foucauldian approaches, including **Leonard (1997)**, **O'Brien and Penna**. **(1998, Ch 4)** and **Watson (2000)**. The key text in this context by **Foucault** himself is *Discipline and Punish* **(1977)**. For some examples of the application of a Foucauldian approach in social policy research and analysis see, for example, **Dean (1988/9)**; **Squires (1990)**; **Henman and Adler (2003)**; **McDonald and Marston (2005)** and **Morgan (2005)**. There is a considerable literature specifically on surveillance: useful general texts include **Lyon (2001)** and **Hier and Greenberg (2007)**. **Fitzpatrick (2005, Ch 8)** and **Henman and Marston (2008)** bring a social policy perspective to surveillance.

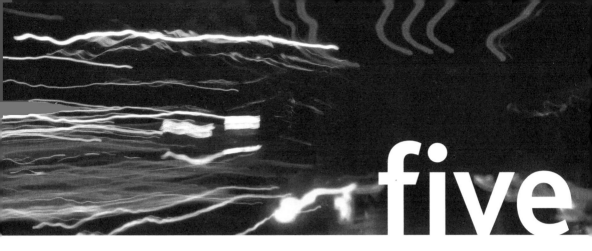

five

What's the problem?
Social constructionism

Social constructionism is a theoretical perspective, influential in sociology and social psychology, which has been applied in social policy particularly in relation to the study of social problems. The first part of this chapter introduces you to social constructionism and to its interpretation by Carol Bacchi (1999) in her 'What's the problem?' approach to the analysis of the representation of policy problems. The second part illustrates social constructionism through an exploration of various ways in which the problem of poverty has been constructed in contemporary political debate through the discourses of the 'underclass', 'welfare dependency' and 'social exclusion'.

Social constructionism and the 'what's the problem?' approach

Box 5.1: What is social constructionism?

Social constructionism has been defined as 'a perspective that explores the assumptions embedded in the labelling of people and places and emphasizes the importance of social expectations in the analysis of taken-for-granted or apparently natural social processes' (Clarke, 2001a, p 266). It is often contrasted with 'naturalist', 'realist' or 'essentialist' approaches, which assume that an 'external, objective world exists outside our categories of perception and interpretation' (Sandvoss, 2006, p 569).

Clarke explains the distinction in a social policy context:

A naturalist or realist perspective in the social sciences treats social problems as though they are given: phenomena about whose existence we can all agree. The social constructionist perspective insists on the necessity of taking a step back from this view and asks instead, who says this is a social problem – and what sort of social problem do they think it is? (2001a, p 266)

A further distinction can be made between 'strong' and 'weak' forms of social constructionism (Lupton, 1999, pp 28-35). Strong forms would reject the existence of an objective reality that constitutes a social problem. Weak forms 'do not deny there is a "real world" of pain, loss, poverty, hunger and so on, but they are concerned with how we come to know about and construct this world, or more accurately worlds' (Featherstone, 2009, p 70). It is the weaker form that is more influential in social policy and that will be explored here.

Social constructionism, with its preoccupation with the meanings attached to social phenomena, is one example of the 'cultural turn' in social policy, discussed in the Introduction. It also takes us back to the observation in the Introduction that theory encourages scepticism towards 'common sense' understandings of society.

As explained in ***Box 5.1***, according to social constructionism, phenomena only exist as 'social problems' insofar as they have been defined or constructed as such. That does not mean that there are not troubling conditions such as poverty: what is important is the process by which they become defined and labelled as a social problem. In the next section, we look in turn at three elements in that process, namely the ways in which:

- private troubles become defined as social problems;
- certain social phenomena become defined as problems in particular societies at particular points in time;
- social problems are defined as such and how they are understood.

We will then explore the importance of language, power and discourse to the social constructionist approach to social problems.

The process of defining a social problem

The notion of a 'social problem', as understood within a social constructionist framework, rests on a distinction made by the sociologist C. Wright Mills between 'personal troubles' and 'public issues' (1979, pp 7-10). Personal troubles may be experienced by individuals, families or even groups of people; not all of them emerge as 'public issues' where some form of public intervention is deemed appropriate. 'Social construction implies an active process of definition and redefinition in which some issues are widely understood to be social problems, while others are not' (Clarke and Cochrane, 1998, p 9). This process can take a number of forms. It may represent a top-down process in which government names a social problem to be tackled. In some cases, this might be in response to media and/or pressure group representations, which have helped to identify the problem. Such representations may, in turn, reflect a more bottom-up process of 'claims-making' (explored further in Chapter Six with regard to needs). One social constructionist account, which uses the notion of claims-making, refers to '*the activities of individuals or groups making assertions of grievances or claims with respect to some putative conditions ... The central problem for a theory of social problems is to account for the emergence, nature, and maintenance of claims-making and responding activities*' (Spector and Kitsuse, 2001, pp 75-6, emphasis in original). These forms of processes may operate singly or, more commonly, in various combinations.

Social constructionism is interested in the factors that determine which issues do and do not come to be widely understood as social problems. These factors will lie partly in the claims-making process and partly in government responses or initiatives. So, for example, a social constructionist analysis might ask why some of the 'private' issues identified by feminists as problematic (for instance domestic violence against women [see Radford, 2001]) have been recognised as social problems in many societies, while others (such as the domestic division of labour and time) have not.

> ***Question:*** Can you think of other examples of private troubles which became constructed as social problems in recent decades and also of private troubles, which have not emerged as social problems?

An important aspect of social constructionism, which it shares with postmodernism (see Chapter Three), is its focus on particular societies at particular points in time. The point here is that many of today's social problems were not defined as such in earlier time periods but remained personal troubles, and the same personal trouble may be recognised as a social problem in some societies and not others. As already suggested, domestic violence against women is a prime example. Moreover, some aspects of social change are articulated as a social problem in some societies but not others. The treatment of lone parents illustrates this last point and, as we will see, also a number of other aspects of social constructionism. In the UK, there is a tendency to take for granted the 'problem' status of lone parenthood, for this has been a consistent theme in British social policy. Yet lone parents are not treated as 'a problem' in all countries. In particular, in the Nordic countries lone parent families are not singled out as different from other families.

Similarly, the ways in which a social problem is constructed vary over time and between societies. Social constructionism asks questions not only about the issues that become identified as social problems but also about the nature of that identification: how is the problem defined and understood? Again, the example of lone parents is illustrative. The nature of the problem that lone parents, and in particular unmarried mothers, are believed to constitute has been constructed differently over time in the UK. Kiernan, Land and Lewis describe how the problem of unmarried motherhood was constructed as a moral as well as a social problem in the 1950s, early to mid-1960s and again for much of the 1990s. 'Only in the late 1960s, 1970s and 1980s was unmarried motherhood constructed as a material problem, at first sympathetically and increasingly negatively during the 1980s as the attack on welfare dependency gathered force' (1998, p 122). During this period, lone mothers generally became constructed increasingly as a threat. They were cast as 'a drain on public expenditure and as a threat to the stability and order associated with the traditional two-parent family' (Kiernan et al, 1998, p 2).

Kiernan, Land and Lewis observe: 'it is striking that the problem of unmarried motherhood has, over what is a relatively short period of time, been so completely reconstructed time and again with touching faith that each successive construction constituted truth' (1998, p 123). Among unmarried mothers, teenage mothers have been particularly problematised: 'public discourse in Britain sees teenage motherhood as a pernicious social problem where mothers, their children and society generally will all suffer' (Duncan, 2007, p 307; see also ***Box 5.2***). Interestingly, in contrast, in the US, there have been signs recently of the celebration of teenage parenthood among members of the anti-abortion lobby (*The Observer*, 14 September 2008).

Box 5.2: The social construction of teenage parenthood

Three recent social policy studies have examined the construction of teenage mother/parenthood. The first, by Wilson and Huntington, explores how representations of motherhood in the US, UK and New Zealand have 'shifted over the past few decades to position teenage mothers as stigmatised and marginalised' (2006, p 59). It observes that 'concerns about teenage motherhood are articulated through the discourses of welfare dependency and social exclusion', which are discussed later (2006, p 62).

The second, by Simon Duncan, analyses the dominant construction of teenage parenthood and contrasts it with research findings about its actual impact. He writes that:

> teenage parenthood in Britain, and elsewhere in Western Europe and North America, is typically depicted as a calamity for individual young women and as a severe problem for society ... The policy understanding of teenage parents as a social problem ... has become linked in public debate with a wider 'social threat' discourse. Teenage pregnancy is taken as a particularly significant indicator of the gathering 'breakdown of the family'. (2007, p 306)

He underlines the significance of labelling (to be discussed later):

> When they use the term 'teenage mother' politicians, the media and even voluntary organizations invoke a particular categorical representation of a type of person. 'Teenage mother' is seen to stand for an a priori, unitary, fixed, coherent, inherent and essentialized set of attributes and characteristics – which in Britain and the USA easily become a negative stereotype as social victim or threat. (2007, p 327)

He then points out how the research cited in his paper indicates that 'most teenage parents do not fit this caricature' (2007, p 327). Instead, it

> shows that teenage childbirth does not often result from ignorance or low expectations, it is rarely a catastrophe for young women, and that teenage parenting does not particularly cause poor outcomes for mothers and their children. Indeed ..., expectations of motherhood can be quite high and parenting can be a positive experience for many young men and women. Furthermore, becoming a teenage parent can make good sense in the particular life worlds inhabited by some groups of young women and men. Policies about teenage parenting, however, assume the opposite. (Duncan, 2007, p 328)

Duncan's study is a good example of how dominant social constructions can misrepresent the nature of a social problem. This has implications for policy. Whereas 'most studies recommend the policies should be redirected towards support for teenage parents', the balance of policy has in practice favoured prevention of teenage parenthood (Duncan, 2007, p 328).

The third study, by Lisa Arai, echoes the earlier research in challenging the assumption that teenage pregnancy is necessarily a problem. It found that in some cases 'young motherhood can be life-enhancing' even though this does not fit the dominant 'story' (2009, p 181). She argues that 'policymakers (and researchers) need to be careful about the dangers of creating representations of teenage pregnancy which contribute (inadvertently or otherwise) to the pathologisation of young parenthood' (2009, p 181). Young mothers themselves are very aware of the stigma attached to their status, Arai observes.

Increasingly, during the late 20th century, many of society's ills were imputed to the damaging impact on children of lone parenthood more generally, with particular reference to the absence of fathers from their lives. Today, in the UK, 'social threat and social problem discourses on lone motherhood still dominate policy debates on family change, emphasising risks for gender socialisation, children's development, welfare dependency and rates of child poverty from increasing numbers of lone mother households' (Churchill, 2007, pp 172-3).

> **Question:** What have been the implications of these changing social constructions of lone parenthood for policies towards lone parents?

Ideology, discourse, language and power

Social constructionism works with a number of concepts and analytical tools in trying to understand the factors behind the identification of social problems and the effects of such identification. One such concept is **ideology** (discussed in the Introduction). Clarke and Cochrane introduce it in order to deal 'with the question of why some conditions become identified as problems and why some sorts of social constructions are in widespread use' (1998, p 30). Social constructionism is particularly interested in the ways in which ideology legitimates particular social arrangements and interpretations of them as 'common sense'.

To return to the example of lone parents: the construction of lone parenthood as a 'problem' can be understood as reflecting familialist and patriarchal ideologies, which uphold the traditional nuclear family and women's traditional place within it. An alternative explanation lies in neo-liberal ideology, which constructs lone parenthood as part of the problem of 'welfare dependency' (to be discussed later). The two ideological positions both construct lone parenthood as a 'problem' but they tend to point to different solutions. Commentators subscribing to the familialist/patriarchal ideological position look to bolster traditional family patterns by, for instance, pursuing policies to strengthen marriage, whereas the welfare dependency ideological position points to policies designed to encourage or force lone parents into paid work.

Language and **discourse** are at the heart of much social constructionist analysis. Earlier social constructionist works, most notably Berger and Luckmann's classic *The Social Construction of Reality* (1967), were concerned with the role of language in labelling certain groups or forms of behaviour as problematic. 'How we name things affects how we behave towards them. The name, or label, carries with it expectations … [Social constructionism] starts by exploring the assumptions associated with the naming or labelling of things' (Clarke and Cochrane, 1998, pp 26, 30). For example, from a social constructionist perspective, lumping together and labelling diverse forms of behaviour as 'anti-social' has created the problem of 'anti-social behaviour'. Squires underlines the 'pejorative' and pathological nature of the language used to describe the problem: 'The language of demonization is never far away when ASB features in the tabloids: "mindless thugs", "lager fuelled yobs", "feral children" or "neighbours from hell". Indeed, rather disappointingly, the same language is employed in a large number of the Home Office's own press releases' (2006, pp 163, 150).

Some social policy analysis has focused on how language is used in the policy process to shape perceptions of a social problem and therefore of appropriate solutions to it (see ***Box 5.3***). This approach has taken on particular significance under New Labour, whose 'way of governing … is in part a way of using language' (Fairclough, 2000, p 12).

Box 5.3: An example of social constructionist linguistic analysis of a social policy document

Annette Hastings provides a detailed linguistic analysis of a 1988 policy document, *New Life for Urban Scotland*, published by the Scottish Office. The document was significant in shaping subsequent urban policy. Her investigation examines 'the causal model of urban change constructed' in the document and how 'linguistic strategies ... distribute agency between the main protagonists involved in *New Life*'s tale of decline and renewal' (Hastings, 1998, p 198). To illustrate the latter point, Hastings quotes a section about initiatives that have contributed to the transformation of Glasgow. The document lists central and local government, public bodies and the private sector, all of which are 'portrayed through a number of verbs of action: to work together, to focus, to deploy, to make available; giving them the status of deliberate, conscious actors' (1998, p 206). In contrast, the residents are absent from the narrative and 'elsewhere they appear as passive victims "suffering from multiple deprivation" (para. 12) or ... as the objects rather than the subjects of action' (1998, p 206).

As well as demonstrating how urban policy is constructed on assumptions about a 'culture of dependency', the analysis illustrates how 'further elements of a pathological discourse may be present. Moreover it demonstrates how the use of language is involved in making the pathological explanation of decline credible to the reader' (1998, p 198). Hastings concludes by making the case for linguistic analysis of this kind as an important tool for social policy research:

> ... it allows consideration of how language works, particularly of how it constructs credible, persuasive versions of reality and of how these accounts relate to broader social processes and practices. Understood and used in this way, a discursive approach to policy analysis can be part of the critical, democratic agenda in policy studies. If discourse analysis can identify *what* kind of knowledge is promoted through policy and *how* it is promoted through language use, then it provides the opportunity for discourses to be both scrutinised and challenged. (1998, p 209, emphasis in original)

Hastings moves beyond language to talk also about discourse. She explains that 'constructionist perspectives are either explicitly or implicitly underpinned by the broadly Foucaultian notion that language, knowledge and power are fundamentally interconnected at the level of discourses' (1998, p 192). Clarke and Cochrane clarify how the concept of discourse is applied differently to that of ideology in social constructionism. Whereas the concept of ideology is used to analyse 'constructions as a means through which social groups promote or legitimate their interests', that of discourse directs attention to the ways in which social constructions shape rather than reflect 'social identities and interests' (Clarke and Cochrane, 1998, p 29). For instance, with reference to our example of lone mothers, examination of patriarchal ideology might reveal how the interests of men are promoted or legitimated, while the analysis of discourse in **Box 5.2** illustrates how it shapes the social identity of a category labelled as teenage mothers.

As we saw in Chapter Three, discourses act as frameworks which shape how we think and talk about things. With regard to the social construction of social problems, discourses 'define what the problem is; they say what is worth knowing and what can be said ... Discourses shape and become institutionalized in social policies and the organizations through which they are carried out' (Clarke and Cochrane, 1998, p 35). As we will see in the second part of this chapter, if we use the language of the 'underclass' or 'welfare dependency', then that structures the way we think about poverty and the solutions to it, leading to rather different social policies than a traditional discourse of poverty. This example illustrates further a point made in Chapter Three: discourses have **material effects**. As already indicated, the same is true of the social construction of social problems (see also ***Box 5.4***).

Box 5.4: The effects of social constructions

Esther Saraga (1998b) identifies three kinds of consequences of social constructions in a social policy context. These are for:

* How people see themselves and their position and how others see it. Consider the effect of the discourse of the 'welfare scrounger' on how social security claimants might see themselves and how others regard them.
* Patterns of social inclusion and exclusion in different social groupings including the 'nation' itself. Consider here the impact of the discourse of the 'bogus asylum-seeker' on the inclusion of asylum-seekers and refugees in social, economic, political and cultural life. Or the discourse of 'local homes for local people' promoted by Gordon Brown, when Prime Minister – the (false) implication is that housing shortages are caused by immigrants jumping the queue (*The Independent*, 30 June 2008).
* 'Concrete policies and practices, which in turn reinforce (or solidify) the social construction on which they are based' (Saraga, 1998b, p 204). Take, for example, the combination of 'welfare dependency' and 'lone mothers as problem' discourses reflected in welfare-to-work policies, which reinforce the social construction of lone mothers not in paid work as 'passive dependants'.

The material effects of social constructionism reflect wider power relations. As the earlier quotation from Hastings indicates, social constructionism links language and discourse to **power**. Gail Lewis identifies two kinds of power involved in the process of the social construction of social problems. The first is 'discursive power'. This enables some social groups to impose their view of which issues become defined as social problems and the ways in which they are constructed as problems. Second is the 'institutional or practical power ... to determine and implement the kinds of institutional practices developed in the attempt to "solve" these social problems' (Lewis, 1998b, p 266). Lewis sees these two kinds of power as different 'sides of the same coin' of 'social power' (1998b, p 266). At an institutional level, the media wield discursive power and governments institutional or practical power.

As discussed in Chapter Four, power invokes **resistance**. Social constructionists may point to how dominant social constructions become 'solidified' as taken-for-granted 'common sense', which then shapes policy (Clarke, 2001a). Nevertheless, they also emphasise that there is not just one common sense and what constitutes common sense can be contested. Similarly, dominant social constructions can be resisted. In recent years, various new social movements have struggled for the reconstruction of social problems (see also Chapter Nine). For instance, whereas in the past dominant constructions identified homosexuality as a social problem, today, thanks to the struggles of the gay and lesbian movement, the problem is recognised to be homophobia.

> ***Question:*** Can you think of any other social problems that have been reconstructed in similar fashion, thanks to the struggles of social movements?

What's the problem?

One of the most fully worked accounts of social constructionism in a social policy context can be found in Carol Bacchi's *Women, Policy and Politics* (1999). Bacchi adopts a 'what's the problem?' approach, which is shorthand for 'what's the problem represented to be?' (1999, p 1). This is a way of analysing policies, in which nothing is accepted as given. She sums it up: 'it directs attention to problematizations rather than to problems, which can only be understood with reference to the ways in which 'they are problematized' (1999, p 199). The approach is based on the assumption that every policy contains an explicit or implicit interpretation and diagnosis of a problem, which she calls 'its problem representation' (1999, p 1). Problem representations often vary between societies and over time, as we saw with the example of the social construction of lone parenthood earlier.

Bacchi suggests that, as a first step, 'proposals need to be screened for problem representations and these then need to be analysed in terms of their effects, practical and discursive' (1999, p 206). A useful move here is 'to examine when and how a particular topic achieved social problem status' (1999, p 206), since the problem representations are likely to be clearest at that point. ***Box 5.5*** outlines a series of questions through which Bacchi recommends the 'what's the problem?' approach that can be applied to any particular policy, either actual or proposed. They bring together some of the points made earlier.

Box 5.5: Application of the 'what's the problem?' approach using the example of lone parenthood

Bacchi (1999, pp 12-13) provides a step-by-step guide to applying the 'what's the problem?' approach. We indicate briefly how it might be applied to the example of lone parenthood used earlier in this chapter:

- 'What is the problem [of 'x'] represented to be' in either a specific policy debate or proposal? For example, the 'problem' of lone parenthood is typically represented as one of family breakdown, female sexual behaviour or welfare dependency.
- What assumptions inform this representation? We might here want to explore the assumptions about: sexuality; the reasons for lone parenthood and its effects on children; the proper role of mothers and fathers; and the effects of reliance on welfare, which inform the representation of lone parents.
- 'What effects are produced by this representation?' For example, what are the effects of dominant representations on how lone parents view themselves and how others view them; and what are the material effects on lone parents? And who gains or loses as a result of these representations?
- 'What is left unproblematic' in the dominant representations? For example, if lone parenthood is represented in terms of the negative impact of family breakdown or 'welfare dependency', lone parents' poverty is left unproblematised.
- How might policy responses be different, if the 'problem' were represented in an alternative way? For instance, if lone parenthood were represented as a problem of poverty, the response might be a significant improvement in benefit levels.

Notice how Bacchi's questions are designed not simply to identify representations but also to evaluate them in terms of their effects.

In addition to questioning the way in which social policies construct specific social problems, Bacchi suggests that a 'what's the problem approach?' can 'also be used to clarify the assumptions and implications of understandings of an issue offered by those who *deny* an issue 'problem' status' (1999, p 13). It thus also asks questions about those 'troubling social conditions [that] fail to achieve the status of a "social problem", or only achieve this status at particular times' (1999, p 58). So, for instance, we might use the 'what's the problem approach?' to ask why social security fraud tends to get problematised in a way in which tax fraud rarely is in dominant representations of the tax–benefit system.

Moreover, Bacchi argues that a 'What's the Problem approach offers a way to think beyond single issues, and questions the kind of separation implied by listing a number of discrete policy areas. In contrast to many studies of policy, [it] encourages us to think about the interconnections between policy areas' (1999, p 2). She is critical, for instance, of 'the reduction of multi-faceted programmes of change to single issues, like "domestic violence" or "pay equity"' (1999, p 166). With regard to the latter she points to how 'consistently, feminists have been at pains to show that pay equity is part of a package', which needs to include a wide range of reforms that go beyond the labour market itself (1999, p 91). Yet this understanding is lacking in dominant problem representations.

The social construction of poverty

We have explored the key facets of the social construction of social problems in the first part of the chapter. In the second part we use the social construction of poverty as a case study. Poverty is a major social problem in many societies. How it is constructed varies between societies and over time. Clarke's social constructionist analysis of poverty is summarised in *Box 5.6*.

Box 5.6: John Clarke's social constructionist analysis of poverty

If we take poverty as a social problem, it is possible to see how the constructionist perspective might force us to reconsider how poverty becomes a social problem – and how it is treated as a social problem. Poverty (as it is conventionally understood as a social problem) is constructed round a binary distinction between 'normal' people (those who are not poor) and 'deviant' people (those who are poor). It involves the construction of normative boundaries (the continuing debate about what counts as being poor or, more accurately, definitions of what you have to lack to be counted as poor). Poverty is then 'produced' or 'constructed' by applying those normative distinctions to groups of people, marking some as poor … This constructionist perspective does not involve denying that people will, in practice, lack the means of subsistence – but that only some people, at some times, and in some places, will be defined or labelled as being in poverty. (2001b, p 7)

Clarke points to how this constructionist perspective on poverty opens up a number of issues:

- the importance of how poverty is defined;
- the wide social and historical variation in how it is 'defined, constructed and responded to';
- the effects of the application of the label of poverty to individuals and groups on how they are treated and on how they see themselves (see also Lister, 2004a);
- the possibility of alternative constructions, such as the long radical tradition, rooted in a structural analysis of inequality. This 'suggests there is not a binary distinction between the poor and not-poor but a structure through which resources are unequally distributed between different groups or classes' (2001b, p 8).

At the level of explanation, Clarke and Cochrane (1998, pp 16–18) identify three broad 'common-sense' constructions of poverty as:

- natural and inevitable – the idea that 'the poor will always be with us' because some people will inevitably be more successful than others and the consequent inequality is necessary as an incentive to work hard and get on;
- caused by the characteristics or behaviour of people living in poverty themselves – examples are lack of aspiration or ability, lack of interest in working, or inability to budget;
- attributable to economic or political causes such as low pay, unemployment or inadequate social security benefits.

> **Question:** Each of these constructions of poverty points to different policy solutions. What do you think these might be?

Clarke and Cochrane's analysis illustrates 'the way in which discourses of poverty shape what can be said about poverty, whether in everyday conversations, academic research or political debate' (Saraga, 1998b, p 202). We will turn now to explore the ways in which three dominant discourses have shaped understandings of poverty in recent years. These are the discourses of the 'underclass', 'welfare dependency' and social exclusion. They constitute ways of constructing the problem of poverty that are very different from the radical tradition identified by Clarke in *Box 5.6*.

The 'underclass'

The 'underclass' is probably the most contentious of the labels attached to people in poverty and the one which is most clearly socially constructed:

> The concept of the 'underclass' is not about a lived social reality, but is a social construction: an attempt to portray the poor – or at least certain groups of the poor – in certain ways. It is about the construction of a set of assumptions and a way of looking at the poor that above all else sets them apart from everyone else, and constitutes them as a new and distinct 'social problem.' (Novak, 1997, p 226)

The concept has its roots in earlier labels for those at the very bottom of society. Kirk Mann explains that the 'underclass':

> may simply be a new term for an old intellectual activity. From at least the beginning of the 19th century, and probably earlier, British commentators developed a succession of labels for the poorest strata of society ... Unfortunately there is always something unsavoury about the underclass, whether it has been called the residuum, the dangerous class, the relatively stagnant population, the lumpen-proletariat, or whatever happens to be the fashion of the day. Seen in this light the idea of an underclass is simply the most recent label for a class of failures. (1994, pp 80-1)

Although the term 'underclass' has been around for some time, it was popularised in the US during the 1980s and imported to the UK by Charles Murray (Lister, 1996). It subsequently became a dominant popular construction of poverty in the UK during the 1990s. Although it is not quite so prominent today, it is still used casually by the media and some politicians to describe many groups in poverty, particularly those not in paid work. Typically, the adoption of the discourse of the 'underclass', together with that of 'welfare dependency', marks a redefinition of the problem of poverty from being primarily about a lack of resources to being primarily a problem of behaviour, in particular, crime, drug-taking, failure to work, illegitimacy and family breakdown. The political nature of the process of social construction involved is detailed by David M. Smith (see **Box 5.7**).

Box 5.7: The 'underclass': a political process of social construction

Smith observes how the new right

> was acutely aware that social problems are socially constructed and that the problems and solutions can be changed through an effective manipulation

of public debate. The historical evolution of the underclass debate illustrates that maintaining a particular definition of reality is essentially a political process: a confrontation between competing definitions of reality, in which certain groups can impose their definition on others. The role of 'primary definers' (those structurally dominant groups who can alert the media to a particular event or problem) played a crucial role in defining the new 'common sense' surrounding issues of welfare and poverty in the 1980s. (2005, pp 51-2)

He points to the role of right-wing think tanks in disseminating the idea of the 'underclass' and how it was used to justify 'political critiques concerning the corrosive effects of over-generous welfare systems and the need for a "law and order" response to check the tide of rising crime and antisocial behaviour' (Smith, 2005, p 52).

Smith's analysis chimes with those of Mann and Lydia Morris who suggest that the discourse of the 'underclass' is a reflection of anxieties about social change. Mann argues that its usage 'says more about the observers than those who are observed' and that 'one feature of the underclass which recurs in virtually every account, particularly the US literature, is the apprehension this class provokes in others' at a time of growing inequality (1994, pp 82, 85). For Morris, 'the anxiety evoked by the image of an underclass in 1990s Britain and its political purchase are rooted in the growing instability of two traditional building-blocks of social life – secure full-time employment for men, and the nuclear family household' (1998, p 228). Changes in gender relations are thus at the heart of many of the anxieties evoked in the concept of the 'underclass'. There is also a racial dimension, which is particularly prominent in the US, where the threat of the 'underclass' has been explicitly racialised (see Chapter Two).

The discourse of the 'underclass' represents 'an exercise in conceptual containment' (Morris, 1996, p 161). It provides a seemingly simple explanation by locating the problem of poverty in the behaviour of marginalised individuals rather than in unequal class, gender and 'race' relations and structural causes. 'The poor,' not poverty, are constituted as 'the problem'.

Murray himself acknowledges that 'underclass is an ugly word' (1996, p 23). He and others use the language of disease and contamination to describe it: words such as 'plague' and 'a cancer'. It is not a label with which anyone wants to identify. The 'underclass' is, thus, a very good example of the discursive power of such discourses. The 'underclass' is represented as a threat and as the 'other', different from 'us' (Lister, 2004a). It leads to a set of policy prescriptions for addressing anxiety-provoking social changes, which are more likely to be about social control than social welfare. 'The "underclass" is a convenient ideological tool for either abandoning any commitment to the poor and disadvantaged, or cultivating popular support for more coercive measures' (Williamson, 1997, p 80).

Welfare dependency

The concept of 'welfare dependency', which is often used in tandem with 'the underclass', reinforces this construction of the problem of poverty as a problem of the behaviour of 'the poor'. An American report, which was very influential at the time, states that 'at the heart of the poverty problem … is, then, the problem of behavioural dependency' (Novak, 1987, p 72). The idea of behavioural dependency was taken up by the new right in the late 1980s and subsequently by New Labour. Even a casual reading of ministerial speeches and policy documents reveals frequent use of the discourse of 'welfare dependency' and the 'dependency culture' (see **Box 5.8**).

The notion of a 'dependency culture' is an example of how culture is used as an explanation of social problems (see Introduction). The main focus of blame here is the social security system. It is reconstructed as a cause of poverty rather than as part of the policy solution, by equating receipt of benefit with dependency. In other words, the argument is that benefit receipt encourages people to become dependent on benefit and give up efforts to become self reliant through paid work. As Marsland articulates it, from a new right perspective: 'The most damaging impact of the Welfare State is on the character, motivations and behaviour of the individual men and women subjected to its comprehensive expropriation of their capacity for free and independent action, for self-reliance, for enterprising initiative and for moral autonomy' (1996, p 109). Although the research evidence does not support this view, it now has a very powerful hold on popular beliefs about poverty. It means that policy prescriptions are focused on moving as many people as possible off benefits into paid work rather than on improving benefits themselves. This social construction of poverty is reinforced by a discourse of 'active' as opposed to 'passive' welfare (see **Box 5.8**).

Box 5.8: Government discourses of dependency and passive/active welfare

[The welfare system] chains people to passive dependency instead of helping them to realise their full potential ... cash hand outs alone can lead to a life of dependency.(Department for Social Security, 1998, pp 9, 19)

A welfare state that is just about 'social security' is inadequate. It is passive where we now need it to be active. It encourages dependency where we need to encourage independence, initiative, enterprise for all. (Blair, 1999, p 13)

We must do more than just alleviate poverty by increasing welfare payments. We must continue to drive it down by tackling the corrosive effects of dependency and, where necessary, change culture and behaviour. (Blunkett, 2006, p 4)

[Previous Labour prime ministers] would have been horrified to see how the notion of personal responsibility gradually became obscured over the decades as parts of our welfare system trapped people between the twin vices of benefit dependency and poverty ... The clear link between benefit dependency and poverty is shown by the simple fact that half of the most severe pockets of deprivation ... are contained within the hundred parliamentary constituencies with the highest numbers of incapacity benefit claimants. So by creating a welfare state where rights properly match responsibilities we have the potential to end the ignominy of a system that traps people in benefit dependency. (Hutton, 2006)

Social justice through independence, not a socially regressive culture of dependency [is] the idea of welfare that, as Secretary of State, I will seek to promote. (Purnell, 2008)

In an influential article, Fraser and Gordon underline the discursive power of the language of dependency and how it reconstructs the problem of poverty in lone parent families:

> 'Dependency' is the single most crucial term in the current U.S. debate about welfare reform ... Few concepts in U.S. social policy discussions do as much ideological work as 'dependency'. The term leaks a profusion of stigmatizing connotations ... It alludes implicitly to a normative state of 'independence', which

> will itself not withstand critical scrutiny. Naming the problems of poor solo mothers and their children 'dependency', moreover, tends to make them appear to be individual rather than social problems, as much moral or psychological as economic. (1994, p 4)

Their article traces the historical roots of the discourse of welfare dependency and the shifting connotations of dependency. They point out that in the economic sphere 'its meaning has shifted from gaining one's livelihood by working for someone else to relying on charity or welfare for support; wage labor now confers independence' (Fraser and Gordon, 1994, p 21). In attempting to formulate an alternative approach, they start from 'the insight that all versions of the opposition between dependence and independence are ideological' (1994, p 22). Who decides what constitutes dependence or independence? They and others argue the need to 'rehabilitate dependency as a normal, even valuable, human quality' (1994, p 23). We are all dependent at some stage in our lives:

> Dependency, whether it be upon the market, the family or the state, is the universal condition of all social beings, and ... it represents a central axis for the exercise of power throughout the whole of our social fabric. At the level of discourse, 'dependency' tends to be regarded quite universally as if it is some undesirable aspect of the human condition. It is regarded as a pathological feature of or within western culture, as something to be avoided where possible ... The ideological, theoretical and discursive contortions which have focused upon 'dependency' have in the process turned welfare state dependency in particular into something which is uniquely problematic. (Dean and Taylor-Gooby, 1992, p 150)

Dean and Taylor-Gooby's reference to dependency as 'a central axis for the exercise of power' hints at how some forms of dependence can be harmful in the context of unequal power relations. From a feminist perspective, Fraser and Gordon distinguish between harmful forms, such as women's economic dependence on men, which are rooted in unequal power relations, and 'socially necessary' forms such as the need for others' care, which is 'an inescapable part of the human condition' (Fraser and Gordon, 1994. p 24). However, some of the assumptions underpinning such distinctions have themselves been challenged by some disability theorists. They criticise the way in which a discourse of dependency is often used to construct disabled people as lacking autonomy and to undermine their citizenship (see Chapter Nine).

In place of the dependence-independence dichotomy, many critical theorists argue for recognition of human interdependence. So, for example, instead of constructing lone mothers as dependent on the state, we might examine how non-resident fathers may depend on lone mothers to bring up their children. Or, we might emphasise the relations of interdependence revealed in 'most studies of disabled women's lives and experiences [which] have shown how they view themselves not just as passive recipients of care but as part of reciprocal networks of care – as mothers, daughters, spouses, friends and relatives who give and receive support in a variety of ways' (Rummery, 2007, p 179).

Social exclusion

The term 'social exclusion' originated in France where it was used to describe marginalised groups who had fallen through the net of the French social insurance system. It led to policies to promote 'insertion' and integration in society. It was taken up by the European Commission in the late 1980s and spread more widely through Continental Europe during the 1990s. It is now firmly embedded within European Union social policy discourse. Initially it was seen as a more Continental European concept in contrast to Anglo-Saxon preoccupation with the 'underclass', but it was taken up as a central social policy concept by New Labour shortly after coming to power in preference to the 'underclass'. New Labour's concern with social exclusion was institutionalised in the early establishment of the Social Exclusion Unit (SEU) at the heart of government.

Ruth Levitas' analysis of social exclusion illuminates how it is socially constructed (see *Box 5.9*). She explains that it is 'a powerful concept, not because of its analytical clarity which is conspicuously lacking, but because of its flexibility' (2005, p 178). This flexibility means that it can be used by both politicians and analysts in widely differing ways. We will focus on its political usage here (see Lister [2004a] for a full discussion of social exclusion as an analytical concept). Within the political arena, Levitas distinguishes three competing discourses within which the concept of social exclusion is embedded (see *Box 5.9*)

Box 5.9: Ruth Levitas' deconstruction of the concept of social exclusion

Levitas contends that:

> The term social exclusion is intrinsically problematic. It represents the primary significant division in society as one between an included majority and an excluded minority. This has implications for how both included and excluded groups are understood, and for the implicit model of society itself. Attention is drawn away from the inequalities and differences among the included. Notably, the very rich are discursively absorbed into the included majority, their power and privilege slipping out of focus if not wholly out of sight. At the same time, the poverty and disadvantage of the so-called excluded are discursively placed outside society ... Exclusion appears as an essentially peripheral problem, existing at the boundary of society, rather than a feature of a society which characteristically delivers massive inequalities across the board and chronic deprivation for a large minority. The solution implied by a discourse of social exclusion is a minimalist one: a transition across the boundary to become an insider rather than an outsider in a society whose structural inequalities remain largely uninterrogated. (2005, p 7)

The three discourses of social exclusion, which she identifies, are:

- RED: a redistributive, egalitarian discourse, which embraces notions of citizenship and social rights. Its primary objective is social justice.
- MUD: a moralistic discourse, which deploys the language of the 'underclass' and 'dependency culture'. Its primary objective is to change the behaviour of 'the poor'.
- SID: a social integrationist discourse, which emphasises social cohesion and defines social inclusion primarily, and sometimes exclusively, with reference to paid work. It ignores the value of the kinds of unpaid work discussed in Chapter Two. Its primary objective is to move people into paid work (Levitas, 2005, pp 9-28).

Levitas sums up the three discourses in terms of what 'the excluded' are seen as lacking: money (and we might add power) in RED; morals in MUD; and paid work in SID.

Today, RED is by far the weakest political discourse. The New Labour government's construction of social exclusion has been primarily that of

SID, with splatterings of MUD. As deployed by New Labour, the discourse of social exclusion constructs the problem of poverty as primarily one of lack of paid work, reinforced by welfare dependency. The definition of social exclusion contained in the former Social Exclusion Unit's remit was 'a shorthand label for what can happen when individuals or areas suffer from a combination of linked problems such as unemployment, poor skills, low incomes, poor housing, high crime environments, bad health and family breakdown' (Levitas, 2005, p 148). While this definition does not confine social exclusion to lack of paid work, it nevertheless foregrounds it. Moreover, the definition represents social exclusion as a series of discrete, albeit connected, problems and this was reflected in the remit given to the SEU. Such a representation reinforces the kind of fragmented individual 'problem' approach, criticised by Bacchi (1999). It also obscures any 'explanatory logic which tries to go beneath appearances to find explanations, including cause/effect relations between different problems and agencies' (Fairclough, 2000, p 53).

On the basis of a cross-European study of discourses of social exclusion Hilary Silver warns of its possible policy implications:

> though the idea of exclusion could be useful to reformers who wish to point to the inadequacies of existing welfare states ...by ghettoizing risk categories under a new label and publicizing the more spectacular forms of poverty requiring emergency aid, policies to combat exclusion may make it easier to re-target money on smaller social categories, like the homeless or the long term unemployed. It may even undermine the universal social insurance schemes that traditionally protected the working and middle classes. (1994, p 572)

Summary

- Social constructionism provides social policy with a critical analytical tool for the study of social problems.
- It problematises the process through which certain troubling conditions do or do not come to be defined as social problems and the ways in which social problems are represented.
- Social constructionism deploys ideology, language, discourse and power as key concepts and analytical tools in the study of the representations of social problems and the effects of these representations.
- Bacchi's 'what's the problem?' approach is an example of the application of social constructionism to social policy.

• The chapter ends with an exploration of the social construction of poverty through the contemporary discourses of the 'underclass', 'welfare dependency' and 'social exclusion'.

Further reading

The classic sociological social constructionist text is **Berger and Luckmann (1967)**; **Burr (2003)** provides a useful introduction from a psychological perspective. For the application of social constructionism to social policy analysis see **Lewis (1998a)**, **Saraga (1998a)**, **Bacchi (1999)** and **Clarke (2001b)**. A more political analysis of the use of language, with implications for social policy, can be found in **Fairclough (2000)**.

Part Three
Concepts

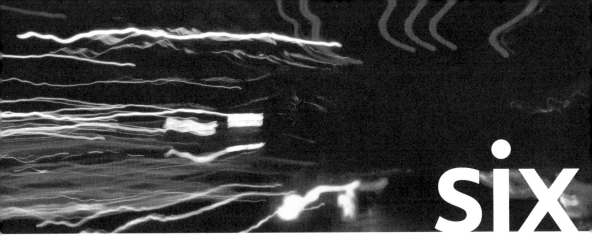

Needs

This is the first of three chapters that focus on key concepts in social policy. Each of these concepts is contested in the sense that their meanings and implications for policy are the subject of political and theoretical debate. We will explore how some of the theoretical perspectives discussed in Part One (and to a lesser extent Part Two) are reflected in these debates. The concepts are also inter-connected in a number of ways, with implications for the kind of society in which we live and for alternative visions of society.

We start with the concept of needs. According to Nick Manning, 'the identification of needs remains at the heart of ideological differences over welfare' (2007, p 80). Indeed, the concept has been described as lying 'at the heart of social policy' (Liddiard, 2007, p 121) and as 'arguably the single most important organising principle in social policy' (Dean, 2010, p 2). Some social policy analysts argue that attention to needs is what differentiates the state from the market as an allocator of resources and also the welfare arms of the state from its other arms (such as social control). According to Howard Glennerster, 'the starting point for the study of social policy is: how have societies evolved ways of meeting the basic needs of their populations?' (2003, p 2). An understanding of needs is critical in assessing the effectiveness of welfare policies and proposed reforms to them and also in the formulation of alternatives. In other words a key question to be asked is: how well does or will any specific social policy meet the needs of those to whom it is directed?

Despite (or perhaps because of) its centrality, the concept of 'needs' was largely taken for granted in social policy analysis until the 1980s. The challenge to the welfare consensus from the 1970s onward, from both left and right, led to the politicisation of the 'needs' concept and to its much closer theoretical scrutiny. Nevertheless, the very familiarity of the notion of needs can get in the way of appreciating the issues it raises. Some of these are introduced by Clarke and Langan in **Box 6.1**.

> ## Box 6.1: The significance of the concept of needs
>
> One reason for the significance of the idea of need is that it links common-sense understandings of the social world with the language and ways of thinking (discourses) of social policy and technical expertise. We all think of ourselves – and other people – as having needs ... There are points of connection and overlap between our everyday usage of the idea of need and the more formal discourses of social policy. These discourses define specific forms of need (for health or social care) and how they are to be addressed by welfare-providing organizations. In some respects these overlaps or connections make it harder to disentangle the processes of social construction that are at stake in the identification, attribution and meeting of need. But these processes are fundamental ones in the organization of social welfare. Though the condition of being in need may be regarded as self-evident, the question of how the needs of different individuals, or groups of individuals, are met in our society is not so straightforward ... It is immediately apparent that there is considerable scope for conflict over the ways in which society defines and meets the needs of particular individuals or sections of society. (Clarke and Langan, 1998, pp 260-1)

In this chapter, we will begin at the more 'common-sense' level of what it means to need something. We will then explore the issues raised by the considerable literature on needs under two main headings:

- ways of thinking about needs, including, in particular, the contested question as to whether it is possible to understand needs as universal;
- 'the politics of needs interpretation', which refers to the kinds of processes described in **Box 6.1**. The key question here is: who decides who needs what? It reflects the kind of social constructionist perspective discussed in Chapter Five.

What is a need?

It is common to answer the question 'what is a need?' by contrasting it with 'wants' and 'preferences'. You will be able to think of many examples for yourself of how needing something and wanting something are not necessarily the same thing. On the one hand you may need something that you do not want: for example you may need medical treatment without knowing that you need it and therefore without wanting it, or your tutor may tell you that you need this book to complement your theory lectures but you may not want to read it! On the other hand, you may want something that you do not need: for example you may want to eat out at expensive restaurants, but you do not actually need to; what you do need is to eat something.

These examples are informed by the idea that need is something that can be determined more or less objectively by other people, most notably 'experts', without necessarily asking the person concerned. In fact, it is not as straightforward as that. (As you will have realised, theory is rarely straightforward!). One study of needs observes that the boundary between needs and wants is 'contested and changes over time. Needs surrounding the Internet and digital technologies are a good example: is Internet access a need in the UK today? What about having a mobile phone? Clearly the answers to these questions change' (Young Foundation, 2009, p 24). Some theorists argue that where any particular line is drawn between needs and wants is in part determined by ideology (see, for instance, Hewitt, 1992). Moreover, as we shall see in our discussion of the politics of needs interpretation, whose expertise decides what counts as a need is contested.

Nevertheless, the implication remains that for something to be accepted as a need in social policy making, it has to be recognised as such by others, especially policy makers. According to Michael Ignatieff, 'to ask what our needs are is to ask not just which of our desires are strongest and most urgent, but which of our desires gives us an entitlement to the resources of others. This natural pairing of the idea of need with the idea of duty and obligation is what distinguishes need from desire' (1990, p 27).

Ignatieff's formulation leaves open the question of which desires do imply such an obligation on others because they have been accorded the status of needs. For many needs theorists the key criterion in distinguishing a need from a want or a desire relates to the implications of it not being met. This can be established by asking for what purpose something is needed or wanted. Thus, the factor that decides whether something is a want or a need is what it is for: in the formula A needs B for C it is C that is critical in determining whether B is a need or a want. Turning the formula into a concrete example, where B is, say, a winter coat: if A does not possess a coat, C = in order to be warm outside in winter; but if A already has a perfectly serviceable warm coat, C might = to look nice, to keep up with fashion or for variety, in which case it represents a want rather than a need. Implicit in this example is the belief that there are certain Cs that justify Bs as needs and others that do not.

Underlying this belief is a more philosophical argument about the nature of need. This is rooted in the idea that a need implies that, unless it is met, a person will be harmed in some way: 'that there is a certain state of human flourishing or welfare, and if a person fails to achieve this state he [sic] will ail or will be harmed. Needs are what are necessary to achieve this condition of flourishing'

(Plant et al, 1980, pp 33-4, cited in Doyal and Gough, 1991). Indeed, some commentators, such as the psychologist Oliver James, argue that the pursuit of wants over needs is, in itself, harmful to human flourishing (see **Box 6.2**).

Box 6.2: Needs and wants

In a reflection on the credit crunch, James underlines 'one fundamental implication':

> to prioritise meeting real needs over confected wants ... We *need*, let's say, emotional intimacy or antibiotics for our children if they are sick, whereas we only *want* a Starbucks or widescreen television. As money becomes tight, every time we are about to purchase something we should automatically start asking ourselves, 'Do I need this, or do I just want it?' One of the great boons that will follow from this sudden collapse of neoliberalism will be that needs will no longer be so conflated with wants, a process caused by advertisers and marketers ... Pursuing wants rather than needs is very bad for mental health. It creates an inner emptiness, a constant hunger for more ... If we cut down on *having*, we can begin to focus on *being*. (James, 2008, emphasis in original)

Other commentators, such as Benjamin Barber, locate the distortion of the distinction between wants and needs squarely within capitalism itself:

> Capitalism's success means that too many goods are now chasing too few needs. Yet capitalism requires us to 'need' all that it produces in order to survive. So it busies itself manufacturing 'needs' for the wealthy while ignoring the wants of the truly needy ... [It shapes consumers' 'wants'] and invent[s] new 'needs'. (Barber, 2007, p 14)

However, in consumer societies capitalism is shaping the needs of 'the needy' also, most notably through increasing commercial pressures on children (Piachaud, 2008a). Research shows how children from low income families do not 'fit in' and are often bullied for not being able to display designer labels and the latest fashion accessories: 'the social imperative' among children and young people 'is increasingly to present a visible display of ownership of consumer goods' (Ridge, 2002, p 144). Low income parents who buy designer goods for their children often face criticism for spending money that could otherwise be spent on 'needs' rather than 'wants'. Yet, in today's consumer society, who is to say that meeting their child's psychological need to 'fit in' is not as important for the child's welfare as meeting her more obvious needs for food and basic clothing?

Question: Can you think of any goods or services that you talk about needing that would be classified as wants according to the distinction made in this section?

The other distinction made in the literature (especially economics) is between needs and preferences. Preferences are revealed through the exercise of choices, usually through the purchase of goods or services. Some new right theorists argue that it is only through the exercise of such choices that individuals can make known what they want or need. Therefore it is illegitimate to contend that need can be determined separately from the expression of preferences. Counter arguments put by social democratic theorists, among others, are that some people do not have the money required to express preferences in the market place and that those needs of which a person is not aware (for example certain medical needs) cannot be expressed in this way. Moreover, preferences can be 'adaptive', which means that members of marginalised groups can adjust their expressed preferences to what they are familiar with and think is possible. In this way, expressed preferences can be depressed by the low expectations borne of experience. The concept of need therefore remains pivotal to social policy.

Thinking about needs

The literature contains numerous taxonomies or classifications of needs. One report (Vale et al, 2009) lists eight, together with two that relate specifically to children's needs. These taxonomies typically address the question of 'need for what?' They tend to list a range of physiological, material, emotional, psychological, social and cultural needs. Examples include: subsistence or food, water and shelter; belonging or love; self-esteem; participation; and leisure.

Some of these taxonomies are hierarchical. The most famous of these is Maslow's (1943) hierarchy of basic needs. This is built on the belief that basic physiological needs have to be met first before turning to more psychological or social needs in a fixed order. Another influential taxonomy is that of Manfred Max-Neef and colleagues. They argue, in contrast to Maslow, that 'all human needs are interrelated and interactive. With the sole exception of the need of subsistence, to remain alive, no hierarchies exist…On the contrary, simultaneities, complementarities and trade-offs are characteristics of the process of needs satisfaction' (Max-Neef et al, 1989, p 19). This is also the position taken by Doyal and Gough, whose work we will discuss in greater depth. They argue that human needs are 'interwoven like a web' (1984, p 11). A study of needs in the UK provides empirical support for their view. It found that 'most people now think of needs in terms of psychological wellbeing as well as material factors. It also shows that there is no simple hierarchy of needs: for some people, whether refugees or unemployed teenagers, a mobile phone may be as important or a higher priority than having a square meal' (Young Foundation, 2009, p 15). How people classify needs in practice depends on a number of factors, 'not least the context or situation they find themselves in.' (Young Foundation, 2009, p 26). Examples of how material and sociopsychological needs are interwoven can also be found in the poverty literature, where people in poverty often express a need for recognition, respect and social participation as urgently as they do supposedly more basic material needs (Lister, 2004a).

As well as taxonomies, which classify particular needs, there are also broader, sometimes overlapping, categorisations, which differentiate types of need. Two, which are particularly prominent in the social policy literature, distinguish between basic universal and relative needs and between thin and thick needs. As we shall see, there is considerable overlap between these two categorisations.

Universal and relative needs

The fundamental question addressed by many needs theorists is whether there are certain needs that we have irrespective of when and where we live and of cultural or other differences. In other words, can needs be understood as universal?

> **Question:** Can you think of any needs that you have that you would have regardless of the century or part of the world in which you lived?

The most important and thorough exploration of this question can be found in Doyal and Gough's *A Theory of Human Need* (1991). Their starting point is to engage with various theoretical approaches that, in different ways, dispute the notion of universal needs in favour of the idea that needs are historically and culturally determined. We too will look briefly at how some of the theoretical perspectives discussed in earlier chapters address the nature of and distinction between universal and relative needs before outlining Doyal and Gough's own theory.

Emphasising the relative

Need is an important concept in **Marxism**, as reflected in its censure of capitalism's failure to meet human needs and the ideal of 'from each according to his ability, to each according to his needs', popularised by

Marx in the *Critique of the Gotha Programme* (1875). There is not the space here to do justice to Marx's various writings on needs (see, for instance, Hewitt, 1992, 1998; Dean, 2010). The key point, in this context, is that while Marxism recognises a basic universal biological need for survival, its main emphasis is on the historical variation in how people experience their needs. This variation is shaped, in particular, by the economic means of production, social institutions and the state of technology. 'Marx proposes an historically relative definition denoting what is needed by people and capable of being satisfied by productive forces within society at a specific time' (Hewitt, 1992, p 74). He wrote in *Capital*:

> [the individual's] natural needs, such as food, clothing, fuel and housing vary according to the climatic and other physical peculiarities of his country. On the other hand, the number and extent of his so-called necessary requirements, as also the manner in which they are satisfied, are themselves products of history, and depend therefore to a great extent on the level of civilisation attained by a country; in particular they depend on the conditions in which, and consequently on the habits and expectations with which, the class of free workers has been formed. (Marx, 1976, p 275, cited in Hewitt, 1992, p 74)

Marxism also criticises the ways in which capitalism creates supposed needs out of wants in the drive to sell more commodities, in particular through advertising. A key figure in 20th century Marxism, who developed this argument, was Herbert Marcuse. According to Marcuse, 'the intensity, the satisfaction and even the character of human needs, beyond the biological level, have always been pre-conditioned' (1964, p 21). He distinguishes between 'true and false needs' and maintains that only true needs 'have an unqualified claim for satisfaction'; these are 'vital ones – nourishment, clothing, lodging at the attainable level of culture' (1964, pp 21, 22). False needs 'are those which are superimposed upon the individual by particular social interests in his [sic] repression: the needs which perpetuate toil, aggressiveness, misery, and injustice' (1964, p 21). Modern industrial society and technology create these 'false' needs as a form of social control.

Elements of Marcuse's critique are shared by many non-Marxists (see **Box 6.2**). In a widely publicised book on the 'turbo-consuming society', for instance, Neal Lawson (2009, p 3) argues that capitalism sells us anything – togetherness, individuality, control and identity – through the advertising of consumer goods as a means of satisfying psychological needs. This repudiation of capitalism's manufacture of needs is also reflected in **environmentalism**, which rejects material consumption as the main measure of needs satisfaction (Cahill, 2007). Bill Jordan makes the connection:

> capitalist production seeks to expand people's perception of their personal needs and the material goods on which their sense of well-being depends. All this encourages high levels of use of materials, and especially fossil fuels and other non-renewable sources of energy production, as intrinsic features of capitalist development. (2006, p 242)

In contrast, environmentalism emphasises the importance of non-material sources of human well-being (discussed later) and environmental needs over consumer goods. **Post-Fordist** writers maintain that a key element in the shift from Fordism to post-Fordism is the replacement of standardised needs and products to meet them with a huge diversity of products customised to individual 'needs' through niche marketing.

The most fundamental challenge to the idea of universal needs comes from **postmodernism**. As we saw in Chapter Three, postmodernism questions the very idea of the universal. It argues that all needs and how they are met 'are always culturally and historically conditioned, and anyone who argues otherwise is guilty of generalising from an ethnocentric and temporally local conception of human nature and its needs' (Soper, 1993, p 114). In other words, the argument is that it is not possible for us to generalise about needs from within our own specific historical and cultural situation. Needs are relative. Moreover, postmodernists and Foucauldians reject the idea of needs as given. Instead, they focus on the ways in which needs are talked about and the processes through which they are constructed:

> Here the question may be asked what notions of power, control, normalization and self-regulation are involved in producing the concept. Once the social is understood as the site where needs become politicized, contested and interpreted, then what is important are the processes by which certain needs are politicized and others are not. Needs can no longer be taken as given and simply waiting to be expressed and satisfied. (Watson, 2000, p 73)

This approach takes us back to the social constructionist position discussed in Chapter Five and will be explored further in the second part of this chapter. The postmodernist theorisation of needs also resonates with some **anti-racist** and **feminist** positions, which assert the specificity of the needs of women and of different ethnic groups. Thompson and Hoggett make the connection. They observe how postmodernists reject 'the existence of a set of basic, culturally universal needs, based on an account of intrinsic human nature. By contrast, some theorizations of social movements of sexuality or ethnicity stress the particularity of their … needs' (1996, p 26).

In a more extreme version of this position, it is argued that only members of a particular group, be it defined by 'race'/ethnicity, gender or sexual orientation, can understand the needs and perspectives of that group. Some radical feminists, in particular, assert that fundamental differences exist between women's and men's needs. In a less extreme version, the argument might be that if we assume the universality of needs, as social policy has tended to do, there is a danger that policies fail to pay attention to those needs that are particular to specific groups and to variations in the ways in which needs are experienced. In Chapter Two we saw how the cultural and other needs of minority ethnic groups are often overlooked by welfare state services (see **Box 2.16**). With regard to women, Hewitt suggests that 'if the different needs claimed by feminists are taken seriously, then notions of common human needs and universal rights to welfare become highly problematic' (1998, p 66).

> **Question:** Can you think of examples of needs which might differ between women and men or between ethnic groups?

Hewitt contrasts feminist concern with gendered differences in needs with the **social democratic** understanding of basic needs as 'universal and by implication common to one single human nature' (1998, p 66). This does not mean, however, that social democratic/democratic socialist thinking allows no space for thinking of needs as relative. Paul Wetherly, for instance, identifies need 'as a key socialist value' and argues that views as to what constitutes the adequate satisfaction of needs 'will vary between cultures' (1996, pp 45, 58). Moreover, the social democratic conception of poverty, highly influenced by the work of Peter Townsend, is founded on a notion of needs as relative rather than absolute (Lister, 2004a). This is in two senses: first, that we can only judge whether someone is in need or in poverty relative to other people living in the same society at the same historical moment; and second that needs are themselves socially and culturally shaped. For instance, the need for food or clothing will be met in very different ways in urban Britain and rural Africa. This means, as we shall see, that there are disagreements as to what constitutes a need that society should ensure people can meet.

Doyal and Gough's theory of universal needs

Having rejected those approaches that treat needs as primarily relative, Doyal and Gough (1991) make the case for a universal conceptualisation of basic human needs. This is premised on a definition of basic human needs as 'the universal pre-requisites for successful … participation in a social form of life' (Gough, 1998, p 53). These universal pre-requisites are identified as physical health and autonomy. Physical health involves more than just survival; it also means good-enough physical health to enable social participation. Autonomy refers to 'autonomy of agency – *the capacity to make informed choices about what should be done and how to go about doing it*', which, is identified as 'the definitive attribute of human beings' (Gough, 1998, p 53, emphasis in original). Doyal and Gough articulate a social rather than individualistic understanding of autonomy as involving inter-dependence rather than independence: 'we can only acquire the ability to act from the positive actions of others and they from others and so on' (1991, p 76; see also Tao and Drover, 1997).

Physical health and autonomy of agency are, according to Doyal and Gough, necessary in any culture before any individual can effectively participate in order to achieve any other valued goals. However, these basic needs are formulated at a very general level. They are not, therefore, on their own, a very good guide for social policy. They do not tell us what social policy must provide in order to satisfy these basic needs. Doyal and Gough therefore add another layer of 'intermediate needs'. These represent 'derived or second-order goals which must be achieved if the first-order goals of health and autonomy are to be attained' (Doyal and Gough, 1991, p 157). The criterion for inclusion in the list of intermediate needs (*Box 6.3*) is universal and positive contribution to physical health and autonomy.

Box 6.3: Doyal and Gough's list of intermediate needs

Nutritional food and clean water
Protective housing
A non-hazardous work environment
A non-hazardous physical environment
Appropriate health care
Security in childhood
Significant primary relationships
Physical security
Economic security
Appropriate education
Safe birth control and child-bearing. (Doyal and Gough, 1991, pp 157-8)

The list of intermediate needs is still fairly general in that it does not tell us how these needs are to be met. It is therefore necessary to introduce a further level:'specific needs satisfiers'.The notion of needs satisfiers refers to the ways in which needs are met in a specific social context. Intermediate needs provide 'the crucial bridge between universal basic needs and socially relative satisfiers' of those needs (Doyal and Gough, 1991, p 157). In other words, while Doyal and Gough's theory sets out to establish that there are certain basic, universal human needs, how those needs are satisfied will vary according to social, historical and cultural context. So, while nutritional food is a universal intermediate need, essential to ensure the fundamental needs of physical health and autonomy, the specific satisfiers that meet this need are different today than they were in earlier centuries and vary between cultures.To take a simple example: what constitutes an appropriate breakfast, required to satisfy the need for food in the morning, differs widely between cultures.

Despite their emphasis on universal needs and rejection of relative conceptualisations, Doyal and Gough also accept that:

> there is a sense in which particular groups have specific needs. Obvious examples are women, groups subject to racial oppression and people with disabilities. Members of each group are commonly subject to additional threats to their health and autonomy over and above those which we have already outlined. As a result they require additional and specific satisfiers and procedures to address and correct them.The fact that this is the case, however, does not entail that the basic needs of members of such groups are any different from those of all other persons. (1991, p 74)

In this way Doyal and Gough combine their universalist stance with acknowledgement of the kind of 'particularist' perspectives more usually associated with postmodernism (although their theory focuses very much on the former).Thompson and Hoggett explain that 'at a general theoretical level, it could be said that, while forms of *universalism* seek to apply the same standard to all individuals, *particularist* theories contend that different standards are appropriate in different circumstances for different individuals and groups' (1996, p 22, emphasis in original; see also Hewitt, 1998).This is a theme to which we will return in Chapter Seven in our discussions about citizenship.

> *Question:* Look at the following list of needs and classify them according to whether they represent intermediate needs or socially specific satisfiers. The list is taken from items deemed necessities by a majority of the British population in a survey of poverty and social exclusion (Gordon et al, 2000):
> - damp-free home;
> - two meals a day;
> - fresh fruit and vegetables daily;
> - warm, waterproof coat;
> - meat, fish or vegetarian equivalent every other day;
> - washing machine;
> - carpets in living rooms and bedrooms.

Thin and thick needs

The notion of 'thin' and 'thick' needs is another way in which the literature distinguishes between more abstract, universal intermediate needs and concrete, particular needs satisfiers. The distinction was first made by Nancy Fraser (1989). She uses the example of the needs of homeless people to illustrate it. It is easy to agree on the 'thin' need of homeless people for some form of shelter in order to live. 'However, as soon as we descend to a lesser level of generality, needs claims become far more controversial. What, more "thickly", do homeless people need in order to be sheltered from the cold? What specific forms of provision are entailed once we acknowledge their very general, thin need?' (Fraser, 1989, p 163). Options include a bed in a temporary shelter, a room in a hostel or bed and breakfast, or a tenancy for a flat or house. All these are thick needs and their articulation will vary according to cultural and social context. Drover and Kerans endorse Fraser's distinction, 'largely because it evokes a continuous spectrum rather than a dichotomy' (Drover and Kerans, 1993, p 11). This reflects the complementary rather than oppositional nature of the thin–thick distinction.

Hartley Dean (2010, Ch 6) develops the thin and thick distinction in a rather different way in order to introduce the increasingly fashionable notion of well-being (see *Box 6.4*) into his account of human need. Part of his argument is that, from the perspective of promoting well-being, thin needs require satisfaction in order to prevent harm and to be well enough; thick needs enable the achievement of more ambitious goals such as human flourishing and social quality (see *Box 6.4*). Underlying this distinction are two different conceptions of the human subject (see Introduction): a rational economic actor, maximising his interests, and an embodied human being embedded within social relationships.

Box 6.4: Well-being and social quality

Well-being is an ideal that is increasingly being advocated in policy debates, particularly by environmentalists (see Chapter Two). Some theorists argue that it is what social policy is all about (Dean, 2006). This view is reflected in *Towards an African Regional Social Policy*, a draft framework for social policies in Southern Africa, drawn up by ministers and senior civil servants from 13 Southern African countries. It states that 'social policies are interventions which are about promoting the well being of all citizens' (cited in Noble et al, 2007, p 10).The French President, Nicolas Sarkozy, established an International Commission on the Measurement of Economic Performance and Social Progress, involving some of the world's leading economists, to propose measurements of social progress. Their widely publicised report identifies the promotion of well-being as critical to social progress (www.stiglitz-sen-fitoussi.fr).

In the UK, politicians across the political spectrum have taken up the idea and a local index of child well-being for England has been developed by the government (www.communities.gov.uk/publications/communities/childwellbeing2009). The new economics foundation (nef) has been a leading proponent. In 2004 it published *A well-being manifesto for a flourishing society*. This defined well-being as 'more than just happiness. As well as feeling satisfied and happy, well-being means developing as a person, being fulfilled, and making a contribution to the community' (Shah and Marks, 2004, p 2). The distinction is similar to that made by Dean between thin and thick needs. The manifesto argues that 'one of the key aims of a democratic government is to promote the good life: a flourishing society where citizens are happy, healthy, capable, and engaged, in other words with high levels of well-being' (Shah and Marks, 2004, p 4).

The nef has subsequently developed the aim of 'well-being for all as the primary objective of sustainable social justice ... It's about flourishing – physically, socially and psychologically – not just now but in the medium and long term' (Coote and Franklin, 2009, p 12). The nef has also proposed how national well-being might be measured to complement narrow measures of economic growth through:

> a radical proposal to guide the direction of modern societies and the lives of people who live in them. It says that national governments should directly measure people's subjective well-being: their experiences, feelings and perceptions of how their lives are going. These measures should be collected on a regular, systematic basis and published as National Accounts of Well-being. (Michaelson et al, 2009, p 8)

The related concept of '**social quality**' has been developed by a group of European social scientists. It is defined as 'the extent to which citizens [and other residents] are able to participate in the social and economic life of their communities under conditions which enhance their well-being and individual potential' (Beck et al, 2001, p 7)

Another concept, often associated with well-being, is that of **capabilities**, articulated most fully by Amartya Sen (1985, 1999; see also Dean, 2009 for a critique). Sen, together with Martha Nussbaum (1995), has made explicit links between the capabilities approach and the notion of well-being; they focus on the positive of the kind of life we want people to be able to achieve in order to flourish and the choices and opportunities open to them in leading that life. Sen introduces the terms 'capabilities' and 'functionings' to express this idea. 'Capabilities' denote what a person can do or be, that is, the range of choices that are open to her. 'Functionings' refer to what a person actually manages to do or be; they range from elementary nourishment to richer aspects of well-being such as participation in the life of the community and the achievement of self-respect. Functionings are achieved through 'commodities' or goods and services. This is another way of bringing together conceptualisations of needs as universal (at the level of capabilities) and relative (as expressed through more concrete commodities). Indeed, Doyal and Gough integrate Sen's framework into their own, with some modifications.

The British Equality and Human Rights Commission have also adopted the capabilities approach in the development of an 'equality measurement' framework (see Chapter Eight). Following extensive consultation, the framework is presented as reflecting consensus on 'a list of fundamental things people need in order to thrive in life': 'those things in life that people say are important for them to actually *do* and *be*.' (EHRC, 2009a, p 1, emphasis in original)

The politics of needs interpretation

A third categorisation is between what Dean describes as 'notions of need which are *inherent* to the human individual and *interpreted* needs which are creatures of policy processes and debates' (2002, p 25; 2010, Chs 2 and 3). Elsewhere this distinction has been framed as between 'intrinsic' and 'procedural' approaches (Hewitt, 1992, Tao and Drover, 1997). Again, there is some overlap with the categorisations we have already discussed. So far the discussion has, for the most part, implicitly treated needs as inherent; we have taken for granted that people have particular needs and have discussed different ways of categorising such needs. However, as Drover and Kerans point out, a thick understanding of need 'relies on interpretive methods to grasp the full particularity of the meaning of … need … in its everyday context … A thick notion of need, therefore, focuses on the politics of needs interpretation, since it foresees that [needs] claims … will be contested' (1993, pp 12-13). The idea of thick needs therefore acts as a bridge to the question of needs interpretation.

As explained earlier, the notion of needs as interpreted reflects postmodernist and social constructionist thinking, in which needs are understood as 'socially constructed, historically specific and contested' (Langan, 1998b, p 7). In other words, the assumption is that needs can be understood only in terms of how they are constructed by different groups in a specific time and place. Unlike approaches that treat needs as inherent, an understanding of needs as interpreted does not take them as given but problematises the processes involved in the articulation, interpretation and satisfaction of needs. The term 'the politics of needs interpretation' conveys a dynamic political process in which needs have to be interpreted by a range of social actors before any decision can be made as to whose needs for what should be met and by which institutions.

The idea of 'the politics of needs interpretation' was first articulated by Fraser (1989). Her focus is discourses about needs rather than needs themselves. The aim is 'to bring into view the contextual and contested character of needs claims' (Fraser, 1989, p 163). Fraser's statement introduces the idea of 'needs as claims' or a process of claims-making in which individuals and groups attempt to get their needs established as worthy of being met. As Paul Spicker observes, since 'the concept of "need" is not decisive in the allocation of resources … [It] has to be understood as a form of claim-language' (1993, p 7). He explains that 'the establishment of priorities between greater and lesser needs depends on the strength of the claim which the needs present, and the context in which services operate, rather than on intrinsic comparisons between different levels of need' (1993, p 7). What the notion of the politics of needs interpretation adds to the idea of claims is an understanding that 'what is central is the *struggle* over the interpretation of needs' (Drover and Kerans, 1993, p 6, emphasis added). This struggle also involves concepts that will be the subject of the following two chapters: citizenship, liberty, equality and social justice.

Fraser (1989) identifies three 'moments' of the politics of needs interpretation: the establishment of the political status of needs; the practical interpretation of needs; and the satisfaction of needs. Although they are separated out for analytical purposes, they are interrelated in practice. She emphasises the significance of competing kinds of 'needs talk' or discourses in shaping the politics of needs. Ignatieff makes an even more fundamental point about the importance of language: 'Our needs are made of words: they come to us in speech, and they can die for lack of expression. Without a public language to help us find our own words, our needs will dry up in silence' (1990, p 142). For example, before women had developed a language in which to articulate the need for protection against sexual harassment in the workplace, it was impossible to place this need on the political and policy agenda (Bacchi, 1999).

Establishment of the political status of needs

The first moment in the politics of needs interpretation 'is the struggle to establish or deny the political status of a given need, the struggle to validate the need as a matter of legitimate concern or to enclave it as a nonpolitical matter' (Fraser, 1989, p 164). This process is very similar to that involved in the identification of social problems. It usually involves translation of a felt need from the private domestic sphere to its articulation in the public political sphere. Social movements such as feminism and the disabled people's movement have been instrumental in the collective representation of needs, which were previously not recognised as such and in challenging dominant interpretations of needs (see Chapter Two and Chapter Nine). Fraser argues that these represent '"oppositional" forms of needs talk, which arise when needs are politicized "from below"' (1989, p 171). Indeed the very process of developing oppositional needs discourses and politicizing needs in this way can help to crystallise emergent collective identities, as common needs are identified and named.

> **Question:** Can you think of examples of where the political status of needs has been established as a result of the struggles of the feminist or disabled people's movement or of other social movements?

When social movements or other social groups are successful in getting such discourses heard, they then have to contend with two other kinds of needs discourses. The first are 'reprivatisation discourses'. These are deployed by powerful organised groups and institutions whose interests are served by dominant needs discourses. Reprivatisation discourses 'articulate entrenched need interpretations that could previously go without saying' (Fraser, 1989, p 171). They attempt to deny the political status of the needs identified from below and thereby to 'reprivatise' them. Reprivatisation discourses are also deployed in order to justify the state's retreat from meeting needs. 'They classically take the form of demands to "roll back the state" or to make the individual or family responsible for their own welfare in order to counter "dependency" on public provision' (O'Brien and Penna, 1998, p 126).

Second, as social movements or groups engage with the state they encounter 'expert needs discourses'. It is through expert needs discourses that recognised needs can be translated into 'objects of potential state intervention' (Fraser, 1989, p 173). This brings us to the next moment of the politics of needs interpretation: the actual interpretation of needs in the policy-making and implementation process.

The interpretation of needs

'Expert needs discourses' turn needs into administrative categories such as homelessness so that decisions can then be taken as to how they should be met. O'Brien and Penna spell out their role:

> Expert needs discourses are associated with the major institutions of knowledge-production and application – including universities and think-tanks, professional associations and agencies of the social state. They serve most readily as vehicles for translating politicised needs into objects of state intervention by redefining them into categories of administrative service. This redefining process classically takes the form of translating a particular 'expressed' need into a 'case' of a more generalised social problem – unemployment, disability or homelessness, for example. The effect of the redefinition is ... to depoliticise the conditions which gave rise to its expression in the first place. (1998, p 125)

One increasingly vocal response from user movements to this deployment of expert needs discourses has been to challenge assumptions about the nature of expertise. The disabled people's movement has been in the vanguard (see Chapter Nine). User movements are no longer willing to accept without question the assumption that professionals and bureaucrats know best. Contending interpretations of need emerge 'most notably in the profound tension between "professional" and "lay" standpoints, in which user movements have challenged the objectivism of professional knowledge (and assessments deriving from it). Instead, they have articulated the claim that users – not professionals – are the "experts of their own condition"' (Clarke et al, 2007, p 61). Some of the issues at stake, including where users are not active in user movements, are illustrated in **Box 6.5**.

Box 6.5: Whose expertise?

A Young Foundation report on unmet needs asks:

> Are professionals or experts best able to identify the needs of others? Their views must surely be constrained by their worldview and their professional parameters and what about their distance from those whose needs are being assessed? ... Conversely, there might be good reasons to be sceptical about the utility of focusing solely on individuals' and groups' perspectives of their own needs when these might well be limited by insufficient knowledge of what means of needs satisfaction are available, entrenched powerlessness and resignation about the intractability of the need and dependent forms of coping mechanisms they have developed to adapt to the prolonged existence of the need. (Vale et al, 2009, p 74)

A user perspective is voiced by Simon Stevens, an independent disability consultant. It makes clear some of the complexities involved in needs interpretation. He observes how the professional expert categorisation of needs translates into the labelling of users themselves:

> users' experiences of the social care system are based on the label which has been placed on them ... Once a label has been imposed it will be difficult to remove even if it is inappropriate and can affect people for the rest of their lives. As a young, physically impaired person entering the system in the early 1990s I was labelled 'independent'.

This label has, in his view, meant an assumption that:

> I am able to self-manage many aspects of my impairment and other health needs. This has led to my interaction with services being more based on my own viewpoint rather than any objective assessment. So I have got the wheelchair I want but maybe not the one that is best suited for me. (Stevens, 2009a, p 10)

An account of a Spanish healthy eating project for Romanian immigrant families emphasises the importance of listening to users' own views of what they need (Taylor, 2008). The project was established to address health problems among immigrant families unused to Spanish food. The families were already receiving food parcels but they contained food that Romanians do not eat. A project organiser explained that '"Not many people start from the premise of asking people what they really need," he says. "[Instead], we tend to start from the premise that they need food so we will give them food." By contrast, the Montilla project started by talking to the families about their diet, and looking at what was good about it and what could be added to it' (Taylor, 2008, p 20). This provided the basis for shopping and cooking sessions designed to encourage healthy eating.

The expert needs discourses of different professional, bureaucratic and political bodies may themselves sometimes clash. An example is the interpretation of the needs of rough sleepers in the London Borough of Westminster. Councillors proposed that soup runs for rough sleepers should be outlawed. In a letter to *The Independent* (19 November 2007), the cabinet member for housing put the case. She argued that 'Westminster knows the way to help rough sleepers is to meet their complex needs. Ex-rough-sleepers ... tell us that soup runs keep people on the streets rather than helping them off ... The majority of soup runs are failing rough sleepers by simply handing out food that ensures that people can remain on the streets'. This, she claimed, is 'damaging the health and lifechances of rough sleepers.' A series of letters to *The Guardian* (12 November 2007) from homelessness workers provided a different perspective: 'For many of London's homeless, soup runs are the only readily accessible source of free food. A ban would effectively be starving many of society's most vulnerable people'. 'No regard is given to alternative arrangements for those who require succour – physically and mentally.' The effect 'will be to deepen the isolation suffered by people already struggling in our divided society.' Homeless people themselves protested, arguing that without the soup runs they would starve (*The Independent*, 14 November).

An earlier attempt to express the different ways in which needs are interpreted at this stage of the politics of needs interpretation is Jonathan Bradshaw's (1972) taxonomy of needs. This is widely cited in the literature. He distinguishes between four kinds of need:

- **Normative**. Needs are defined according to professional or expert norms and standards. (*Note:* this is a different meaning of the term 'normative' to that used in the Introduction; it is about setting standards rather than expressing ideals.) How needs should be met is decided by welfare professionals or bureaucrats on the basis of these norms.
- **Felt.** These are needs as perceived and experienced by an individual or group themselves. Professionals sometimes attempt to gauge felt needs by asking individuals (as in the Spanish example in ***Box 6.5***) or collectively through needs audits.
- **Expressed**. When vocalised publicly, felt needs become expressed needs. A need is then translated into a demand (even if it is not expressed in the language of demands).

- **Comparative**. A comparative need reflects a judgement between the needs of different individuals or groups. A decision as to whether an individual's needs should be met is made by comparing them with those of others.

The distinction between normative need on the one hand and felt and expressed need on the other is at the heart of the process of needs interpretation at the level of everyday interaction in the welfare state. Implicit in the idea of comparative need is an assumption that resources are limited to a greater or lesser extent. The politics of needs interpretation is, therefore, in part a process of rationing. In the UK, this rationing is often effected through 'needs assessments', particularly in the domains of health and social care. As the Young Foundation explains:

> needs assessments ... are primarily a resource prioritization targeting tool and it might be argued are being used to disguise the fact that fewer resources are available, that mainstream universal needs are non-priority or low priority and that services and goods will naturally be concentrated on residual categories of people assessed as having 'high', 'priority' or 'special' needs. (Vale et al, 2009, p 74)

In the domain of social care, provision is allocated according to assessment of the needs of both the person in need of care and of their carer. When the policy of community care was introduced, Langan and Clarke (1994) observed that despite a 'user-led' discourse, care managers' performance would be judged primarily on the basis of their use of resources. This has proved to be the case. Care-managers have to stay within budgets and this shapes how they interpret needs, as is made clear in the official guidance to which they work (see *Box 6.6*). The assessment of comparative needs trumps normative, felt and expressed needs at the point of needs interpretation (see *Box 6.6*).

Box 6.6: UK examples of how the interpretation of needs is determined by the rationing of resources or of how comparative needs dominate needs assessments

The covering note to the Department of Health's (2003) guidance on eligibility criteria for adult social care states:

> The framework is based on individuals' needs and associated risks to independence, and includes four eligibility bands – critical, substantial,

moderate and low ... The guidance confirms that when setting their eligibility criteria, councils should take account of the resources locally allocated to adult social care. Because of the different resource positions of councils, the guidance does not require councils to reach similar decisions on eligibility, or to provide similar services, to people in similar needs (www. dh.gov.uk/en/Publicationsandstatistics/Publications).

In other words, resources shape the interpretation of needs at the level of local authority policy making. One consequence is what is sometimes described as a 'postcode lottery' as to which and whose needs are met. A 2008 report from the Commission for Social Care Inspection warned that nearly three-quarters of local authorities in England were planning to confine help to people with 'critical' or 'substantial' care needs (*The Guardian*, 29 January 2008). This excludes people unable 'to carry out several personal care or domestic routines' or sustain several 'social support systems and relationships' or 'family and other social roles and responsibilities' (Department of Health, 2003, para. 16). The implication for individuals was brought home in an earlier editorial in *The Independent* (11 October 2007), which criticised 'the 150 local authorities who have so recast their definition of needs that even those who need help getting out of bed in the morning now find themselves excluded from services'.

Resources also shape the interpretation of needs at the level of the assessment of individual users. Simon Heng, a disabled user, claims that 'increasingly social workers have found that they have become gatekeepers and rationers of resources, which have become progressively thinly spread between ever-increasing numbers of clients, or restricted to those most in need' (2007, p 10). Social workers themselves complain of their inability to respond to expressed need because they are acting as gatekeepers to inadequate budgets. Simon Stevens, another disabled user, describes how his 'desire to live a full and active life was converted into a three-hour-a-day social services contribution to toileting, dressing and meal preparation' once his 'user-led' outcomes were translated 'into needs and the dreaded eligibility criteria' (2009b, p 10).

Child protection is another area in which need is a mechanism for rationing. The 1989 Children Act requires local authorities to provide services for children classified as 'in need'. However, the threshold adopted is so high that professionals complain that a child must almost be requiring protection in order to qualify for help, thereby undermining the preventative aspirations of the legislation (Garboden, 2009).

In the domain of homelessness, Rosa Aers vividly describes how her role as a restrictive gatekeeper led her to give up her job as a trainee homelessness caseworker in an inner city borough. Her account also illustrates the earlier point about how need is translated into administrative categories:

> The concept of judging – to determine whether someone is in priority need of assistance, if an applicant is 'less able to fend for themselves than an ordinary homeless person and subsequently at greater risk of harm or detriment' – seemed, and still seems, absurd. I was judging how ill someone was, how vulnerable they were, while all the time feeling that anyone would be rendered vulnerable living on the streets. This was baffling to me on paper. It was later that I would find it more infuriating as it emerged that the agenda of gatekeeping public funds is as powerful a factor in deciding whether someone would be assisted as the statute and case law itself. (Aers, 2008, p 1)

During training Aers was advised that all cases could be condensed to a 'handful of stories':

> Seeing 10 clients a day and working on 15 longer-term cases at any time, reluctantly I began to categorise people's lives this simply. The 33-day deadline within which each case must be resolved became the clock by which we ticked. People became the blue file containing the paperwork of life – the bank statements, payslips, rent books, medical records, passports and address histories that, as investigators on behalf of the state, we trawled through. And the results of these investigations might be to hand out or deny a grotty third-floor flat on a defeated estate. (Aers, 2008, p 2)

She justifies her decision to leave:

> for me, the grind has been enough – the cynicism too overbearing, the resources too scarce, the legislation too punitive, and the relationships established too fleeting and ultimately bureaucratic in nature. (Aers, 2008, p 2)

Until now, we have been talking about the needs of individuals. Another aspect of the interpretation of needs concerns the distinction that can be made between individual and societal needs. Societal needs refer to interpretations of what is required for society as a whole in order for it to function effectively and, some would argue, fairly. Societal needs, as interpreted by politicians and professionals, are often interpreted with reference to public safety or public order. Typically, 'the needs of society as a whole, as interpreted by the state, codified in legislation and enforced by welfare professionals, take priority over the rights [and felt needs] of individuals who are judged to be a danger to themselves or others' (Clarke and Langan, 1998, p 6). Clarke and Langan warn that problems are likely to arise where a 'need is identified as what society needs rather than the individual', particularly 'in societies where there is a high level of social inequality, differentiation and antagonism' (1998, p 6). The 2007 Mental Health Act provides an example (see *Box 6.7*). A similar distinction could be made between individual and environmental needs when they come into conflict.

Box 6.7: Individual vs. societal needs

Following a number of widely publicised cases of homicide committed by people with mental health problems, legislation was introduced in England and Wales to protect the public. The 2007 Mental Health Act makes provision for community treatment orders (CTOs). Subject to certain conditions, these allow mental health professionals to enforce supervised community treatment on people with mental health problems who are deemed a risk to others. One of the criteria is that a CTO 'is necessary for the patient's health or safety *or the protection of other persons*' (section 17A(5), cited in Dawson, 2007, emphasis added).

According to the mental health charity, Mind, one of the concerns voiced by mental health campaigners 'is that an increase in the use of compulsion in the community will be accompanied by an even greater reliance on chemical treatment' as the easy option for over-stretched workers. Mind argues that 'stopping medication is often a rational decision which can lead to an improved quality of life' (Dawson, 2007, para 4.2).

Rather than forcing 'people to use services which feel unattractive or irrelevant to their needs under a threat of readmission [to hospital], Mind and the Mental Health Alliance believe that the resources being diverted to the introduction of supervised community treatment would be better focused on developing services such as early intervention services that would help prevent the need for readmission' (Dawson, 2007, para 4.5).

The example underlines how societal needs, as interpreted by the government, and the needs of individuals with mental health problems, as interpreted by mental health campaigners, can clash.

> **Question:** Can you think of other policy areas where what the government interprets as societal needs clash with the felt needs of particular individuals or groups of individuals?

Needs satisfaction

We have discussed the processes involved in the establishment and interpretation of needs. The third stage in Fraser's politics of needs interpretation is the satisfaction of needs. This raises a set of questions, which are implicitly or explicitly at the centre of many political debates around welfare.

The first question concerns where responsibility lies for meeting a particular need. The Young Foundation talks about 'the need economy', comprising the state, the market, civil society (including the third or voluntary sector) and the household (or family). It suggests that 'the nature and make up of each, and the boundaries between them are constantly shifting and changing. The shifting boundaries are partly determined by the political process' (Vale et al, 2009, p 28). We saw in Part One how the boundaries between the responsibility of the state and other parts of the 'need economy' are drawn differently by the various political ideologies that have shaped post-war social policy. The dominant trend in recent decades has been for the market, third sector and household or family to play a larger role in needs satisfaction, reflecting both new right and third way thinking. In some cases this has meant the 're-privatisation' of needs (Fraser, 1989). In the UK, an important issue is the role of the third or voluntary sector, which is often identified as best placed to articulate the needs of marginalised groups (see *Box 6.8*).

Box 6.8: The role of the voluntary or third sector in satisfying needs

Jeremy Kendall uses the term 'voluntary welfare' to refer to 'the contribution of organizations between the market and the state to social well-being' (2008, p 212). These organisations are involved in 'an extraordinarily diverse range of activities', many of which 'allow needs to be met in society that would otherwise go unrecognized and unmet' (2008, p 212). He observes that:

> many other countries with long track records of liberal democracy also have their own rich traditions of voluntarism, although the form and shape they take varies dramatically from country to country. But increasing policy recognition of these groups in the UK has now reached such a level that

they may be considered 'mainstream'. The key drivers for this development include policy-makers' beliefs that voluntary organizations can be more responsive, cost-effective or responsible than the alternatives [and] can exhibit greater sensitivity to the needs of socially excluded constituencies ... This is all against a backdrop of a loss of faith in market and state solutions. (Kendall, 2008, pp 212-3)

Question: Can you think of policy areas where the third or voluntary sector is increasingly engaged in the process of needs satisfaction?

Even where it is accepted that a need should be met by the state, a number of questions arise (discussed in more detail in Lister, 2008a). These include:

- *Should the need be met for everyone on a universal basis or should it be met only for particular targeted groups?* Democratic socialist advocates of state welfare provision have, for instance, argued for *universal* policies such as child benefit on the grounds that this is the most effective way of meeting the needs of children. At the same time, new right supporters of the market also sometimes use a needs discourse to justify *selective* welfare. The argument goes that this enables the targeting of resources on those in greatest need, usually through some form of means-testing. In other words, meeting need is an argument used to justify very different policy approaches.
- *Should the need be translated into a clear right or should it be satisfied on the basis of professional or bureaucratic discretion?* A key theme of new right thinking has been opposition to the translation of needs into rights. In the UK the role of discretion in the social security system was a major focus of debate in the 1960s and 1970s. Discretion was criticised for putting too much power into the hands of individual officials, leaving claimants unsure as to what they might receive and without any rights to back up their claim. Gradually the scope of discretion was reduced but it was revived in the mid-1980s in the form of the social fund, which replaced the right to grants to meet one-off needs with a combination of loans and grants for which there is no clear right in law. Discretion was, in this instance, introduced explicitly as a rationing mechanism and it operates as such in the social care system (see ***Box 6.6***). More recently, the 'unambiguous' trend towards greater discretion in the social security system, associated with the 'personalisation' of welfare-to-work services, has been justified by government ministers in the name of flexibility (Griggs and Bennett, 2009, p 43).

Unmet needs

The three stages of the politics of needs interpretation represent a kind of filtering process, the outcome of which decides whether or not a felt need is met. Inevitably some needs remain unmet, not least because 'human need is not always visible' (Young Foundation, 2009, p 13). A key issue then concerns the implications for the people whose needs are not met and for the wider society. The Young Foundation has investigated unmet needs in the UK. The research refers to:

> needs that remain unsatisfied or partially satisfied due to some blockage, obstacle or constraint, either internal or external to the person who feels that need. It is in these situations, where there is a barrier to meeting need and so that need endures, that harm or suffering occurs and in these situations a moral imperative for some part of society to meet that need comes into play. (Vale et al, 2009, p 16)

One of the main findings is that:

> against a backdrop of enduring, severe and intergenerational material needs for an adequate income and the material resources an adequate income facilitates access to (like housing, transport etc), the extent of unmet psychological need (for self-esteem, autonomy, significant relationships and competence) is severe, and intensifying through social change. This is especially important to recognise given the pivotal role psychological needs play in well-being. Current systems in place to meet need are better at identifying and satisfying material needs, whereas psychological needs are harder to identify and satisfy. (Vale et al, 2009, pp 8-9)

The Foundation used unmet need as a 'lens' through which 'to make sense of modern British society' (Vale et al, 2009, p 8). The project's final report suggests that 'perhaps the most important premise of all studies of need is a moral one: that needs matter and that a good society is aware of itself, aware of who is thriving and who is not, and of who is in need of care and support' (Young Foundation, 2009, p14). The project thus underlines the argument with which we started this chapter: the centrality of the concept of need to social policy.

Summary

- The concept of social need stands at the core of social policy.
- Needs are typically distinguished from wants and preferences.
- Some classifications of need treat them as hierarchical; others as interrelated.
- Two key, overlapping, categorisations of different types of need are between universal and relative and thin and thick needs.
- Various theoretical perspectives emphasise the relative nature of needs.
- In contrast, Doyal and Gough's theory of human need focuses on its universal aspects. These are identified as the basic human needs of physical health and autonomy and a set of intermediate needs, which are met through specific needs satisfiers in varying cultural contexts.
- The idea of thin and thick needs represents a similar attempt to distinguish between more abstract universal needs and more concrete relative forms of needs satisfaction. In another interpretation, the distinction is associated with the related concepts of well-being, social quality and capabilities.
- A social constructionist approach to needs understands them as 'interpreted' rather than as inherent to individuals.
- The idea of the 'politics of needs interpretation' identifies three key processes involved in 'needs claims': the establishment of the political status; interpretation; and satisfaction of needs.
- One outcome of these processes is that some needs remain unmet, with potentially significant harmful implications for individuals and the wider society.

Further reading

The two key social policy texts on the concept of needs are **Doyal and Gough (1991)** and **Dean (2010)**. For a social constructionist perspective, see the expositions by **Langan (1998a)** and **Fraser (1989)** of the politics of needs interpretation. **Tao and Drover (1997)** offer a Chinese, Confucianist perspective on notions of need. For an example of the application of ideas about need in a social policy research programme, see **Vale et al (2009)** and **Young Foundation (2009)**.

Citizenship and community

Citizenship is a concept that is at the heart of many current social policy debates, either implicitly or explicitly. This chapter will use some of these debates to illustrate some of the issues raised by the theorisation of the concept. It will also introduce you to two concepts related to citizenship: community and human rights. Our starting point is the definition of citizenship. The rest of the chapter explores in more detail the different elements of this definition. As the definition is underpinned by the idea of membership of a community, we explore here the concept of community itself as well as the meaning of membership. We then discuss citizenship rights, together with human rights, followed by duties or responsibilities. The final section explores the notion of citizenship as an ideal.

The significance and meaning of citizenship

Before introducing a working definition, we need to consider what kind of concept citizenship is in order to understand its significance. First, as already signalled in Chapter Six, it is a contested concept. This is reflected in Chantal Mouffe's observation that 'the way we define citizenship is intimately linked to the kind of social and political community we want' (1992, p 225). In contemporary social policy and politics, its contested nature can be seen most clearly in debates around the nature of and relationship between rights and responsibilities.

Second, citizenship has also been described as a 'contextualised concept'. In other words, although at one level, citizenship represents an abstract, universal concept, it 'is interpreted and articulated in specific national social and political contexts, reflecting historical traditions and institutional and cultural complexes' (Lister et al, 2007, p 1). So, for example, the British literature on citizenship has tended to emphasise the relationship between the individual and the state; the Scandinavian literature pays more attention to the relations between citizens as a collectivity. This difference reflects the respective strength of, on the one hand, individualistic liberal and, on the other, solidaristic social democratic traditions of political thinking.

Third, recognition of citizenship as a contextualised concept is also crucial to understanding it as a lived experience. The notion of 'lived citizenship' refers to 'the meaning that citizenship actually has in people's lives and the ways in which people's social and cultural backgrounds and material circumstances affect their lives as citizens' (Hall and Williamson, 1999, p 2). Here we are talking not just about national contexts but also the local contexts in which people live and the ways in which the experience of citizenship is shaped by factors such as age, social class, gender, ethnicity, sexuality and (dis)ability (Lister et al, 2007). ***Box 7.1*** summarises some of the findings of a study of young people's experiences and understandings of citizenship.

Box 7.1: Young people talking about citizenship

A study of 64 young people in Leicester over three years explored how they negotiated the transitions to full citizenship. The young people revealed three main understandings of citizenship:

- a universal status in which everyone is a citizen by virtue of membership of a community or nation. For some this represented a thin status, of little significance; in other cases the young people drew on thicker notions of belonging;
- 'respectable economic independence', embodied by a person who has a job, pays taxes and has a house and family;
- 'constructive social participation', which denotes a constructive and responsible stance towards the community. This model played a particularly important role in the young people's own experiences and practices of citizenship (Smith et al, 2005).

In addition, smaller numbers subscribed to either a 'social contractual' model of rights and responsibilities or a notion of the 'right to a voice', involving the right and a genuine opportunity to have a say and be heard. How the young people understood and experienced citizenship varied to some extent according to their social status, gender, ethnicity and age (Lister et al, 2003).

Question: What does citizenship mean to you and what are the main ways in which you feel that you have experienced it?

The contested and contextual nature of citizenship means that defining it is not a straightforward exercise and that there is considerable disagreement and debate around its definition. Nevertheless, many theorists use as a broad working definition that provided by T.H. Marshall. Marshall is a key figure in the development of citizenship theory. His lecture, *Citizenship and Social Class*, given in 1949, provides a starting point for most post-war thinking about citizenship in many countries. Marshall regards citizenship as:

> a status bestowed on those who are full members of a community. All who possess the status are equal with respect to the rights and duties with which the status is endowed. There is no universal principle that determines what those rights and duties shall be, but societies in which citizenship is a developing institution create an image of an ideal citizenship against which achievement can be measured and towards which aspirations can be directed. (1950, pp 28-9)

If we unpack this definition, the key elements are: membership of a community; rights; duties; equality of status and an ideal. We shall look at each in turn, other than equality of status, which we will discuss in the following chapter.

Membership of a community

To understand the notion of 'membership of a community' we need to consider both the meaning of 'membership' and of 'community'. In exploring the latter we will stray beyond the strict confines of citizenship to discuss community as a concept in its own right.

Membership

Like citizenship, membership means different things to different people. As suggested in **Box 7.1**, it can have a thin meaning, with little or no significance for a person's identity and actions, or it can have thicker meaning, associated with belonging, as expounded in **Box 7.2**.

> **Box 7.2: A thick understanding of membership of a citizenship community**
>
> Membership of a citizenship community ... involves a set of social and political relationships, practices and identities that together can be described as a sense of belonging. Belonging is not a fixed state, nor just a material one; it involves also emotional and psychological dimensions. Young people, immigrants and marginalized groups, in particular, have to negotiate belonging and different groups experience belonging to the citizenship community in diverse ways. An important element of belonging is participation. (Lister et al, 2007, p 9)

In and beyond the nation state

The reference to membership of a citizenship community begs the question as to what constitutes a citizenship community. The community to which Marshall refers is primarily the national community, created by the nation state. This is the community that confers legal citizenship on its members, symbolised by possession of a passport. Contemporary critical citizenship theory problematises Marshall's assumptions by shifting the emphasis from the inclusionary to the exclusionary face of citizenship and by introducing a multi-tiered analysis. We will discuss each in turn.

First, Marshall's concern is with what happens inside nation states rather than at their borders. This means that the focus is on whether citizens who are already members of nation states enjoy full membership in terms of rights, duties and the ability to participate. Citizenship is represented as essentially a force for *inclusion*. In contrast, many contemporary critical citizenship theorists emphasise the ways in which citizenship can operate as a force for *exclusion* at the borders of nation states. Their focus is the many people crossing the borders of nation states – migrants, asylum-seekers and refugees. As the numbers have increased, many Western nation states have responded with tougher immigration controls, harsher interpretations of the rights of asylum-seekers and more exclusionary residence qualifications for welfare benefits and services. In the UK, it has been proposed that immigrants should be required to 'earn' citizenship through a new points test, based on factors such as behaviour, skills and language abilities. They will have to complete a new 'probationary citizenship' phase of up to 10 years. During this period, they will be required to be entirely self-supporting without access to most social security benefits or housing assistance. This represents a deliberate reinforcement of citizenship's exclusionary impact.

Second, while in Marshall's account the citizenship community is coterminous with the nation state, increasingly citizenship is being theorised as spatially multi-tiered or multi-layered (Lister, 2007a). This is clearest in accounts that go beyond the nation state. These are responding, in particular, to: the development of supra-national citizenship communities such as the European Union (EU); the impact of globalisation in its various forms (see Introduction); and growing concern about environmental harms, which are no respecter of national borders (see Chapter Two and the discussion of environmental citizenship later in this chapter).

The idea of European citizenship has been promoted by the European Commission since the mid-1980s as a way of capturing the loyalty of EU citizens; the status of 'Citizens of the Union' was formally enshrined in the 1993 Maastricht Treaty, which granted to these citizens the right to vote in local government and European Parliament elections in their EU country of residence, regardless of their nationality. European citizenship has been identified by some theorists as a form of post-national membership of a citizenship community. More nebulous, but nevertheless an important element in the contemporary citizenship literature, is the idea of global citizenship (see *Box 7.3*). In a speech in Berlin, prior to his election as president, Barack Obama introduced himself as 'a fellow citizen of the world' and spoke of how 'the burdens of global citizenship continue to bind us together' (*The Independent*, 25 July 2008).

Box 7.3: Global citizenship

Although a modern concept, the idea of global citizenship draws on cosmopolitan thinking (the idea that we are all citizens of the universe), which dates back to ancient Greece and Rome. Nigel Dower (2003, p vii) argues that global citizenship involves both an 'ethical' and an 'institutional' component. He identifies three key aspects of what it means to claim to be a global citizen:

- A 'normative claim' that 'we have certain duties that in principle extend to all human beings anywhere in the world and that all human beings have a certain moral status of being worthy of moral respect' (2003, p 7).
- An 'existential claim' to membership 'of some kind of global community'. This existential claim means that 'whatever else a global citizen is, a global citizen is the bearer of human rights' (2003, p 54).
- An 'aspirational claim' to create a world 'in which basic values are realised more fully' and which 'requires the strengthening' of, for instance, trans-national institutions of global governance (2003, p 7).

Dower paints a portrait of 'a typical "active" global citizen' who acts on the basis of the belief that 'all human beings have certain fundamental rights and all human beings have duties to respect and promote these rights' (2003, p 7). 'Her ethical perspective provides her with both a basis for criticising what governments and companies do and also a basis for personal commitment actively to pursue an agenda in some chosen area such as poverty alleviation, protecting the environment, working for peace and against the denial of human rights' (2003, p 7). She acts not just as an isolated individual but 'sees herself as part of some kind of global community of like-minded people and those whose problems she shares' and 'generally, she acts with others and through organisations that advance her causes' (2003, p 8). This is a portrait of an active, self-identified global citizen. Dower also acknowledges that, at another thinner level, global citizenship can be understood simply as a universal status.

Question: Would you identify yourself as a global citizen? Do you recognise yourself at all in the portrait of the active global citizen painted by Dower? Do you think there is anything missing from that portrait?

A multi-tiered analysis also identifies citizenship communities below the level of the nation state in regions, cities and neighbourhoods. Rogers and Muir (2007) point to evidence of an increase in identification with a person's locality during the 1990s in the UK and elsewhere. They argue that 'the potential of local identities as a source of common belonging has been much neglected. These are by far the most popular territorial identities and there is much that could be done at the local level to promote a common sense of local citizenship' (2007, p 6). It is in neighbourhoods, or 'local communities' that citizenship as lived experience is most likely to be meaningful for members of marginalised groups in particular. The young people in the study described in *Box 7.1* frequently made reference explicitly or implicitly to the local community, especially when discussing 'constructive social participation' and the practice of good citizenship. We will therefore make a slight diversion at this point to discuss 'community' itself.

Community

Community has been described as 'one of the most important yet ill-defined concepts in social sciences' (Fremeaux, 2005, p 265). It is typically described in the literature as 'slippery', 'elusive', 'ambiguous', 'value-laden' and also 'persuasive' and 'seductive'. These adjectives reflect both the varying meanings attached to community as a theoretical concept and the ideological work that it does in political and policy discourses. As Jeremy Brent warns, community 'infiltrates much everyday thought and action, and is bandied about in local and national politics and policy making as well as being the subject of a wide range of academic discourse. As such a ubiquitous term, however, it does have to be given a health warning: "handle with care"' (2009, p 21). We will begin with the way in which community is 'bandied about' in political and policy discourses. We will then consider the different meanings attached to it and the main arguments as to why it should be 'handled with care' as both a political and theoretical concept. This leads into attempts to develop a more pluralist conceptualisation of community by critical scholars.

The ubiquity of community in political and policy discourses is, in part, attributable to its 'emotional appeal to both an imagined past and to an idyllic future' (Hughes and Mooney, 1998, p 58). This appeal typically results in the conflation of community as an ideal and a reality and it infuses the concept with a high degree of 'ideological elasticity' (Shaw, 2007, pp 27, 34). As Phil Cohen observes,

> There is probably no word in our political vocabulary which spans the whole ideological spectrum from extreme individualism to ultra collectivism with such ease, and whose rhetoric embraces so many conflicting reality principles. Not surprisingly then, the term has become a byword for conceptual confusion and political duplicity. (1997, p 30)

Community has been:

- identified as 'a defining value of socialism' (Skillen, 1995, p 77);
- appropriated by New Labour as a central building block of the third way, representing 'the hangover cure to the excess of Conservative individualism' and a socially cohesive antidote to 'the market culture of self-interest' (Driver and Martell, 1997, p 27);
- invoked as a source of self-help, against the state, by the new right;
- the central animating concept of communitarianism (see ***Box 1.1***).

It is not surprising, therefore, that community has been described as 'a fundamentally political concept' and 'a continually contested term' (Hoggett, 1997, p 14). From a policy perspective, Mae Shaw observes that 'there is almost no area of social policy that is immune from the community treatment' (2007, p 24): examples include community policing, community safety, community care and community health. Critics tend to dismiss the use of the community label in this way as spray-on 'cynical and superficial gloss', designed to create a warm, progressive glow (Craig, 2007a, p 336).

Community's elusiveness as a concept lies also in the range of meanings attached to it. One review of the literature identified several hundred meanings, connected only by reference to 'social interaction' (Craig, 2007a, p 336). Within these meanings, there are two broad interpretations of community. The first, and most common, refers to community as a geographical locality: 'a collection of people living within a fairly well-defined physical space – a discrete housing development, a neighbourhood, a rural village or a refugee camp' (Craig, 2007a, p 337). This meaning is how the term has been used historically and is also often deployed to invoke a largely imaginary, romanticised ideal of the past, particularly with respect to working class communities (Mayo, 2000). The second main meaning attributed to community is based on common identity or shared interests. This meaning has become more common in recent years, with frequent reference to, for instance, the 'black and minority ethnic community' (assuming shared identity) or the 'business community' (based on shared material interests). Jeffrey Weeks explores the idea of a community of identity through the notion of a 'sexual community' (see **Box 7.4**). Electronic communications have facilitated the development of communities of identity and interest and have even given birth to digital communities, whose members communicate through email and social networking sites.

Box 7.4: The idea of a sexual community

Weeks argues that 'the social relations of a community are repositories of meaning for its members, not sets of mechanical linkages between isolated individuals. A community offers a "vocabulary of values" through which individuals construct their understanding of the social world, and of their sense of identity and belonging' (1996, p 72). From this understanding he identifies four key elements of 'a sexual community' and illustrates them with reference to 'the best documented sexual community, the lesbian and gay community' (1996, p 73):

- *Community as a focus of identity*. Identities and a sense of belonging are both forged and sustained through the social relations of the lesbian and gay community. 'Community here stands for some notion of solidarity, a solidarity which empowers and enables, and makes individual and social action possible' (Weeks, 1996, p 76).
- *'Community as ethos or repository of values'* (1996, p 76). Weeks gives as an example: 'the dense interconnections, networks, relationships, experiments in living, new forms of loving and caring (above all in response to the HIV and AIDS

epidemic), which have been the outstanding achievements of gay and lesbian politics since the 1960s, provide the grounds on which new values systems are developing' (1996, pp 77-8).

- *Community as social capital*. The networks to which Weeks refers also involve the development of social capital (social networks based on reciprocity and trust) through 'collective activity' and 'collective self help' (1996, p 79).
- *Community as politics*. Weeks refers here to the gay and lesbian community as a social movement (see also Chapter Nine). He suggests that, as a radical sexual community, it embraces both 'transgression', which challenges 'the traditional or received order of sexual life' (and is often articulated as 'queer' politics) and 'citizenship', which fights for inclusion and equal civil rights (1996, p 82).

Weeks emphasises that he uses the term community in a 'critical' way to denote 'a necessary fiction' (1996, pp 73, 83). He warns, though, that radical communities of identity 'can be as exclusive and stifling as traditional ones' (1996, p 84). This warning echoes two key criticisms made of conventional conceptualisations of community, particularly those that locate community in particular geographical spaces.

Weeks' charge of exclusivity parallels the argument made earlier about citizenship: in including some people community excludes others. Paul Hoggett refers to 'the process of boundary construction which distinguishes insiders from outsiders, those who can be trusted and those who can not' and to the emotions of 'anger, jealousy, pride and longing', which can fuel that process (1997a, p 15). Shaw makes a similar point: 'security for some may be achieved only by the exclusion of others; the "belongingness" associated with solidarity may be constituted through the not-belonging of others' (2007, p 28). She cites as examples the exclusion by local communities in the UK of unpopular groups such as asylum-seekers and suspected paedophiles. Moreover, the growing number of 'gated communities' in both the global North and South represents an attempt among the privileged to build community behind walls in order physically to exclude the deprived.

The other main criticism made of community is that it is typically presented as an organic, homogeneous entity in which members share a sense of belonging and commitment to shared goals and values based on common interests. This rosy picture stands in contrast to the actual 'heterogeneity and complexity of communities' (Hoggett, 1997a, p 15). It glosses over the social divisions within communities, such as those of gender and age, and the power relations associated with them. As Shaw warns, 'without an adequate understanding of the ways in which power relations construct and constrain community life, we are left clutching at the straws of idealized and sentimental versions' (2007, p 28). Hughes and Mooney cite the example of Southall Black Sisters, a group of black feminists who have 'struggled against a sense of community that effectively ignored domestic violence and sexual harassment' (1998, p 69). Rahila Gupta, a member of Southall Black Sisters, describes how:

> the state more or less enters into an informal contract with the more powerful leaders in the minority community. In practice community leaders maintain power over family, cultural and religious affairs of the community with the effect of concealing power relations between men and women and legitimising women's subordination within minority communities. (2003a, pp 18-19)

The community about which Gupta writes can be understood as both a geographical community and a community of identity. Within geographical communities, age can be an important source of division, with young people's behaviour often represented as a threat to the community (Brent, 2009). Communities of identity are also divided. Weeks, for instance, acknowledges that his account of the gay and lesbian community 'presupposes a unity which is not necessarily there ... There is no reason to think that people who share one characteristic necessarily share others' (1996, p 72). A group of British Jews launched Independent Jewish Voices in 2007 in order to challenge the idea that there is a single Jewish community on whose behalf the Board of Deputies and the Chief Rabbi can speak (Klug, 2007).

Hughes and Mooney adopt a critical stance towards community yet acknowledge that it 'can also be a source of support and collective solidarity' for marginalised groups (1998, p 69). Communities can be forged and strengthened through struggle. In his autobiography, President Obama explains how images of the civil rights movement told him that

> I wasn't alone in my particular struggles, and that communities had never been a given in this country, at least not for blacks. Communities had to be created, fought for, tended like gardens ... In the sit-ins, the marches, the jailhouse songs, I saw the African-American community becoming more than just the place where you'd been born or the house where you'd been raised. Through organizing, through shared sacrifice, membership had been earned. (2007, pp 134-5)

Women in particular have been able to organise in the space provided by community even if community has also been a source of their oppression (Dominelli, 2006). 'In this sense', Hughes and Mooney continue, 'community is contradictory' (1998, p 69). Brent too argues that community represents 'a form of resistance within asymmetrical relations of power' (2009, p 261). Others emphasise the value of principles such as cooperation and mutualism, which can be promoted through notions of community in opposition to individualism. Such observations lead to a position in which critical theorists argue, not for the abandonment of community but for its re-articulation on more radical, pluralist lines (Hughes and Mooney, 1998, pp 87-98). Such a conception of community would not assume unity and it would acknowledge the ways in which communities are shaped by power relations. Fremeaux concludes that:

> the debate revolves around the necessity of a more fluid understanding of the concept of community in order to open a space for all citizens to evolve in society without being … reduced to a specific and institutionally defined identity, which inevitably constrains the development of all groups, but most of all the most deprived ones. (2005, p 273)

> *Question:* One aspect of the kind of fluid understanding called for by Fremeaux is recognition that we all belong to a number of different communities. What communities do you consider that you belong to?

Two citizenship traditions

While membership of a community is, in some form, an integral component of any definition of citizenship, political philosophies differ in the relative weight that they attach to the community and to the individual citizen. Communitarians, as the name implies, place the community above the individual (see *Box 1.1*). They draw on a tradition of thinking about citizenship called **civic republicanism**. Civic republicanism's origins lie in ancient Greece, where citizenship represented a civic duty to participate in the political life of the community. Duties towards the wider community are prioritised over the rights of individuals. This is reflected in third way thinking, although, as we shall see, there it tends to be work obligations, and to a lesser extent civic responsibility, such as voluntary work, rather than political participation, which are emphasised.

The other main approach to citizenship derives from the **liberal** political tradition, which prioritises the individual over the community. As a consequence, in the liberal tradition, rights represent the essence of citizenship. However, as we shall see, classical and social liberalism differ in their conceptualisation of rights (see also *Box 1.1*).

These two citizenship traditions frame contemporary thinking about citizenship (Dwyer, 2004, Ch 2; Lister et al, 2007, p 7). Another way of thinking about them is to distinguish between citizenship as a 'status', or what a person is, and the rights that accrue to that status, and citizenship as a 'practice' or what a person does (Oldfield, 1990). A similar distinction is implicit in Dower's differentiation between global citizenship as a universal status and the active global citizen (see *Box 7.3*). In practice, citizenship as status and practice are interrelated. We turn now to discuss rights and obligations separately.

Rights

Marshall (1950) identifies three types of rights: civil, political and social. This distinction is now widely used as a starting point for thinking about citizenship rights.

- *Civil* rights refer to 'the rights necessary for individual freedom – liberty of the person, freedom of speech, thought and faith, the right to own property and to conclude valid contracts, and the right to justice. The last is a different order from the others, because it is the right to defend and assert all one's rights on terms of equality with others and by due process of law' (Marshall, 1950, pp 10-11). Keith Faulks suggests that Marshall's exposition, in fact, embraces two different kinds of rights: genuine civil rights associated with freedom and liberty and 'market rights', which exist 'to serve the interest of the market and capitalist society' in particular with regard to property (Faulks, 1998, pp 29-30; 2000).

    Question: Which of the rights identified by Marshall represent 'market rights'?

- *Political* rights represent 'the right to participate in the exercise of political power, as a member of a body invested with political authority or as an elector of the members of such a body' (Marshall, 1950, p 11). Examples include the right to vote and to stand for political office.
- *Social* rights are described by Marshall as 'the whole range from the right to a modicum of economic welfare and security to the right to share to the full in the social heritage and to live the life of a civilised being

according to the standards prevailing in the society' (1950, p 11. Examples include social security, the British National Health Service and education.

Marshall presents the development of these rights as a historical progression. Civil rights were associated with the 18th century, political rights with the 19th century and social rights with the 20th century, especially the period following the Second World War. Each set of rights provided a platform for the next set. However, this formulation has been criticised on three main grounds. First, it represents an Anglocentric view. The account of the historical progression reflects British experience, which is not necessarily valid for other countries. For example, in Germany social rights preceded political rights; indeed they were introduced in a deliberate attempt to pre-empt demands for political rights. Second, Marshall's account ignores group differences. In particular, the sequence has often been different for women. For instance, in Western societies women often achieved political rights before full civil rights. Examples include the US, where women were excluded from jury service even after they had won the vote, and many countries, including the UK, where female citizens enjoyed inferior rights under nationality and immigration laws and married women did not exist as individuals for taxation purposes until late in the 20th century.

The third criticism of Marshall's account is that it underplays struggle. By presenting the development of rights as a simple evolution, it obscures the extent to which each set of rights was achieved as a result of political struggles. Such an evolutionary account can also blind people to the danger that established rights can be vulnerable to attack. There are many examples of social rights being eroded and in both the UK and the US various civil and political rights have been curtailed in the name of national security, post 9/11.

> ***Question:*** Can you think of specific examples of civil, political and social rights that have been eroded or removed?

One lesson from the vulnerability of rights to attack is that rights are not passive entitlements: 'to have a right is to have something to be claimed, asserted and if necessary fought for' (Dower, 2003, p 55; Lister, 2003a). This is an example of how citizenship as a status and a practice are interrelated. Struggles around rights also serve as a reminder of the contested nature of citizenship. This is reflected in the disagreement about the nature of rights between some of the theoretical approaches discussed in Part One. We will focus here on the dispute between new right and social democratic theorists and make reference too to the distinctive positions taken by Marxism and feminism.

Disagreements about the nature of rights

The dispute between **new right** and **social democratic** approaches to rights can be traced back to the earlier differentiation between **classical** and **social liberalism** (see *Box 1.1*). Classical liberalism argued for civil and political rights as the means by which a limited state guarantees the freedom and formal equality of the individual, who is sovereign (see also Chapter Eight). Social liberalism extended the idea of rights to embrace social rights, which it regarded as necessary to ensure that individuals had the material resources required to exercise their freedom. From within the classical liberal tradition, neo-liberals on the new right dispute the validity of extending citizenship rights beyond civil and political rights. They argue that the role of government should be limited to protecting individual citizens from coercion and interference (described as 'negative freedom', see Chapter Eight). They also assert that civil and political rights are categorically different from social rights because the latter imply a claim on resources.

The social democratic case against this position and for social rights has been put most cogently by Plant (1988, 1990). He suggests that if we ask what negative freedom is for, the obvious answer is: to protect individual autonomy, that is to enable individual citizens to pursue their own ends. If this is the case, negative freedom cannot be separated from the ability to pursue those ends. This introduces the notion of 'positive freedom' (see Chapter Eight), which depends on the kind of material resources guaranteed by social rights. Plant also denies that there is a categorical difference between civil and political rights on the one hand and social rights on the other. He points out that the protection of civil and political rights also implies a claim on resources through, in particular, the costs of maintaining the legal and political systems.

Another key social democratic argument in favour of social rights is that they help to promote the effective exercise of civil and political rights by groups who are disadvantaged in terms of power and material resources (Lister, 1990, 2003a). This idea is encapsulated in the increasingly influential notion of the 'indivisibility' or inter-dependence of rights. Take, for instance, homeless people who, without a home and associated address, find it very difficult to vote. Or think about people on low incomes who are unable to assert their civil rights through the legal system without financial assistance from the state. Furthermore, social citizenship rights help to reduce people's reliance on the market for their livelihoods. They promote the 'de-commodification' of labour by decoupling to some extent the living standards of individual citizens from the value they can get by selling their labour in the market. This is another reason why neo-liberals oppose social rights.

The de-commodification argument also draws implicitly on Marxist thinking (see *Box 2.2*). However, **Marxism** (and, more recently, neo-Marxism) has traditionally dismissed the idea of citizenship rights as an individualistic, bourgeois charade designed to obscure fundamental economic and social class divisions and the power of capital over labour. Moreover, as observed in Chapters Two and Four, Marxists are often critical of the welfare state and the social rights it provides as representing part of the apparatus of social control and oppression. Dean sums up their case against social rights: 'first, that in ameliorating the exploitative impact of capitalism they help ensure its survival; second, that social rights provide a powerful mechanism for state/ideological control' (2002, p 65; see also Dwyer, 2004, pp 56-8). In practice, many Marxists today are willing to engage in a rights discourse, in acknowledgement that it can be used to argue for meeting human needs and for a reduction in inequalities. Their stance reflects Marxists' deeper ambivalence about the nature of the welfare state itself, discussed in Chapter Two.

Radical **feminists** take a position on rights that in some ways mirrors that of Marxists but with reference to patriarchy in place of capitalism. Thus they tend to dismiss rights as merely the expression of patriarchal values and power. Postmodernist feminists are sceptical, 'maintaining that unitary categories of woman reify individuals into abstract categories, ignoring their diversity of experience. They view rights-based claims as contingent, temporary and relative' (Hobson and Lister, 2002, p 30). Among feminists writing in a socialist tradition there is a concern about the individualistic nature of rights, although many are nevertheless willing to use the language of rights in framing their demands. This reflects how, 'throughout the history of feminism, the discourse on rights has been central to women's claims: such basic rights to education, property, to custody of children and to suffrage' (Hobson and Lister, 2002, p 27). Rights talk has been particularly audible among some feminists in the US. It is at the heart of liberal feminists' claims, most notably as deployed in demands for equal rights. Overall, while critical feminists caution against placing too much faith in individual rights, they also counsel against outright rejection, in acknowledgement of the law's potential as an agent of emancipation as well as oppression.

Beyond traditional citizenship rights

Feminists have also argued for new forms of rights, most notably reproductive rights and rights to bodily integrity. Such rights include the right to contraception and abortion so that women have control over their own bodies. This is an example of how the demands of social movements have been framed with reference to rights which go beyond the classic civil–political–social rights triad. Other examples include cultural rights or rights of recognition in multi-cultural societies and sexual rights (see **Box 7.5** and also Chapter Nine).

Box 7.5: Sexual rights

In **Box 7.4** we explored Weeks' notion of a sexual community. He refers to the lesbian and gay movement's fight for equal civil rights as part of citizenship. Weeks is also one of a number of theorists who have developed the idea of 'sexual citizenship' (1998; see also Lister, 2002). One element of sexual citizenship is the notion of sexual rights, which we describe here as an example of new forms of rights claims. Diane Richardson (2000) identifies three kinds of sexual rights claims based on conduct or practice, identity and relationships.

- *Practice-based sexual rights* claims refer to the rights to participate in sexual activity, to sexual pleasure and to sexual and reproductive autonomy. They sometimes overlap with civil rights. The right to sexual activity is a particular issue for 'sexual minorities' and for disabled people.
- *Identity-based sexual rights* represent claims to public recognition by lesbian, gay, bisexual and transgender citizens as opposed to private toleration of particular sexual acts. They involve the right to self-definition and self-expression.
- *Relationship-based sexual rights* claims concern the rights of consent, such as the age of consent; to choose sexual partners; and to conduct publicly recognised sexual relationships. Particularly controversial is the right to same-sex marriage, which exists in very few countries.

The right to participation in decision-making is another type of citizenship right that increasingly is being promoted, including by user movements in relation to welfare services. The right to participation in decision-making is also invoked in human rights discourses, particularly in anti-poverty politics. We discuss briefly human rights and their relationship to citizenship rights in **Box 7.6**. Participatory rights act as a bridge between citizenship as a status and citizenship as a practice.

Box 7.6: Human rights

Human rights can be defined as 'basic universal rights that belong to every human being, regardless of their circumstances. By acting as a set of minimum legal standards that states must respect in how they treat people, human rights serve to make real and meaningful core values such as human dignity and worth, equality, respect, freedom and democracy' (BIHR et al, 2008, p 14). Modern human rights were first codified as principles in the 1948 *Universal Declaration of Human Rights*. These principles were turned into binding international human rights law in the form of two covenants, agreed in 1966: the *Covenant on Civil and Political Rights* and the *Covenant on Economic, Social and Cultural Rights*. These various rights are regarded as indivisible. Regional human rights law, such as the 1950 *European Convention on Human Rights*, and its incorporation into domestic legislation, have developed in parallel.

'The universality of human rights means that by definition they are not "given" or "endowed" by states – only respected and protected by states or claimed by those who hold them' (BIHR et al, 2008, p 14). Herein lies a key distinction between human and citizenship rights. Citizenship rights *are* given or endowed by states. Whereas human rights reside unconditionally in individuals as humans, regardless of where they live or their citizenship status, citizenship rights are enjoyed by citizens of individual states and can be subject to conditions. Thus, human rights and more narrowly drawn citizenship rights can come into conflict with each other, as in the case of migrants and asylum-seekers when nation states try to exclude them from citizenship rights. By the same token, migrants and asylum seekers can appeal to their human rights in support of their claims.

Human and citizenship rights are nevertheless related and share a common language and many common elements. In some ways, citizenship rights could be said to represent the specific interpretation and allocation by individual nation states of the more abstract, unconditional and universalisable human rights. At a global level, as we saw in **Box 7.3**, human rights law represents 'an essential ingredient of global citizenship' (Dower, 2003, p 62).

In the UK, human rights are playing an increasingly important role in social policy. The introduction of the 1998 Human Rights Act, which incorporates most of the European Convention on Human Rights, and the subsequent establishment in 2006 of the Equality and Human Rights Commission (EHRC) were significant milestones. In its human rights strategy, the EHRC states that human rights 'abuses take place whenever people are not treated with the dignity and respect that everyone irrespective of age, disability, gender, gender identity, race, religion or belief, or sexual orientation, deserves' (EHRC, 2009c, pp 18-19). A Human Rights Inquiry, carried out by the EHRC, concludes that:

> the human rights framework, backed by the legal underpinning of the Human Rights Act, has had a positive impact in the delivery of public services. A human rights approach can provide an ethical framework for the actions of public authorities. Properly understood and applied, it can have a transformative function, transforming the organisation itself, the services delivered, and ultimately the lives of the people receiving these services. (EHRC, 2009b, p 14)

The Inquiry's report provides examples of 'everyday situations in which the Human Rights Act might apply'. Social policy examples include: 'provision of facilities or food which do not meet religious or cultural needs'; 'not respecting gay and lesbian partners as next of kin and inheritors of tenancies'; 'not being sufficiently protected from domestic violence'; and 'curfews preventing law-abiding young people from going out at night' (EHRC, 2009b, p 3).

A widespread criticism of the Human Rights Act is that it excludes economic, social and cultural rights (Johnson, 2004; Joint Committee on Human Rights, 2008). In a consultation document on a new Bill of Rights and Responsibilities to complement the Human Rights Act, the Ministry for Justice rejects arguments for guaranteeing such rights as human rights in domestic law. It does, however, open the door to articulating as constitutional principles 'certain social and economic guarantees' (Ministry for Justice, 2009, p 43).

Economic and social rights are an important element in the growing interest in a human rights approach to poverty reduction, influenced by thinking in the global South (Lister, 2004a; Killeen, 2008; Donald and Mottershaw, 2009). In the UK, a number of anti-poverty and human rights organisations are collaborating (BIHR et al, 2008). 'At the most basic level, the starting point for both is a deep commitment to human dignity and the imperative of realising this for every human being' (BIHR et al, 2008, p 5). The adoption of a human rights discourse by some anti-poverty activists in a number of countries, including the US, can be understood as a way of: thinking about poverty; talking about poverty; and articulating concrete demands such as social and economic rights and the right to participate in policy debates and decision-making (Lister, 2004a, 2009b).

Recent theorisation of human rights, which the EHRC has drawn upon, emphasises the links with the capability approach discussed in Chapter Six. Vizard and Burchardt, who helped to develop the EHRC's position, argue that 'the capability approach and human rights can be mutually reinforcing and supportive' (2007, p 11); in particular, human rights standards and principles can be used to apply the capabilities approach, as demonstrated by the EHRC's Equality Measurement Framework (EHRC, 2009a).

Duties

Marshall's account of citizenship is remembered for his exposition of the nature of citizenship rights. It is often forgotten that he also made a number of references to 'the corresponding duties' of citizenship (1950, p 70). Today, the nature of the relationship between the social rights and duties of citizenship is at the heart of many political debates about social policy. In line with the predominant reading of Marshall, the post-war period in the UK has frequently been characterised as an era dominated by a rights citizenship paradigm (even though, as we saw in Chapter One, middle way politicians did not favour too great an emphasis on rights). While there is a tendency to exaggerate the strength of such a rights culture, it is certainly true that it has been challenged since the 1980s. In its place, there has been growing use of a 'duties discourse … in contemporary political and ideological debate' (Roche, 1992, p 49).

As Maurice Roche observes, 'both the Right and the new social movements have made equal, if distinct and different, contributions to this duties discourse' (1992, p 49), as have subsequently supporters of the third way. Roche singles out feminism and environmentalism as social movements that have contributed to the new 'duties discourse'. We will do the same, but first we discuss the ways in which dominant political ideologies of the new right and third way have promoted a duties discourse, often using interchangeably the language of obligation and responsibility.

The social right of social security has been the central policy site on which the debate about the relationship between rights and obligations has been waged. In the late 20th century, in the US and UK in particular, **new right** thinkers argued for the intensification and extension to new groups of the work obligations associated with entitlement to social security. Lawrence Mead was amongst the most influential, with his message that work obligations are 'as much a badge of citizenship as rights' (1986, p 229). Subsequently, in a UK context, he claimed that 'responsibility cannot be the assumption of policy, but it must be the goal. So I say: the poor must become responsible for themselves. That requires that government define the obligations of citizenship to include employment, and to expect the dependent to fulfil them – with some help' (Mead, 1997, p 130; see also Deacon 2002).

Some **democratic socialist** theorists, such as Plant (1988), accept the case in principle for attaching work obligations to entitlement to benefit for unemployed people in the context of decent benefits and training and job opportunities. Indeed, this is very much the philosophy pursued in the social democratic Nordic welfare states. However, others appeal to liberal principles to oppose any link between the rights and duties of citizenship. Jordan, for instance, contends that 'the first principle of liberalism – strong unconditional rights, weak and conditional duties – is breached if rights are hedged about with restrictive obligations' (1998, p 82).

As we saw in Chapter One, responsibility is a central value of the **third way**. Tony Blair asserted, when Prime Minister, that 'for too long, the demand for rights from the state was separated from the duties of citizenship and the imperative for mutual responsibility on the part of individuals and institutions' (1998, p 4). New Labour has developed a contractual understanding of citizenship, involving a contract between the state and individual citizens in which social rights are conditional on specified obligations (see **Box 7.7**). This was reflected in the subtitle of its first welfare reform policy document: 'A new contract for welfare' (Department for Social Security, 1998). Policies in many welfare states have been primarily directed towards activation of benefit claimants into paid work. In addition, in the UK, a number of social security policies have aimed to encourage desirable behaviour more widely (for instance staying on at school after the leaving age) and to discourage undesirable behaviour (such as anti-social behaviour).

> *Question:* Can you think of other examples of social policies where obligations are being attached to rights?

Box 7.7: A welfare contract

The UK government-appointed Social Security Advisory Committee commissioned a paper on *Rights and Responsibilities in the Social Security System* (Griggs and Bennett, 2009). The paper explores the increased emphasis on conditional social rights and on the idea of a contract between social security claimants and the state. It attributes this emphasis in part to the influence of communitarianism on New Labour thinking about citizenship.

The authors point out that, in the benefits system, the contract is rather 'one-sided' because of the unequal power relationship between the individual citizen and the state (Griggs and Bennett, 2009, p 67). They therefore discuss proposals for a 'fair welfare contract' put forward by White and Cooke (2007), which builds on

Stuart White's (2003) earlier theoretical work on welfare contractualism and the appropriate balance between rights and responsibilities. White and Cooke propose four requirements for such a contract: fair opportunity (with reference to the level of social mobility and of inequalities within society); fair reward for labour; universality of the contributions expected from members of society; and sensitivity to the diversity of contributions made (including unpaid care work). White and Cooke conclude that these requirements are not met in the UK. Griggs and Bennett add the requirement of adequate benefit levels, since 'both access to rights and the fulfilment of responsibilities are dependent upon resources' (2009, p 68).

As well as specific obligations attached to rights, British politicians frequently extol the virtues of more general civic responsibilities. One example is the Conservative Leader David Cameron's espousal of the value of social responsibility, mentioned in Chapter One. Another appears in a report commissioned by Prime Minister Gordon Brown from Lord Goldsmith QC. The report considers how to strengthen civic participation, particularly among young people, as a means of 'enhancing the bond of citizenship' and 'our shared sense of belonging' (Goldsmith, 2008, p 88). Civic participation, through voluntary work and other forms of constructive social participation, represented the essence of good citizenship for many of the young people in the study referred to in *Box 7.1*. It also forms a key element of the points-based citizenship test proposed by New Labour, mentioned earlier.

Broader understandings of citizenship responsibility such as these are in some ways more in tune with the duties discourse developed by new social movements than are narrow contractual definitions, which elevate paid work as *the* citizenship obligation. One strand of **feminist** citizenship theory, in particular, is highly critical of the equation of citizenship obligation with paid work. Instead, it emphasises the importance to society of unpaid work in the home and the local community. Care, it argues, should be recognised as a responsibility of citizenship (Hobson and Lister, 2002; Lister, 2003a, 2007e). Another strand in citizenship theory echoes some of the themes of civic republicanism by emphasising the importance of political participation as a responsibility of citizenship (Voet, 1998).

As we saw in Chapter Two, environmentalism echoes the critique of paid work as the primary citizenship obligation. It also shares with some strands of feminism a more general concern with the responsibilities of citizenship. According to Roche:

> if anything, the ecological movement, even more clearly than
> feminism, is concerned with the politics and morality of duty

> ... It asserts the importance of human duties, indeed it asserts
> their primacy in some respects over human rights ... It requires
> us to consider the inter-generational dimension of our sociality
> and of our moral and citizenship duties. (1992, pp 52-3)

Environmentalism also, Roche observes, expands the sphere of citizenship
'beyond the nation state level to the global level and to other ecologically
relevant levels from the global to the local' (1992, p 53). The notion of
ecological citizenship has since been developed further (see ***Box 7.8***).

Box 7.8: Ecological citizenship

Andrew Dobson is among those who have explored the notion of ecological
citizenship in depth. He makes a distinction between two complementary concepts:
'environmental citizenship', which 'deals in the currency of environmental rights'
and 'ecological citizenship', which 'deals in the currency of non-contractual
responsibility' (2003, p 89). 'The idea of obligation' is, he explains, 'central to ...
a defensible articulation of ecological citizenship' (2003, p 85). 'The principal
ecological citizenship obligation is to ensure that ecological footprints make a
sustainable, rather than an unsustainable, impact' (2003, p 118-9). He continues:
'Ecological footprints are an expression of the impact of production and
reproduction of individuals' and collectives' daily lives on strangers near and far. It is
these strangers to whom the obligations of ecological citizenship are owed' (2003,
p 119). Moreover, they 'are strangers not only to each other, but to each other's
place and even time. The obligations of the ecological citizen extend through time
as well as space, towards generations yet to be born' (2003, p 106).

Citizenship as an ideal

The final element of Marshall's definition of citizenship refers to 'an
image of an ideal', which represents a yardstick against which progress
can be measured and aspirations directed. One of the contributions of
contemporary citizenship theory is to demonstrate why this cannot be
treated as a fixed, unchallengeable, yardstick. In this spirit, John Hoffman
describes citizenship as a 'momentum concept'. Momentum concepts, he
explains, '"unfold" so that we must continuously rework them in a way that
realizes more and more of their egalitarian and anti-hierarchical potential'
(2004, p 138). In this final section, we return to the tension between
citizenship's exclusionary and inclusionary sides. We discussed earlier
exclusion at the borders of nation states. Here we turn to the struggle for

inclusion *within* nation states, which has contributed to the 'unfolding' of citizenship. This struggle has been an important theme in citizenship theory and activism (Lister, 2007a). ***Box 7.9*** reproduces an inspiring attempt at articulating 'an image of an ideal citizenship', framed in terms of the values underpinning inclusive citizenship, some of which are discussed in greater depth elsewhere in this volume. We then look at how citizenship theory has been influenced by some of the critical perspectives discussed in Parts One and Two, especially feminism and postmodernism.

Box 7.9: The values underpinning inclusive citizenship

Naila Kabeer has articulated four values of inclusive citizenship, 'viewed from the standpoint of the excluded' (2005, p 1). They are derived from a series of case studies with excluded groups, mainly in the global South. She proposes that, despite the very different contexts and experiences of these groups, 'their testimonies and actions suggest there are certain values that people associate with the idea of citizenship which cut across the boundaries that divide them' (2005, p 3). The values that emerged from these testimonies are:

- *Justice*, articulated in terms of 'when it is fair for people to be treated the same and when it is fair that they should be treated differently' (2005, p 3; see also Chapter Eight).
- *Recognition* 'of the intrinsic worth of all human beings, but also recognition of and respect for their differences' (2005, p 4; see also Chapter Nine).
- *Self-determination* or 'people's ability to exercise some degree of control over their lives' (2005, p 5). This value also emerges particularly strongly in disability theorists' accounts of citizenship, which detail the concrete barriers to self-determination and also participation faced by disabled people (Morris, 2005; see also Chapter Nine).
- *Solidarity*, that is 'the capacity to identify with others and to act in unity with them in their claims for justice and recognition' (2005, p 7; see also Spicker, 2006). This value emphasises the collective nature of citizenship.

In Chapters Three and Six we referred to the relationship between the 'universal' and the 'particular'. This has also been an important theme in critical citizenship theory. Citizenship has always been understood as a quintessentially universalist concept. In other words, the theory is that all citizens are deemed to be of equal status and therefore should be treated the same, enjoying the same rights and with the same obligations. This is the essence of Marshall's definition.

However, feminists have demonstrated how it has been a false universalism embedded in citizenship, which has served to exclude women and other marginalised groups from full citizenship (Lister, 2003a, 2007e). The citizen has traditionally been understood as an abstract, disembodied individual, rising above the claims of the body, of the private domestic sphere and of particular interests, able to apply rationality and reason in a dispassionate way. The problem is that these are qualities which have historically been associated with the male and the opposite, devalued, qualities have been associated with the female. So it was no accident that women have been excluded from (full) citizenship. Feminists have exposed how women's exclusion from, and partial inclusion in, citizenship have been rooted in the public-private divide, discussed in Chapter Two (see **Box 2.5**). In doing so, they have opened up the private sphere and personal lives as areas of relevance to citizenship (Lister, 2003a, 2007a, 2007e; Lewis, G., 2004).

Not only is the abstract citizen seen to be a male citizen, but he is also a white, able-bodied heterosexual male who sets the universal norm or standard against which citizenship has been measured. Thus, anti-racist, queer and disability theorists have also developed critiques of traditional conceptualisations of citizenship. They, together with feminists, are theorising from 'particular' standpoints. In other words, they are arguing that particular groups have specific needs and perspectives, which cannot simply be subsumed into a general, universalist ideal of citizenship.

Stuart Hall and David Held pose the question: is there an 'irreconcilable tension' between, on the one hand, the ideals of equality and universality embodied in the very idea of the citizen and, on the other, the 'variety of particular and specific needs, of diverse sites and practices which constitute the modern political subject?' (1989, pp 176-7). As we saw in Chapter Three, postmodernism challenges the very idea of such universal ideals. Nevertheless, there are some theorists who have attempted to combine postmodernist insights with more traditional ideals of justice and to reconcile universalistic and particularistic approaches.

Thompson and Hoggett, for instance, contend that 'any justifiable universalism or egalitarianism must take particularity and difference into account; and any legitimate particularism or politics of difference must employ some universal or egalitarian standard' (1996, p 23). Their argument is that the genuinely universal is made up of a myriad of particular positions that cannot therefore be ignored. At the same time, the claims of particular groups have to be made with reference to a universal benchmark, which transcends them, in order to link one particular position with another and to provide a common reference point for their citizenship claims. Thus we still work with a common ideal of citizenship but that ideal has to take account of the particularities of the groups that make up the citizenry. This does not resolve the tension between the universal and the particular, but it turns it into a creative tension (Lister, 2003a). These are difficult theoretical arguments but they might make more sense when you read the concrete examples in **Box 7.10**.

Box 7.10: Combining the universalist standard of citizenship with particularist claims

These are some examples of where marginalised groups have used the universal standard of citizenship as the focus of particularist claims; they are 'particular' groups who are demanding simultaneously to be treated as equal citizens and to be recognised as different.

- The disabled people's movement has often articulated its demands as a struggle for full and equal citizenship but through the assertion of disability as a 'different' social and political category (see also Chapter Nine).
- Some parts of the gay and lesbian movement have used the discourse of equal citizenship and citizenship rights but have included the right to assert their difference from the heterosexual norm in public places (see also **Boxes 7.4** and **7.5**).
- In France, some Muslim schoolgirls argued the right to wear the headscarf in schools, which is not allowed in the secular French education system. This was a struggle to assert their particular cultural identity, but the arguments they used were couched in a discourse of universalistic human rights.

In addition, a good example of a political statement that combines the universal and the particular in its articulation of citizenship can be found in the Northern Ireland Peace Agreement, 1998. This statement was very much the work of the Northern Ireland Women's Coalition, who self-consciously drew on contemporary critical theorising about citizenship. Article 1(v) of the Agreement states that power:

> shall be exercised with rigorous impartiality on behalf of all the people in the diversity of their identities and traditions and shall be founded on the principles of full respect for, and equality of civil, political, social and cultural rights, of freedom from discrimination for all citizens, and of parity of esteem and of just and equal treatment for the identity, ethos and aspirations of both communities. (full text of Agreement available via www.taoiseach. gov.ie/eng/Publications/)

As well as attempting to reconcile the universal and the particular, critical citizenship theorists have sought to refashion the yardstick of citizenship so that it no longer represents a false universalism. Examples include: the attempt by some feminists to build care into the meaning of citizenship and the construction of citizenship responsibilities; and the conceptualisation of a multi-cultural model of citizenship, which does not take the majority culture as the ideal to which 'minorities' should aspire but which builds in different cultures, giving them equal status.

Some critics have questioned whether citizenship has any value for a progressive social policy and politics, given its roots in a false universalism. Others argue that the examples of social movements' deployment of a discourse of citizenship to press their claims suggests that it does have a value, particularly when combined with the concepts of social justice, equality and liberty, which we explore in the next chapter. You might like to reflect on this question yourself.

Summary

- Citizenship has been described as a 'contested' and 'contextual' concept. It also represents a 'lived experience'.
- Key elements of citizenship are: membership of a community; rights; duties; equality of status. Moreover, it represents an ideal or yardstick.
- As well as legal membership of the nation state, citizenship theory has articulated citizenship above and below the nation state, including through the notion of 'global citizenship'.
- 'Community' is a ubiquitous term in political and policy language. It has two main meanings, based on a geographical place and on shared identity or interests. Two key criticisms are directed at rosy expositions of community that ignore how it serves to exclude non-members and to gloss over internal power relations and associated divisions and conflicts. This had led some critical theorists to develop more pluralist and fluid understandings of community.
- Contemporary understandings of citizenship reflect two broad traditions of citizenship: liberalism and civic republicanism. They represent citizenship as a status and a practice.
- The rights of the individual stand at the heart of the liberal tradition. As well as the triad of civil-political-social rights identified by Marshall (1950), social movements have articulated claims to new rights such as sexual rights.
- A duties discourse, which prioritises the community over the individual in line with the civic republican tradition, has become increasingly dominant in political debate. It embraces both a narrow definition of the obligation to undertake paid work as a condition of the right to social security (new right and third way) and broader

conceptualisations, which include care (feminism) and a sustainable ecological footprint (environmentalism).

- Contemporary citizenship theorists have articulated principles of inclusive citizenship and have integrated universalist and particularist perspectives in an attempt to re-fashion citizenship as an ideal or yardstick that is not built on a false universalism.

Further reading

There is a huge literature on citizenship. Two useful, wide-ranging introductory texts are: **Faulks (2000)** and **Dwyer (2004,** 2nd edn 2010).**Bellamy et al (2004)** and **Lister et al (2007)** offer a cross-national, contextual account. **Dower (2003)** provides an accessible introduction to global citizenship and **Dean (2004, 2008)** provides a critical account of human rights and social policy. **Jones (1994)** contributes a detailed introduction to rights more generally. **Deacon (2002)** and **Roche (1992)** provide an overview of recent debates around the citizenship obligations attached to social citizenship. All of these themes are explored from a feminist perspective by **Lister (2003a, 2007e)**. The idea of inclusive citizenship is developed by **Kabeer (2005)**, in the context mainly of the global South, and by **Lister (2007a)**. Three useful social policy texts about the concept of community are: **Hoggett (1997b), Hughes (1998a)** and **Brent (2009)**.

Liberty, equality and social justice

Liberty, equality and social justice are all normative concepts: embedded in them is an ideal, a value. They are central concepts in political theory and in social policy. Perhaps more than any of the other concepts discussed in this volume the positions taken on them act as a differentiator between some of the dominant perspectives covered in Chapter One. For instance, typically, the new right is represented as pro-liberty and anti-social justice and equality, whereas democratic socialism is represented as prioritising social justice and equality over liberty or even as anti-liberty. Here, liberty stands on the one side and social justice and equality on the other, in opposition to each other.

In fact, as we shall see, the relationship between the three concepts and some of the political positions taken on them is more complex and less intrinsically antagonistic than such formulations imply. Some commentators would argue that 'equality and liberty are only in opposition when either is pushed to an extreme' (Barker, 1996, p 5). It tends to be theorists of the right who treat the two values as in opposition. An example is provided by the conservative author Ferdinand Mount: 'Equality often conflicts with liberty ... The government cannot engineer greater equality in economic relations without damaging the freedom of the more thrusting citizens to get ahead' (2008, p 4; see also **Box 8.12**). Social democratic and democratic socialist theorists are more likely to emphasise the interrelationship between the two values.

Stuart White, for instance, rejects claims as to the inevitable 'incompatibility of liberty and equality' as 'misguided'. He maintains, instead, that 'theorists and activists of the left have always sensed that there is in some fundamental way a real complementarity between the struggles for freedom and equality' (2002, p 35). For Brighouse and Swift 'achieving social justice is essentially about getting the right balance between equality and liberty' (2008, p 139).

This balance is explored in a volume on the future of liberalism entitled *Beyond Liberty*. One conclusion reached is 'that promoting individual liberty and social justice must go hand in hand' (Margo et al, 2007, p 239). This is acknowledged by one of the contributors, the British Liberal Democrat MP, Steven Webb: 'just as a truly fair society has to be one in which personal freedom is respected and cherished, so a free society must be one where fairness and justice reign' (2007, p 143).

The relationship between social justice, equality and freedom is addressed in Sen's treatise on justice. In it, he observes that 'every normative theory of social justice that has received support and advocacy in recent times seems to demand equality of *something*'; at the same time, he underlines 'the importance of freedom in different forms in theories of justice' (2009, pp 291, 301, emphasis in original). He also cautions against 'the adoption of some narrow and unifocal view of equality or liberty', which does not have regard to their various meanings (2009, p 317). Sen's approach emphasises both the richness and the inter-connectedness of the three concepts. We will discuss liberty and equality in turn before tackling the more overarching concept of social justice.

Liberty

For liberals, and in particular classical and neo-liberals (on the new right), liberty (or freedom) is the supreme value. We here use the terms 'liberty' and 'freedom' interchangeably.

'Negative' freedom

In classical liberal thought, from which, as we saw in Chapter One, new right theory draws, liberty has three essential elements:

• freedom from coercion or the imposition of someone else's will without consent;
• property rights as inherent in an individual's 'natural rights' (which derive from being human), so that protection of property (defined broadly to include income and savings) is central to guaranteeing individual freedom;
• maximum freedom of choice.

In the context of welfare this classical liberal conceptualisation of freedom adds up to a perception of the welfare state as a threat to freedom. The welfare state is coercive and undermines property rights in that it taxes what people have rightfully earned – it is theft from their property; and it reduces choice through its provision of benefits and services in place of the market. True freedom resides in the market. Without the market, Marsland argues, people are serfs and where the market is restricted, as in welfare state societies, they are 'half-free, half-slave' (Marsland, 1996, p xii). The freedom associated with markets has been used by neo-liberals to justify the inequality created by markets – an example of where liberty and equality are set against each other.

This conceptualisation of freedom is often described as 'negative' freedom: it is about freedom from constraints and coercion. Spicker (2006) identifies three aspects:

- *non-interference from other people*: 'the protection of freedom means that the freedoms of each person have to be circumscribed, so that they do not infringe the freedoms of other people' (2006, p 8);
- freedom from *coercion by other people* or 'the use of power by one person to determine the behaviour of another' (2006, p 10);
- freedom from *coercion by government* through regulation (for example employment protection or age of consent laws), restriction of action (for example through criminal law) and mandatory activity (such as jury service or paying tax). It is freedom from coercion by government, which particularly exercises classical and neo-liberals.

As Spicker's account of non-interference implies, negative freedom raises the question: how much freedom? 'Unless we think that people should be free to do absolutely anything – to others as well as to themselves – there cannot be a right to freedom without qualification' (Jones, 1994, p 122). Thus, for instance, as the philosopher Onora O'Neill observes, 'even committed liberals don't seriously think that rights to free speech are unlimited or unconditional, although they seem to be unsure about which limits should be set' (2006). The right to freedom of speech or expression does not include the right to libel or slander; more controversial is whether it should include the right to 'hate speech', which encourages hatred of oppressed groups (see *Box 8.1*).

Box 8.1: Examples of controversies around the limits to freedom of speech

There have been a number of controversies around the limits to freedom of speech in recent years, many of them concerning 'race' or religion.

- The decision by a Danish newspaper to print cartoons of the prophet Mohammad in 2005 provoked a huge international controversy. The decision was taken in the name of reaffirming the right to free speech and expression, in the knowledge that it would be offensive to Muslims, for whom representations of the prophet are forbidden. The stereotypical images of Islam depicted in the cartoons compounded the offence. Supporters of the decision to print the cartoons invoked the sanctity of the principle of free speech; critics responded that the right does not extend to the vilification of powerless and marginalised minorities and should be exercised responsibly (see, for instance, Hensher and Younge, 2006; Klug, 2006).

- Adolf Hitler's *Mein Kampf* has been banned in West Germany since the end of the Second World War. The desire to eradicate all traces of Nazism was considered more important than the liberal principle of free speech. Controversially, there is now a move to allow its publication, with a critical commentary, which has the support of the Central Council of Jews (*The Independent*, 10 August 2009).
- In the UK, there was considerable public debate in 2007 around a proposal to extend laws banning incitement of racial and religious hatred to cover homophobia. Again, the debate concerned the limits of freedom of speech with reference to a marginalised minority group.

Question: Can you think of any other examples of debates where the right to freedom of speech has been countered by the right of minority groups not to be subjected to hate speech?

Just where one draws the lines that qualify freedom is an issue of importance to a number of areas of social policy. The positions taken form a spectrum. Libertarians, who argue for the maximum possible freedom, stand at one end. They would, for instance, argue that all drug use should be legal on the grounds that individuals should be free to do what they want with their bodies. Authoritarians and paternalists are found at the other end. They maintain that the state should lay down detailed rules about what individuals can or cannot do in the name of the good of the wider community as well as, in the case of paternalists, the protection of individuals themselves. Paternalist arguments are typically couched in terms of the individual's own welfare. Paternalism is also sometimes justified, paradoxically, in the name of freedom: 'If people's actions forestall choices, for example through drug addiction or alcoholism, intervention will help them to preserve their independence and freedom' (Spicker, 2006, p 36).

What the question about the limits to freedom underlines is that freedom is not the only good to be valued and in the development of social policy it is constantly being weighed against other goods, such as collective security, community cohesion, health and welfare and ecological needs (see **Box 8.2**). This need to balance liberty against other policy goals, as well as the liberties of different members of society, is reflected in speeches made by both New Labour Prime Ministers, Tony Blair and Gordon Brown. When launching the Respect Action Plan to deal with anti-social behaviour, Blair presented the measures as part of 'a genuine intellectual debate about the nature of liberty in a modern developed society'. He called for 'a radical new approach' in order 'to restore the liberty of the law-abiding citizen. My view is very clear: their freedom to be safe from fear has to come first' (Blair, 2006). The argument is developed by the then Justice Minister, Michael Wills: 'The Anti-Social Behaviour Order (ASBO) ... has been cited by some as an example of the erosion of liberty. But on the estate where vulnerable pensioners have been terrorised by gangs of thugs, ASBOs have not destroyed the liberty of those pensioners, they have secured it' (Wills, 2009, p 34).

In a speech on liberty, Brown explained that 'precious as it is, liberty is not the only value we prize and not the only priority for government. The test for any government will be how it makes those hard choices, how it strikes the balance.' (Brown, 2007; see also Wills, 2009) He referred in particular to the balance between the 'claims of liberty' and 'the needs of security'. Many commentators argue that the New Labour government has, in fact, compromised 'the claims of liberty' in the name of 'the needs of security' and of fighting crime and anti-social behaviour (see also Chapter Four). Such concerns led to a major Convention on Modern Liberty in 2009. There has been fierce debate in the media about the extent and significance of the erosion of liberty under New Labour.

> **Question:** Can you think of examples of the erosion of liberty in the name of fighting terrorism or crime and anti-social behaviour in the UK or elsewhere?

Box 8.2: Balancing liberty against other public goods

- In a number of countries smoking bans in public places have provoked fierce controversy about the relative weight to be given to the individual's liberty to smoke where she or he wishes and the wider public good of protection against the harmful health effects of other people's smoking. Smoking rights groups in the US have resisted smoking bans as an attack on basic rights of freedom (*The Guardian*, 16 September 2009). Two earlier letters to *The Guardian* (16 February 2006) sum up what is at stake: one claims that the ban is 'an infringement of civil liberties'; the other, from a young woman with a respiratory problem, retorts that 'in all the talk of ... "infringement of smokers' civil liberties", why is it never mentioned that those of us unwilling or unable to tolerate cigarette smoke ... have until now been consistently denied all choice and civil liberties when it comes to socialising?' In Berlin, the British musician Joe Jackson is quoted as claiming that the ban is 'much worse than for other cities, because this city was always a symbol of freedom and tolerance' (*The Observer*, 20 January 2008).

- Liberty can also come into conflict with environmental needs. At the heart of environmentalism is the belief that human beings cannot be free to continue to consume regardless of the costs to the environment and future generations. The argument is put sharply by Mayer Hillman, a policy analyst: 'I've seen pictures of people in Bangladesh with the sea surging, or in Africa with the drought and the famine which has been exacerbated by temperature changes. How dare people then go on saying "Oh you can't interfere with people's freedom if they want to fly to Prague for a stag weekend"' (2007, p 10). As with smoking, the argument can also be articulated in terms of competing freedoms. Lawson, for instance, asks 'How can the freedom to consume whatever you want without restriction be more important than the freedom to live on a habitable planet?' (2009, p 214).

Question: can you think of other policy areas where liberty has been, or in your view should be, restricted in the interests of the wider public good?

'Positive' freedom

The value of freedom is typically closely linked to that of agency and autonomy: the idea that individuals have some control over their lives, 'capable of making choices and reaching decisions which are, in some sense, authentically their own' (Jones, 1994, p 125; discussed also in the Introduction and Chapter Six). Indeed, 'the promotion of autonomy is fundamental to freedom' (Spicker, 2006, p 25). The volume on the future of liberalism mentioned earlier concludes that 'the case that tackling unfairness is central to promoting freedom is greatly strengthened by emerging evidence on what it means to equip individuals with what they need in order to exercise meaningful agency' (Margo et al, 2007, p 239).

This argument and the value of autonomy more generally provide a bridge to the other conceptualisation of freedom, often called 'positive freedom'. This refers to 'freedom *to*' rather than simply 'freedom *from*', as in negative freedom. The distinction was introduced in the previous chapter in the discussion of Plant's defence of social rights. The argument goes: if freedom is about autonomy, then absence of coercion is not enough; what also matters is whether a person is able to exercise that freedom and this partly depends on economic resources. The example frequently given is that we are all, in theory, free to dine at the Ritz but without the money we cannot, in practice, dine there. In other words, from the perspective of negative liberty there is nothing stopping us dining at the Ritz; from the perspective of positive liberty, only those with sufficient money are actually free to do so. One corollary of the idea of positive freedom is that poverty represents a reduction in liberty.

Another example is provided by the American health care system, described by one observer as 'the greatest restriction on personal freedom' she has witnessed: the fear of losing health insurance can discourage people from changing jobs and lack of health insurance can lead to avoidable deaths (Lavender, 2009). In this example the market limits rather than promotes freedom; it is itself a source of coercion. Michael J. Sandel illustrates the point with another example from the US: the volunteer army. He suggests that 'the volunteer army may not be as voluntary as it seems' because of 'the coercion that can occur if economic disadvantage compels young people to risk their lives in exchange for a college education and other benefits' (2009, pp 82, 83-4). 'How free are the choices we make in the free market?' and 'How much equality is needed to ensure that market choices are free rather than coerced?' he asks (Sandel, 2009, pp 102, 84).

Another way of thinking about positive freedom is provided by the capabilities approach (introduced in Chapter Six). The capabilities approach is concerned with:

> a person's capability to do things he or she has reason to value
> … The focus here is on the freedom that a person actually has
> to do this or be that – things that he or she may value doing
> or being … The idea of freedom also respects our being free
> to determine what we want, what we value and ultimately
> what we decide to choose. The concept of capability is thus
> linked closely with the opportunity aspect of freedom. (Sen,
> 2009, pp 231-2)

Sen emphasises that 'since the idea of capability is linked with substantive freedom, it gives a central role to a person's *actual* ability to do the different things that she values doing' (2009, p 253). Some feminist scholars have applied Sen's formulation to the choices that women with caring responsibilities can make: 'if women are to exercise *real* freedom to choose, there must be *equal* freedom on the part of men and women to choose between alternatives (e.g. between work and care)' (Lewis and Giullari, 2005, p 90, emphasis in original).

The essence of substantive freedom is the same as that of positive freedom (Carpenter, 2009b). This broader notion of freedom was promoted by the 'social' or 'new' liberals at the end of the 19th century (see **Box 1.1**). It is rejected as illegitimate by classical and neo-liberals (including the new right) (Plant, 2004). The social liberals built on John Stuart Mill's writings on freedom, which paid more attention to the social dimension than did most classical liberal thought. In turn, social liberalism was influential on middle way thinkers such as Beveridge. The Beveridge Report sets out 'the way to freedom from want' (1942, p 7). Although Beveridge here uses the language of 'freedom from', it is in the spirit of 'freedom to'. Social liberals recognised a collective responsibility to ensure genuine freedom or positive liberty through state intervention. This view was then developed further by democratic socialists.

Freedom and equality

One of the main democratic socialist exponents of positive liberty in contemporary politics has been the former Labour cabinet minister, Roy Hattersley. His book, *Choose Freedom*, is subtitled 'The future for democratic socialism'. It is primarily making the case that liberty and equality are indivisible, if freedom is conceived of in positive as well as negative terms. Published at the height of Margaret Thatcher's term in office, it represents an attempt to counter the new right position, which identifies democratic socialism as anti-liberty.

Hattersley (1987, p 78) cites R. H. Tawney (a key democratic socialist thinker, introduced in *Box 1.3*): 'socialists interpret [freedom] as implying the utmost possible development of every human being and the deliberate organisation of society for the attainment of that objective' (1931/1964, p 167). Here is another exposition of the relationship between positive liberty and individual autonomy and agency. Tawney addresses the relationship between liberty and equality at some length in his treatise on equality, in a way that introduces again the idea of other public goods that need to be weighed against liberty (see *Box 8.3*).

Box 8.3: R. H. Tawney on the relationship between liberty and equality

Liberty and equality have usually in England been considered antithetic ... Equality implies the deliberate acceptance of social restraints upon individual expansion. It involves the prevention of sensational extremes of wealth and power by public action for the public good. If liberty means, therefore, that every individual shall be free, according to his opportunities, to indulge without limit his appetite for either, it is clearly incompatible, not only with economic and social, but with civil and political, equality, which also prevent the strong exploiting to the full the advantages of their strength ... But freedom for the pike is death for the minnows. It is possible that equality is to be contrasted, not with liberty, but only with a particular interpretation of it ... It is a truism that liberty, as distinct from the liberties of special persons and classes, can exist only in so far as it is limited by rules, which secure that freedom for some is not slavery for others. The spiritual energy of human beings, in all the wealth of their infinite diversities, is the end to which external arrangements, whether political or economic, are merely means. Hence institutions which guarantee to men [and women] the opportunity of becoming the best of which they are capable are the supreme political good, and liberty is rightly preferred to equality, when the two are in conflict. The question is whether, in the conditions of modern society, they conflict or not. It is whether the defined and limited freedom, which alone can be generally enjoyed, is most likely to be attained by a community which encourages violent inequalities, or by one which represses them. (Tawney, 1931/1964, p 164)

In Hattersley's formulation, equality is not an end in itself but the means to freedom: 'liberty is our aim. Equality is the way in which it can truly be achieved' (1987, p 23; see **Box 8.4**). A very similar stance is adopted by Neal Lawson, chair of the influential British democratic left pressure group Compass. He contends that 'equality should remain fundamental to the left but only within the wider and more ambitious project to redefine freedom as the inspirational value of socialism'; and that 'the left must accept that socialism is a philosophy of liberty' (Lawson, 2006, pp 6, 21). Echoing Tawney, Hattersley concludes that, ultimately, the real aim, to which both liberty and equality are intermediate objectives, is 'the full flowering of the individual human spirit' (Hattersley, 1987, p 101).

Box 8.4: Achieving greater liberty through greater equality and social (or distributive) justice

According to Plant,

> a liberal state as the defender of liberty has to be concerned with the distribution of resources that will reasonably satisfy the claims of ability and opportunity. Hence a concern with positive liberty will naturally also imply a concern with distributive justice: that is to say, with access to that bundle of resources and opportunities which individuals should have in order to realise positive freedom ... In this way, freedom and social justice go together. (2004, pp 25-6)

White draws out the implications for a policy of the redistribution of income and wealth:

> A distribution of wealth is a distribution of private property rights in resources and, as such, entails a corresponding distribution of liberty ... Thus, when the egalitarian proposes to use state power to redistribute wealth it is quite misleading to picture this as a gain for equality at the expense of liberty. In and of itself, the redistribution of wealth entails a redistribution of liberty: it generates *a more equal liberty*. (White, 2002, p 28)

Equality

Our discussion of liberty has led directly into equality, reinforcing the point made in the introductory section that, depending on how they are formulated, they can represent complementary rather than conflicting values or concepts. According to Andrew Heywood, 'The idea of equality is perhaps the defining feature of modern political thought ... Nevertheless, few political principles are as contentious as equality, or polarise opinion so effectively' (1994, p 225). At the heart of the disputes around the concept of equality lies the question posed by Sen: 'equality of what?' (1992, p 12). Sen (2009) points out that even those political philosophers who argue against the case for material equality believe in some form of equality such as equal rights to liberty. The concept of equality is important for a number of political philosophies discussed in Part One, notably democratic socialism, feminism and anti-racism.

In this section, we will map out the principles which are most commonly deployed to answer the question 'equality of what?' First, though, we give some examples of classifications of equality.

Classifications of equality

The question 'equality of what?' can be answered with reference to different principles of equality or by classifying forms of equality. We focus mainly on the former here, but first **Box 8.5** provides two examples of classifications of equality. You will see that there is some overlap between elements of these classifications and some of the principles of equality.

Box 8.5: Two examples of classifications of equality

White identifies five 'forms of equality' (2007, p 4):

*   *moral equality*: 'each member of the state has equal worth' (2007, p 10). As, White's elaboration implies, this is the same as the principle of equal worth, which we will discuss under principles of equality;
*   *legal equality*: equal treatment before the law (which also represents one element of equal worth);
*   *social equality*: equal status (yet again a variant of the principle of equal worth) and 'the absence of domination in people's everyday social relationships' (2007, p 7);
*   *political equality*: 'those who are subject to the commands of a state should have equal right to participate in formulating the laws on which these commands are based' (2007, p 5; see also Dahl, 2006);
*   *economic equality*: concerns access to and the distribution of, in particular, the material resources of income and wealth in various forms. We will look at some of the principles of economic equality further.

The sociologist, Göran Therborn, offers a rather different classification of *in*equality:

*   *vital inequality*: 'inequality of health and death' (2009, p 20);
*   *existential inequality*: 'denial of (equal) recognition and respect' and 'potent generator of humiliations' of a range of marginalised groups (2009, p 21). Again, this draws on the principle of equality of status;
*   *material or resource inequality*: inequality of access to opportunities and the unequal distribution of material rewards (as in White's economic equality).

Therborn also identifies four mechanisms of inequality:

*   *distantiation*: 'some people are running ahead and/or others falling behind' (2009, p 21);
*   *exclusion*: 'through which a barrier is erected making it impossible, or at least more difficult, for certain categories of people to access a good life' (2009, p 21);
*   *institutional hierarchy*: 'societies and organisations are constituted as ladders, with some people perched on top and others below' (2009, pp 21-2);
*   *exploitation*: 'in which the riches of the rich derive from the toil and the subjection of the poor and disadvantaged' (2009, p 22). As we saw in Chapter Two, exploitation is a key concept in Marxism.

Principles of equality

The main principles of equality, which we will discuss, are: equal worth; complex equality; equality of opportunity, equality of outcome; and equity.

Equal worth

The concept of equal worth can be articulated in both a weaker and a stronger form. The weaker form represents the most basic, minimalist, form of equality and is sometimes referred to as 'foundational equality'. It is a moral principle deriving from our common humanity and it typically underpins the case made for other forms of equality. Even the new right, who, as we shall see, oppose more substantive forms of equality, subscribe to the weak principle of equal worth. In particular, they believe in the equal right to liberty and formal equality before the law, meaning equal treatment without bias or prejudice. In the words of Marsland, 'equality before the law is a foundational principle of any free society' (1996, p 22).

> *Question:* Can you think of societies either today or in recent history where the principle of equality before the law has not applied?

The 'stronger' version of the concept of equal worth tends to be articulated in terms such as 'social equality' or 'equality of status' or 'regard'. According to the political theorist, David Miller: 'Equality of status obtains in a society when each member regards him- or herself as fundamentally the equal of all the others, and is regarded by the others as fundamentally their equal. It involves, then, the reciprocal recognition of equal standing' (1997, p 92). Like the weaker version, it is not a principle of distributive justice, falling within the domain of economic equality. Nevertheless, it goes beyond formal equality to address social relationships and how we live together and it is opposed to social hierarchies. Some theorists would therefore argue that even if the stronger concept of equal worth is not of itself a principle of distributive justice it has implications for it. The argument is that the more unequal the distribution of income and wealth and of economic opportunities, in other words the greater the economic inequality, the less likely we are to achieve genuine social equality. The case is well made by Anne Phillips:

> A society that condones excesses of poverty in the midst of wealth, or arbitrarily rewards one skill with one hundred times the wages of another, is not recognizing its citizens as of equal

human worth ... Strict equality may not be necessary to sustain equality of worth ... but ideals of equal citizenship cannot survive unscathed by great differentials in income and wealth. When the gap between rich and poor opens up too widely, it becomes meaningless to pretend that we have recognized all adults as equals. (1999, p 131)

Sandel elaborates on the connection with equal citizenship. In the context of growing inequality in the US, he warns that 'too great a gap between rich and poor undermines the solidarity that democratic citizenship requires. Here's how: As inequality deepens, rich and poor live increasingly separate lives' (2009, p 266). As a consequence, it is 'difficult to cultivate the solidarity and sense of community on which democratic citizenship depends' (2009, p 267).

The stronger meaning of equal worth draws on a vocabulary of recognition and respect, as in Therborn's notion of 'existential inequality'. This vocabulary is often used by poverty activists to demand respectful treatment by agencies of the state and the media (Lister, 2004a). However, as we shall see in the following chapter, the social justice paradigm of recognition is more often associated with claims for recognition of *difference* (associated with, for instance, gender, 'race', disability or sexual orientation) than with claims for *equality* based on what we *share in common*. This takes up the theme of the tension between universality and equality vs. particularity and difference, already introduced in Chapters Two, Three and Seven.

Complex equality

Miller suggests that the notion of 'social equality' points us towards what the political theorist Michael Walzer (1983) has called 'complex equality'. This notion expresses the idea that there are a number of spheres of distribution such as income, political power and education; these should be kept separate so that if a person does well in one sphere it should not have implications for their position in any other sphere. This means, for example, that money should not be able to buy a person a better education or political power. What is at issue in the notion of complex equality is dominance and power: 'the way that access to one social good has given people the power (or made them believe that they have the right) to claim another' (Phillips, 1999, p 65). This gives rise to relations of domination and subordination, which are inconsistent with social equality.

Walzer is partly arguing that economic inequality does not matter where it does not affect other spheres of equality. The problem, as a number of critics have pointed out, is that in practice economic inequality all too often does affect other spheres. In his treatise on political equality, Robert A. Dahl observes that the economic inequalities generated by a market economy extend 'to information, status, education, access to political elites' and that such resources are 'readily convertible to political resources, resources that can be used to gain influence, authority and power over others' (2006, p 66). The point is illustrated in a study of the US as an 'unequal democracy'. The author, Larry M. Bartels, explains that one of the book's 'most important questions' is 'whether political equality can be achieved, or even approximated, in a society marked by glaring economic inequalities.' He asks, 'when push comes to shove, how impermeable are the boundaries separating the economic and political spheres of American life?' (2008, p 24). His answer is that the boundaries are all too permeable: 'economic inequality clearly has pervasive, corrosive effects on political representation and policy making in contemporary America' (Bartels, 2008, p 284).

Equality of opportunity

The boundaries between economic and educational spheres are also permeable in societies where private education plays a significant role (see **Box 8.12**). One argument used against the permeability of these spheres of distribution is that the ability to purchase a better education undermines the principle of equality of opportunity. The principle of equality of opportunity is articulated in a number of ways.

First, is the notion of 'equal opportunities', which usually refers to the idea that social divisions such as those of 'race' or ethnicity, gender, disability and sexual orientation should not affect an individual's opportunity to succeed. It is often associated with anti-discrimination policies and in the case of gender and 'race' with some forms of feminism and anti-racism (see Chapter Two).

Second, opportunity is also at the heart of Sen's notion of capabilities, which we have discussed earlier. Sen describes the capabilities approach as involving 'a fundamental shift in the focus of attention from the *means* of living to the *actual opportunities* a person has' (2009, p 253, emphasis in original). The Equality and Human Rights Commission's equality measurement framework, which is based on the capabilities approach, states that 'an equal society protects and promotes the central and valuable freedoms and *real opportunities* of each person' (EHRC, 2009a, p 2, emphasis added). It continues that 'in an equal society, central and valuable freedoms and *real opportunities*…are limited by the need to guarantee the same freedoms and *opportunities* for all' (EHRC, 2009a, p 2, emphasis added).

(Note too how equality, opportunity and freedom are used in support of each other in this formulation.)

Third is the concept of equality of opportunity, as typically used in opposition to that of equality of outcome. This is the meaning on which we concentrate before turning to discuss equality of outcome. The distinction between the two has been at the heart of debates about equality associated with the third way and New Labour (see *Box 8.7*). The key principle is that a person's social and economic starting position in life should not affect their ability to succeed, particularly in the fields of education and employment. Typical metaphors are those of the 'level playing field', 'an equal start in the race' and 'ladders' of opportunity. As not everyone can win the race or reach the top of the ladder, the implication is that it is the opportunity not the outcome that matters.

Equality of opportunity is a key principle of the third way. In New Labour politics two models have emerged: meritocracy and 'the new egalitarianism' (see *Boxes 8.6* and *8.7*).

Box 8.6: Meritocracy

The term 'meritocracy' was coined by Michael Young (1961) to denote a society in which merit, defined as intelligence (measured by IQ) plus effort, win out. Those who are intelligent and talented and work hard will rise to the top. Social mobility is one of the watchwords of proponents of meritocracy. Meritocracy and social mobility are generally regarded as desirable. One advocate, Peter Saunders, explains that 'the essence of a meritocratic society is that it offers individuals equal opportunities to become unequal. There is open competition for the most desirable, responsible and well-rewarded positions, and the most able and committed people generally succeed in attaining these positions' (1996, p 76). Saunders observes that this 'seems to be a "good thing", both for the society (for it ensures that the most talented people get into the key leadership positions) and for individuals themselves (for it respects and justly rewards individual achievement)' (1996, p 76). However, he also concedes that 'a meritocracy can be an uncomfortable place in which to live, for it is inherently competitive, and it produces losers as well as winners. For this reason, the meritocratic ideal has many enemies, not least among egalitarians' (1996, p 76; see, for instance, Lister, 2006; Hickman, 2009).

Indeed, it is often forgotten that Young's fictional account of a meritocracy was written as a warning not a utopian vision. He feared that, if achieved, a meritocratic society would be marked by division. It would also legitimate inequality and the privileges associated with it, as implied by Saunders' exposition. More recently Young has warned that 'If meritocrats believe, as more and more of them are encouraged to, that their advancement comes from their own merits, they can feel that they deserve whatever they can get ... So assured have the elite become that there is almost no block on the rewards they arrogate to themselves' (2001).

The meritocratic tendency against which Young warns is satirised by Tawney:

> It is possible that intelligent tadpoles reconcile themselves to the inconvenience of their position by reflecting that though most of them will live to be tadpoles and nothing more, the more fortunate of the species will one day shed their tails, distend their mouths and stomachs, hop nimbly onto dry land and croak addresses to their former friends on the virtues by means of which tadpoles of character and capacity can rise to be frogs. (1931/1964, p 105)

The flip side of Tawney's argument is that those who remain tadpoles or who slide back into the pond are likely to be branded as failures, deserving of their fate. As a Performance and Innovation Unit paper puts it: 'the losers or downward mobile in a meritocracy would have no one to blame for their circumstances but their own lack of ability and commitment' (Aldridge, 2001, para 71). The phrase 'their own lack of ability and commitment' raises the question of how ability and commitment (merit) are defined and measured. Typically they are defined narrowly by proponents of meritocracy. But it is possible to raise questions as to why, for instance, a care worker is rewarded so much less than a City trader (Lister, 2006). An analysis of the value to society of a number of different jobs concludes that 'the least well paid jobs are often those that are among the most socially valuable – jobs that keep our communities and families together', but which are not rewarded well by the market (Lawlor et al, 2009, p 2). Conversely it suggests that the greatest financial rewards accrue to 'some of the professions that are the most socially and environmentally costly' (Lawlor et al, 2009, p 4). As a Fabian Commission explains:

> A broader understanding of the term [merit] would give proper social (and economic) recognition to the contribution that people make to the wellbeing of others in society, e.g. by devoting their lives to caring for others, or servicing basic needs in the form of catering and cleaning work. We need to confront the complacent view that a steep hierarchy in social positions is inescapable. (Fabian Commission, 2006, p 27)

Sandel reminds us that 'Justice is not only about the right way to distribute things. It is also about the right way to value things' (Sandel, 2009, p 261). The point I am making here is that the two are interwoven.

Tawney's parable of the tadpoles (quoted in **Box 8.6**) continues with the observation: 'And what a view of human life such an attitude implies! As though opportunities for talent to rise could be equalized in a society where the circumstances surrounding it from birth are themselves unequal!' (1931/1964, pp 105-6). Similar arguments are made today by democratic socialists who believe that genuine equality of opportunity is impossible in highly unequal societies, where the successful are able to pass on the rewards and privileges they achieve to their children, thereby undermining the idea of an equal start in life. They therefore put the case for greater equality of outcome.

Equality of outcome

Equality of outcome is generally regarded as the most radical approach to equality. It shifts the focus from a concern with starting points to end results and from opportunities to rewards. In its most extreme literal form it would mean that everyone ended up with the same level of material resources. Sometimes opponents of equality of outcome argue as if it is literal equality of outcome, with everyone having the same level of resources, which is advocated. However, in practice very few egalitarians (the label often espoused by proponents of equality of outcome) argue for absolute equality of outcome. Instead they advocate greater equality than prevails at present, particularly in highly unequal societies such as the UK and US.

Someone who comes closest to arguing for a more literal form of equality of outcome is the socialist philosopher G. A. Cohen when he suggests that 'the principle of equality says that the amount of amenity and burden in one person's life should be roughly comparable to that in any other's' (1997, p 37). While Cohen concedes that perhaps no one believes in 'the unlimited sway of the principle', he maintains, that 'I, and many others, certainly believe in it as a value to be traded off against others' (1997, p 38). This trade off is generally made with liberty but also with economic goals such as ensuring people have an incentive to work hard and improve their position by their own efforts.

It is also sometimes argued that equality would stifle diversity and mean uniformity: 'they want to make us all the same' is a typical chant. Tawney's answer to this argument is that 'individual differences, which are a source of social energy, are more likely to ripen and find expression if social inequalities are, as far as practicable, diminished' (1931/1964, p 57). Egalitarians are not arguing that everyone is or should be the same but that 'it is the mark of a civilized society to aim at eliminating such inequalities as have their source, not in individual differences, but in its own organization' (Tawney, 1931/1964, p 57; see also Hattersley, 1987, pp 37-41). Some egalitarians use the term 'equality of condition' rather than 'outcome' in an attempt to avoid the equation of equality with uniformity (Levitas, 2004, p 1; Baker et al, 2004, pp 33-4). The notion of 'equality of freedom' has also been put forward as a means of 'addressing concerns that greater equality is about imposing a dull uniformity on everyone ... Equality of freedom is not about dampening down our dreams and hopes, but ensuring that we all have wings to fly' (Hickman, 2009, p 21).

The respective arguments in favour of equality of opportunity and equality of outcome have been much rehearsed in recent years in the UK in the context of debates about New Labour's political philosophy and programme. The interpretation of the value of equality has been one of the key issues that divide the third way from earlier democratic socialism. New Labour has been accused of a retreat from egalitarianism and in response some New Labour thinkers have developed what they describe as a 'new egalitarianism' (see *Box 8.7*).

Box 8.7: A new egalitarianism?

The claim for a 'new egalitarianism' is made by Patrick Diamond (a former special adviser in the Prime Minister's Office) and Anthony Giddens. It represents an alternative to the meritocratic model of equality of opportunity espoused by many New Labour politicians including Tony Blair. Diamond and Giddens' starting point is to reject as 'misguided' 'the sharp contrast perceived by some between "equality of opportunity" and "equality of outcome". The promotion of equal opportunity in fact requires greater material equality: it is impossible for individuals to achieve their full potential if social and economic starting-points are grossly unequal' (2005, p 101). This is, in fact, the same argument made by more traditional egalitarians who are critical of Labour's espousal of the value of equality of opportunity in place of its earlier commitment to equality (see, for instance, Jackson and Segal, 2004).

In a contribution to Diamond and Giddens' collection, the Cabinet Minister Edward Miliband identifies the debate as being 'between those who thought inequality of opportunity was the most pervasive source of injustice in our society, and those who saw inequality of outcome as more important' (2005, p 47). Diamond and Giddens position 'the new egalitarianism' firmly on the opportunity side of this debate: 'the new egalitarianism focuses primarily on widening opportunities rather than traditional income redistribution – equality of outcome – *per se*' (2005, p 107). It has also been striking, the extent to which New Labour politicians have espoused Sen's capabilities approach as support for the case for equality of opportunity.

The case for equality of outcome and 'traditional income redistribution' has nevertheless been put forcefully in public debate in recent years, not just by those on the left of the Labour Party, such as the pressure group Compass, but also by a number of political commentators, including the journalist Polly Toynbee (Toynbee and Walker, 2008; see also Lister, 2007b). Particularly influential has been an empirical cross-national analysis of the damaging effects of inequality on society (Wilkinson and Pickett, 2009). The growing political concern about inequality is reflected in the establishment in 2008 of a National Equality Panel, which reported in 2010. Its remit included assembling the evidence about the relationships between 'equality strands' (such as gender, ethnicity and disability) and other dimensions such as social class, and employment, income and wealth.

Spicker (2006) outlines the four main ways of achieving greater equality of outcome identified by Douglas Rae (1981):

- *maximin*: maximising minimum levels of resources;
- *least difference* – reducing the range of inequality by limiting both wealth and poverty through redistribution;
- *minimax* – reducing the advantages of the most privileged;
- *reducing the ratio of inequality* – creating a more equal distribution of resources from the top to bottom of society by 'reducing advantage and disadvantage at every point' (Spicker, 2006, p 110).

> **Question:** Can you think of policies that aim to achieve each of these ways of furthering greater equality of outcome?

Equity

The concept of *equity* better grasps the point that people are different and that the best way of achieving a more equal set of outcomes is not necessarily by treating everyone the same. 'An equitable approach means treating people fairly, but differently, in order to ensure that there is some equality between them at the end' (Blakemore and Griggs, 2007, p 23). For example, it is generally regarded as fair or equitable to give extra social security to disabled people in order to help meet the additional costs associated with disability. If disabled people were paid the same as non-disabled in the name of equality, it would be inequitable because their living standards would be lower than those of non-disabled people.

Sen's capabilities approach is, in part, addressing the same principle. He emphasises the fact that 'different people, for reasons of personal characteristics, or the influences of physical and social environments ...

can have widely varying opportunities to convert general resources (like income and wealth) into capabilities – what they can or cannot actually do' (2009, p 261). From this perspective simply ensuring that people have equal resources does not guarantee equitable outcomes because of the variations in the opportunities and ability to convert those resources into outcomes.

Social justice

Social justice is an overarching concept, which, as already indicated, can incorporate liberty and equality (and also the concepts of need and citizenship discussed in the previous two chapters). It is both a highly abstract theoretical concept, which is subject to contested interpretations, and 'an idea that mobilises people to act in order to bring about change' (Newman and Yeates, 2008a, p 2; see also Chapter Nine). Each of the critical political perspectives discussed in Chapter Two draws, explicitly or implicitly, on a notion of social justice when translated into political action (although it should be noted that some Marxists reject talk of justice as a moralistic irrelevance).

In essence, justice is about fairness. We all have a sense of what is fair or unfair in our everyday lives. Sen, drawing on the work of John Rawls, which we will introduce later, describes fairness as 'foundational' to justice and to most theories of justice. He suggests that central to the idea of fairness 'must be a demand to avoid bias in our evaluations, taking note of the interests and concerns of others as well, and in particular the need to avoid being influenced by our respective vested interests, or by our personal priorities or eccentricities or prejudices. It can broadly be seen as a demand for impartiality' (Sen, 2009, p 54).

This account of fairness refers to justice generally and in particular to what is sometimes called procedural justice: the notion that people should be treated fairly and that like cases should be treated alike. This is the notion of justice that underpins the law and the criminal justice system. *Social* justice, while also rooted in notions of fairness, is more than this. In response to the question, 'what's social about social justice?' Newman and Yeates claim that 'social justice is not just about individuals; it is also about 'social groups – recognised collectivities based on class, gender, 'race', and so on – and the systematic patterns of unfairness or inequality that they may experience' (2008b, p 167). They continue that the 'social' in social justice, as a normative concept, also reflects its capacity to summon up 'moral, ethical and political commitments to norms and values about how a society … should be organised' (2008b, p 168).

The dimensions of social justice

It is possible to identify a number of dimensions of social justice (Lister, 2007d, 2008b; Newman and Yeates, 2008c). Broadly these can be grouped within two paradigms of (or ways of thinking about) social justice: the distributional and relational. A commonly cited, straightforward definition of the distributional paradigm is that provided by the political theorist David Miller: 'how the good and bad things in life should be distributed among the members of a human society' (1999, p 1). Distributive justice concerns the moral, ethical and political principles that are used to decide how the cake should be divided among a society's members. It is at the heart of debates about welfare, in particular the tax–benefit system, and is closely linked to most of the notions of equality already discussed. It also underpins the notion of environmental justice – the distribution of environmental goods and bads – discussed in Chapter Two.

The relational paradigm of social justice is concerned with the nature of social and political relations. It involves the dimensions of recognition, respect, discrimination, representation, voice, domination and oppression (Newman and Yeates, 2008c; Lister, 2008b). Some theorists argue that these are more fundamental than the distributive paradigm. The feminist political philosopher, Iris Marion Young, for instance, in her most influential work, *Justice and the Politics of Difference*, contends that 'domination and oppression', that is the 'institutional constraints' on 'self-determination' and 'self-development', rather than 'distribution' should constitute 'the starting point for a conception of social justice' (1990, pp 37, 16). According to another political theorist, Axel Honneth, 'the core of all experiences of injustice' lies 'in the withdrawal of social recognition, in the phenomena of humiliation and disrespect' (2003, p 134). 'Even distributional injustices must be understood as the institutional expression of social disrespect', he argues (2003, p 114). This is because it is, he contends, the experience of disrespect rather than the distribution of resources as such that fuels political claims for redistribution. An alternative perspective is provided by Fraser, who argues that neither the recognition nor distributional paradigm of social justice is reducible to the other. Instead, she has developed 'a three-dimensional account' of social justice, summarised in **Box 8.8**. Fraser's theory of social justice has been influential in the critical social policy literature (Lister, 2007c).

Box 8.8: Nancy Fraser's three-dimensional account of social justice

For Fraser social justice means 'parity of participation', by which she means 'social arrangements that permit all to participate as peers in social life' (2008, p 16). She analyses the three dimensions of social injustice as 'institutionalized obstacles that prevent some people from participating on a par with others, as full partners in social interaction' (2008, p 16). They are:

- *'Distributive injustice or maldistribution'*: 'economic structures that deny [people] the resources they need in order to interact with others as peers' (2008, p 16).
- *'Status inequality or misrecognition'*: 'institutionalized hierarchies of cultural value that deny [people] the requisite standing' (2008, p 16). Elsewhere, Fraser terms this 'cultural or symbolic injustice', which involves: 'Nonrecognition (being rendered invisible via the authoritative representational, communicative, and interpretative practices of one's culture); and disrespect (being routinely maligned or disparaged in stereotypic public cultural representations and/or in everyday life interactions' (1997, p 14). This is very similar in spirit to Therborn's notion of 'existential inequality'.
- *'Misrepresentation'*: 'when political boundaries and/or decision rules function wrongly to deny some people the possibility of participating on a par with others in social interaction – including, but not only, in political arenas' (2008, p 18).

It is only recently that Fraser has added misrepresentation to the dimensions of redistribution and recognition. In doing so, she is acknowledging the political as well as economic and cultural dimensions of social justice. While Fraser articulates the three as 'conceptually distinct' dimensions, she also emphasises that they are interwoven and must therefore be integrated in social justice struggles (2008, p 18).

Principles of social justice

Theories of distributive social justice are often articulated through a series of principles. Most famous and influential is John Rawls' *A Theory of Justice* (1972). Rawls is sometimes described as an egalitarian liberal. From this standpoint, he argues that the just society would seek to balance a fair distribution of resources with individual liberty – 'justice as fairness'. This is achieved through a set of principles, set out in **Box 8.9**.

Box 8.9: John Rawls' principles of social justice

In order to establish what would be fair, Rawls asks us to imagine a contract between citizens and government. We are asked to consider what should be the principles that would decide a fair distribution of resources without knowing what the consequences would be for ourselves. So we would not know, for instance, whether we would be male or female, well or poorly educated or what work, if any, we would do. From this 'original position' behind a 'veil of ignorance', he suggests that people would come up with a just model of distribution. Or to put it more simply: 'the fair division of a cake would be one that could be agreed on by people who did not know which piece they were going to get' (Commission on Social Justice, 1993, p 6).

The principles, which Rawls derives from such an exercise, are:

- Each person is entitled to the maximum degree of liberty subject to the similar liberties of others. This principle takes priority.
- All positions are open to all on the basis of 'fair equality of opportunity' (Rawls, 1972, p 302).
- Any inequality in the distribution of 'primary goods' must be 'to the greatest benefit of the least advantaged' (Rawls, 1972, p 302). This is 'the difference principle'.

He sums up these principles in his 'general conception': 'All social primary goods – liberty and opportunity, income and wealth, and the bases of self-respect – are to be distributed equally unless an unequal distribution of any or all of these goods is to the advantage of the least favoured' (Rawls, 1972, p 303).

Underlying these principles is the premise that in a just society, any inequalities need to be justified. Rawls accepts that some distributional inequality is necessary for the generation of resources but he maintains that justice takes priority over economic efficiency. Nevertheless, one of the criticisms made of the difference principle by democratic socialists is that it could be used to legitimate the 'trickle down theory', which the new right has deployed to justify widening inequality. According to this theory, increasing rewards at the top is justified because it will generate more economic resources, some of which will eventually 'trickle down' to those at the bottom. Hattersley, for instance, expresses the fear that the difference principle can all too easily be deliberately misinterpreted by vested interests, so that it becomes 'little more than a sophisticated justification for a large degree of inequality' (1987, p 52).

Another criticism of Rawls' principles is that they do not translate easily into practical politics and policy. The Commission on Social Justice (1993, 1994), established by the former Labour leader, the late John Smith, therefore drew up a rather different set of principles, which, it believed, would resonate better with the public. These principles were reformulated a decade later by Miller in a volume published to mark the tenth anniversary of the Commission on Social Justice's report (Pearce and Paxton, 2005). They are set out in **Box 8.10**.

> ## Box 8.10: David Miller's reformulation of the Commission on Social Justice's four principles of social justice
>
> Miller suggests that
>
> the core idea of social justice is contained in the following four principles:
>
> - *Equal citizenship*: Every citizen is entitled to an equal set of civil, political and social rights, including the means to exercise these rights effectively.
> - *The social minimum*: All citizens must have access to resources that adequately meet their essential needs, and allow them to live a secure and dignified life in today's society.
> - *Equality of opportunity*: A person's life chances, and especially their access to jobs and educational opportunities, should depend only on their own motivation and aptitudes, and not on irrelevant features such as gender, class or ethnicity.
> - *Fair distribution*: Resources that do not form part of equal citizenship or the social minimum may be distributed unequally, but the distribution must reflect relevant factors such as personal desert and personal choice. (Miller, 2005, p 5)

The last of Miller's principles, like many theories of social justice, raises difficult questions as to when the unequal distribution of resources can be justified. He cites 'relevant factors such as personal desert and personal choice'. What constitutes 'personal desert' is highly contested. Particularly contentious is 'the brute luck principle'. Desert may reflect talent derived from natural ability. But natural abilities are a matter of 'brute luck'. There is disagreement as to whether such luck constitutes a justification for unequal rewards. Many people believe that they do. However, Warren Buffett, the world's second richest man, told the BBC: 'I get paid enormously and at not great credit to me. I was lucky at birth. I shouldn't delude myself into thinking I am some superior individual because of that' (*The Guardian*, 29 October 2009). Even the idea that inequalities can be justified on the basis of the choices and efforts that people make is not straightforward, given that both effort and choices can be constrained by people's circumstances. Political philosophers have ruminated on these questions at great length. See Miller (1997, 1999, 2005) and Sandel (2009) for an elucidation of the competing arguments.

> **Question:** There has been considerable debate following the 2008 economic crash as to whether the huge rewards received by bankers in pay and bonuses constitute a 'fair distribution'. Sandel (2009) uses the example of the widespread sense of injustice at bankers' bonuses following the bailout to explore why rewards are considered to be deserved or not. What do you think are the social justice arguments that can be used to justify and condemn respectively such high bankers' rewards?

Sen's treatise on justice adopts a different stance to that reflected in the principles outlined in **Boxes 8.9** and **8.10**, even though he acknowledges his own indebtedness to Rawls. He characterises the approach taken by Rawls and many other political philosophers as attempts to identify 'the just society' and the rules and institutions required to achieve it. In contrast, the aim of his own theory of justice is more practical: 'to clarify how we can proceed to address questions of enhancing justice and removing injustice' (Sen, 2009, p ix). He contends that 'if a theory of justice is to guide reasoned choice of policies, strategies or institutions, then the identification of fully just social arrangements is neither necessary nor sufficient' (2009, p 15). Drawing on capabilities theory (discussed earlier), Sen argues for a theory of social justice that focuses less on institutions and more on 'the lives that people can actually live' (2009, p 18).

A contested concept

Newman and Yeates emphasise 'how ideas about social justice are both *contested* and *changeable*' (2008a, p 3, emphasis in original). Both its contested and its changeable nature are evident in political and theoretical debates about the validity and nature of the concept of social justice. We have already referred to the debate around the relationship between the distributional and relational paradigms of social justice and to some of the issues raised by principles of social justice elaborated by political philosophers. In this section, we consider the more fundamental challenge to the very notion of distributional social justice.

One volume on social justice and social policy begins 'Everybody is in favour of social justice, almost by definition' (Burchardt and Craig, 2008, p 1). It may appear like that today in the UK, after a decade or so in which social justice has been one of the primary values espoused by New Labour and the Conservative Party has begun to speak the language of social justice. Burchardt and Craig (2008) contrast the approach to social justice taken in the report of the Commission on Social Justice (1994) and in the recommendations of the Conservative Party's Social Justice Policy Group, chaired by its former leader, Iain Duncan-Smith. A key difference between these two political approaches concerns the role of the state in achieving social justice (Lister, 2007d). Such differences notwithstanding, the fact that leading members of the Conservative Party are talking the language of social justice represents a distinct break with the neo-liberal new right, which, following Hayek, disputed the validity of the very idea of social justice.

One of the most influential statements of the new right case against distributive social justice has been made by the libertarian, Robert Nozick (1974). His argument is based on a distinction between 'patterned' and 'non-patterned' forms of justice. Blakemore and Griggs summarise it concisely: 'Patterned justice involves the idea of continual interference in people's lives in order to bring about a particular distribution (pattern) of property, goods and other things of value' (Blakemore and Griggs, 2007, p 18). But such continual interference, Nozick argues, undermines liberty, the supreme value. Instead, 'there is justice in wealth and property being owned in "non-patterned" ways (for instance, according to historical factors and chance)' (Blakemore and Griggs, 2007, p 19; see also Piachaud, 2008b). Nozick thus 'rejects patterned theories of justice in favor of those that honor the choices people make in free markets', without interference from the state (Sandel, 2009, p 63). The state, these authors argue, violates the rights and liberty of those from whom it redistributes the fruits of their labour.

The other main neo-liberal theorist to attack the notion of social justice is Hayek (1976) (introduced in **Box 1.5**). The essence of his argument is that the distribution of resources that results from the market cannot be unjust because it is not the result of deliberate actions: the distributional effects of the market are, like the weather, incidental, unforeseen and not planned. Therefore they can be neither just nor unjust. This means that the notion of social justice has no meaning and that the state has no responsibility to rectify misfortunes that result from the market. As Plant explains it, 'benevolence, charity and altruism are the appropriate personal responses to misfortune, not state action in pursuit of distributive justice' (2004, p 28). Plant (1990) counters this position from a democratic socialist standpoint. He acknowledges that it is true that the distribution of market outcomes is not planned. Nevertheless, he contends, we know enough about what these outcomes are likely to be in order to be able to say that the state should intervene in order to ensure a different, fairer, outcome.

Thus, how we respond collectively can be characterised as just or unjust and justice is a matter not just of how a state of affairs arises but of how we respond to it.

Although the idea of fairness tends to be associated with the idea of social justice, it is also deployed in some new right arguments against the redistribution typically implied by notions of distributive social justice. For example, Sir Keith Joseph and Jonathan Sumption contend that redistribution is 'morally indefensible'; '[i]t is not "fair" to take away from others benefits which they worked to acquire'; and '[t]here is no greater tyranny possible than denying to individuals the disposal of their own talents' (Joseph and Sumption, 1979, pp 19, 82, 125). This is an example of where liberty is seen as in conflict with social justice.

Another new right argument is that since there is no single view of what is just, the state has to impose its own view and this is illegitimate. There is an element of overlap here with the postmodernist position on social justice in the sense that, as we saw in Chapter Three, postmodernism denies the existence of universal principles such as social justice. It is claimed that 'the effect of the postmodernist critique of universalism has been to render any application of the concept of social justice problematic' (Harvey, 1993, p 95). Nevertheless, reflecting a number of contributions to the same volume, Judith Squires reassures us that 'we can accept the weak form of postmodernism and still maintain a legitimate concern with justice' (Squires, 1993, p 10).

Scales of social justice

The discussion hitherto has implicitly taken the nation–state as the context within which discussions of and struggles for social justice take place. However, increasingly, theories of social justice are 'multi-scalar', a term borrowed from geography to denote different spatial scales. This means that injustices can be identified both below and above the nation–state. At one end of the spatial scale, feminists identify the private, domestic sphere as a site of struggles for social justice (Lister, 2007b; see also Chapter Two). At the other end, we move into the arena of what is commonly called 'global justice'. Again, there is considerable debate among political theorists about the validity of translating principles of social justice on to a global scale (see Mandle, 2006 for a discussion). I do not pursue these arguments here but simply introduce you to the concept of global justice in **Box 8.11**.

Box 8.11: The concept of global (social) justice

According to Fraser, 'globalization is changing the way we argue about justice.' (2008, p 12). David Mepham states the case for why this is happening:

> today an exclusively national interpretation of social justice is neither morally defensible nor politically or intellectually tenable. It is not morally defensible because the extent of poverty and human suffering across the world demands a comprehensive moral response. There is now a growing body of political philosophy that addresses 'global justice' and that considers the responsibilities of citizens and governments in developed countries towards poorer parts of the world or towards people in other countries whose human rights are abused. It is not politically or intellectually tenable because global interdependence and interconnectedness are reducing the distinction between domestic and international policy and increasing the number of issues that require a genuinely global response. (2005, p 134)

Two of these issues, which are interrelated, are climate change and poverty. With regard to climate change, there is some overlap between the ideas captured in the concepts of global social justice and environmental justice (discussed in Chapter Two, *Box 2.21*). The idea of a 'climate debt crisis', put forward by the Jubilee Debt Campaign and the World Development Movement, reflects both and makes the link with poverty:

> Development by the world's richest economies has been based largely on a one-way practice of taking natural resources from poor countries, without proportional compensation. This includes a disproportionate use of both national resources such as fossil fuels, timber and minerals; and also includes taking a massive share of the world's common resources, notably the finite capacity for the earth's atmosphere to absorb manmade CO_2 emissions. In fact, it is the poor who continue to pay financially for this injustice ... The signs become ever clearer that a world plagued by persistent social, economic and environmental injustices is one that will not sustain the human race much longer. (Jones and Edwards, 2009, p 4)

With regard to poverty, the philosopher Thomas Pogge argues that citizens of more affluent societies are all implicated in a 'global institutional order', which impoverishes the worst-off. 'The global poor get to share the burdens resulting from the degradation of our natural environment while having to watch helplessly as the affluent distribute the planet's abundant natural wealth amongst themselves' (2004, pp 269, 270).

Immigration is a global social justice issue, with links to both poverty and climate change, as both phenomena propel migrants from the global South to seek better lives in the more affluent North. As Dhananjayan Sriskandarajah observes, immigration

> brings the globalist challenge for the pursuit of social justice closer to home, literally. When the 'outsider' moves in next door, questions of membership and distribution become far more pertinent than when he or she was a television image beamed from a faraway land ... Immigration raises a fundamental question for the pursuit of social justice: is there an equality commitment to the new citizen? (2005, p 159)

There exist a number of different theories of global justice. Jon Mandle's is rooted in the claims of universal human rights and therefore bears some similarities with theories of global citizenship (see **Boxes 7.6** and **7.3**). He maintains that 'duties of global justice are owed across borders, even if people do not share political institutions, precisely because all people are entitled to human rights, and everyone – not only fellow citizens – is bound to respect them' (Mandle, 2006, p 148). It represents a 'realistic Utopia' rather than the world as it is (2006, p 149).

Fraser explores the implications of her theory of social justice (**Box 8.8**) at a global level. She considers the main answers provided in the literature to the question as to 'who' should be covered within the frame of social justice. These are:

- the 'membership principle', which appeals to 'criteria of political belonging' and national citizenship, with all its exclusionary implications;
- the 'principle of humanism', which 'accords standing indiscriminately to everyone in respect of everything';
- the 'all-affected principle', which appeals to 'social relations of interdependence', but which is vulnerable to the interpretation that 'everyone is affected by everything' (Fraser, 2008, pp 63-4).

As an alternative, Fraser proposes 'the all-subjected principle': 'all those who are subject to a given governance structure have moral standing as subjects of justice in relation to it' (2008, p 65). By 'governance structure' she means both states and non-state agencies 'that generate enforceable rules that structure important swaths of social interaction' (2008, p 65). Examples include the World Trade Organisation and International Monetary Fund. Subjection means being 'subject to the coercive power' of such organisations. She explains that 'in today's world, all of us are subject to a plurality of different governance structures, some local, some national, some regional, and some global' (2008, p 66). The appropriate 'frame' of social justice will depend on the issue involved.

> *Question:* What do you believe are the most important examples of social injustice both within your own country and at a global level?

Tension between liberty and equality/social justice

We have now discussed liberty, equality and social justice separately. We return here briefly to the relationship between the three. Hitherto, the main emphasis has been on the social democratic arguments for treating liberty and equality/social justice as complementary values. However, in the introduction to this chapter we also noted that a tension can exist between them. In their reference to getting 'the right balance between equality and liberty' in achieving social justice, Brighouse and Swift acknowledge that 'the problem, of course, is that the freedoms liberals value tend to disrupt the equality egalitarians value' (2008, p 140). *Box 8.12* provides an example of this tension.

Box 8.12: An example of the tension between liberty and equality/social justice

In the UK private education represents an important source of inequality, undermining equality of opportunity and illustrating the nature of complex (in) equality. There is ample evidence of the links between a public school education and subsequent attendance at the most prestigious universities, occupational achievement and political power. Some egalitarians therefore argue for the 'minimax' policy of removing the right to buy a better education in the name of greater equality.

Michael Prowse attempts to answer the question: Why is it that Britain is still 'showing few signs of wishing to confront the social and economic inequality associated with its two-tier educational system?' (1999, p 37). Among the reasons for accepting the status quo, which he reviews, are those that the new right would put forward:

> In a free society, individuals must be permitted to establish private schools and to charge whatever fees they see fit. By the same token, parents must be free to send their children to the schools of their choice. If those with financial means wish to buy a private education for their children, that is their prerogative. It would be totalitarian – a step on the road to serfdom – if the state were to insist on monopoly control of education.

'Education', Prowse observes, 'is one of those unfortunate instances in which two values – liberty and social justice – conflict' (1999, p 38).

Question: Would you give higher priority to liberty or to equality and social justice in formulating policy towards private education? Remember the arguments about positive as well as negative liberty.

Summary

- Liberty, equality and social justice are interrelated concepts; views differ as to whether liberty on the one hand and equality and social justice on the other are complementary or conflicting.
- For liberals, liberty or freedom is the supreme value. It can be understood in terms of both 'freedom from' ('negative' freedom) and 'freedom to' ('positive' freedom). Liberty is not absolute and has to be balanced against other values and public goods.
- In some formulations, genuine liberty can only be achieved through greater equality.
- Equality can be classified in various ways such as moral, legal, social, political and economic equality. The main principles of equality are: equal worth; complex equality; equality of opportunity; equality of outcome; and equity. The debate between proponents of a meritocratic form of equality of opportunity and of greater equality of outcome has marked New Labour's term in office. One, contested, attempt at resolution has been the articulation of 'a new egalitarianism'.
- Social justice is an overarching concept, which has been subject to much abstract theorising but which has also provided a mobilising ideal. In essence, it is about fairness, but goes beyond procedural fairness.
- Dimensions of social justice can be grouped within the two paradigms of distributional and relational social justice. The former is about who gets what; at the heart of the latter are the three 'r's of recognition, respect and representation. Theories of distributive social justice are often articulated through a set of principles, most famously those laid down in the work of Rawls.
- The very notion of social justice is rejected by some new right thinkers.
- Social justice can be understood as 'multi-scalar', with implications at the domestic and the global level. The latter has given rise to the concept of 'global justice'.

Further reading

A number of political theory textbooks and readers provide helpful introductions to some or all of the concepts covered in this chapter: see, for instance, **Heywood (1994); Clayton and Williams (2004)**, on social justice; **Jones (1994, Chapter 6)**, on freedom; **Goodwin (2007)**; and **White (2007)**, on equality. From a social policy perspective, **Spicker (2006)** explores the concepts of liberty and equality and **Pearce and Paxton (2005), Craig et al (2008)** and **Newman and Yeates (2008c)** offer stimulating collections on social justice. **Sandel (2009)** provides a very accessible philosophical account of social justice, grounded in public policy debates (**Chapter 6** in particular is an excellent introduction to Rawls). **Phillips (1999)** and **Fraser (2008)** elucidate the thinking that informs both the relational and distributional paradigms of social justice. **Dench (2006)** provides a flavour of the debates around the idea of a meritocracy.

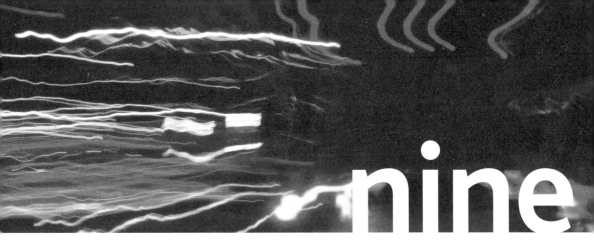

Bringing it all together

> The philosophers have only interpreted the world in various ways; the point is to change it. (Marx, 1888)

> The job of welfare theory is not only to provide the theoretical resources by which critiques of the immediate can be carried out; it is also to stoke the flame of the utopianism that can light the way towards that imaginary horizon, if and when we decide we want to make the journey. (Fitzpatrick, 2001, p 198)

These two quotations will give you a flavour of the main theme of this concluding chapter. It is not a conclusion in the conventional sense of the term, neatly tying together the arguments of preceding chapters. Instead, the aim of this concluding chapter is to reinforce and build on a key message of the Introduction: the relevance and value of theory to the *practice* of social policy as well as the study of it. This message has been a theme – explicit or implicit – throughout the book's overview of a range of theoretical perspectives and concepts, particularly with regard to how theory helps us understand specific social policies or approaches to social policy.

Here we shift the focus to consider how theory can provide both a mobilising and an analytical tool for collective agents of resistance and change, commonly labelled 'social movements'. Social movements carry the 'flame of utopianism' in their attempt to change the world. Moreover, their actions can, in turn, inform theory. My own theorising of poverty, for instance, has been enriched by the work of poverty activists (Lister, 2004a). Taking the example of 'human rights activists and international feminists' who have joined critics of global neo-liberal economic policies 'in targeting injustices that cut across borders' as part of the global justice movement, Fraser observes wryly that 'as usual, theory scrambles to catch up with practice' (2008, p 31)

We return to the global justice movement at the end of the chapter. First, we will explore briefly how some of the theoretical concepts and perspectives discussed in previous chapters are illuminated and drawn on by social movements in general and by social welfare movements and the disability movement in particular. Even more than in previous chapters, this does not claim to be an exhaustive account of what are large and growing literatures. Instead it is illustrative of the central theme of the value of theory.

Social movements

Social movements have been described as 'a quintessentially modern political phenomenon', dating from around the middle of the 18th century (Annetts et al, 2009, p 8). Annetts et al warn against attempting a tight definition, given that 'social movements are heterogeneous, dynamic, constantly evolving social collectivities' (2009, p 7). The key characteristics that they identify from the literature on social movements include:

- a politics of conflict and contest, which strives for fundamental change;
- a shared collective identity, rooted in strong informal networks;
- a degree of longevity, which distinguishes them from shorter term campaigns and protests.

In Chapter Eight, we quoted Newman and Yeates' characterisation of social justice as a mobilising ideal. It is an ideal that has 'informed social and political struggles to bring about a better society – one in which resources, rewards and burdens are distributed more equitably and people are treated with more care, respect and dignity' (Newman and Yeates, 2008b, p 164). These struggles are typically pursued by social movements. Newman and Yeates suggest also that a key challenge for social movements is to expose and explain 'the *social* character of social inequality and injustice. They need to be able to indicate that social organisation and conditions are neither natural, nor necessary, nor inevitable, but the outcome' of specific social, economic and political processes (2008a, p 33, emphasis in original). They give the example of how the North American workers' movement has challenged the closure of factories in the US, justified as the inevitable workings of the market economy, by joining with Mexican workers to contest the movement of jobs across the border to Mexico, where wages are lower.

As well as pursuing a politics of social justice, social movement claims are often framed in the language of citizenship and rights (see Chapter Seven). Indeed, According to Peters et al, 'all social movements concern themselves with citizenship as a process of engagement to challenge and transform established institutional arrangements and the beliefs and value-based systems driving these arrangements' (2009, p 546). Angharad E. Beckett makes the case, therefore, for:

> stronger links between citizenship and social movement theorizing. This may prove to be effective because understanding the way in which citizenship has changed over time is key to understanding the social and political environment in which social movements act. Understanding the nature of contested citizenship is also likely to be key to understanding social movements. (2006a, p 88)

A distinction is sometimes made between 'old' social movements, organised primarily around social class and a social justice politics of redistribution, and 'new social movements', which pursue a social justice politics of recognition (see Chapter Eight). The latter are sometimes represented as pursuing a politics of identity; examples include feminist, anti-racist and lesbian, gay, bisexual and transgendered movements. New social movements' pursuit of a politics of identity often involves a process of consciousness-raising among members of marginalised groups in order to challenge dominant constructions and discourses that contribute to that marginalisation. New social movements have also been represented as challenging the 'microphysics of power' identified by Foucault (see Chapter Four) and as pursuing innovative forms of protest and resistance, such as feminist Reclaim the Night marches and the environmental movement's anti-road campaigns, which have deployed tactics such as tree-sitting (Annetts et al, 2009).

In practice, however, the distinction between old and new social movements is not always that clear-cut. Arguably the materialist struggles of 'old' social movements were also about recognition of human dignity, and the struggles of 'new' social movements for social justice often involve the redistribution of material resources and formal power as well as cultural recognition and a challenge to everyday power relationships. New social movements frame their claims with reference to universalist ideals such as citizenship and human rights as well as particularist concerns associated with identity and embodiment (the needs and desires of physical human bodies). Moreover, 'new' social movements have not replaced 'old' social movements. Instead, as Gail Lewis advises, their 'augmentation of the social inequality agenda has meant that class-based critiques of welfare state practices have to be rethought as pointing to one *among a range* of inequalities attached to the constitution of social differences' (2003, p 90, emphasis in original).

Leonard's description of new social movements, reproduced in **Box 9.1**, draws on a number of aspects of the theoretical concepts explored in previous chapters.

Box 9.1: Peter Leonard on new social movements

The new social movements are, in postmodern conditions, a major means by which people articulate their needs and make welfare claims intended to meet them. In this they are the successor of the old labour movements whose political struggle secured the concessions necessary to establish the welfare state. In defining needs and making claims on the state's resources, the new social movements exercise a significant pressure on social policies and the distribution of scarce government resources. Most importantly, they give voice to those who previously had no voice, those who were excluded and marginalized, and in so doing create new identities, empowered by participation in forms of resistance that produce new knowledge about political systems ... The unmasking of the ideologies and interests of dominant political structures is a necessary step in securing support for a collective demand directed to the state and requires the development of considerable expertise. This is an expertise which does not necessarily depend upon the knowledge of professionals, sometimes regarded with considerable suspicion, but arises directly from engaging in the action itself ... Insofar as the new social movements can be characterized as representing a politics of *identity* – gender, culture, sexuality, age, disability, race – they can be seen paradoxically as a characteristic expression of postmodernism and as its contradiction [because of the boundaries drawn around those identities]. (Leonard, 1997, pp 156-7, emphasis in original)

Question: Can you identify the various theoretical perspectives and concepts, discussed in earlier chapters, which Leonard introduces in this passage in order to make sense of new social movements?

Social welfare movements

Leonard's reference to 'welfare claims' and Lewis's to 'welfare state practices' signal a particular form of welfare movement: '(new) social welfare movements' (Williams, 1992, p 216). One key characteristic is 'oppositional collective action at the point of service delivery', involving at some level 'a challenge to the welfare or regulatory politics of the state' (Annetts et al, 2009, p 10). Whereas social movements generally are not necessarily directing claims at the state, social welfare movements 'perforce ... enter into a conflictual relationship with the state at different levels – local, regional and national' (Annetts et al, 2009, p 249). They typically 'contest the authority of expert knowledge' (Annetts et al, 2009, p 249), most notably as part of the politics of needs interpretation, discussed in Chapter Six.

Social welfare movements span the old/new social movement divide. Annetts et al (2009) point to the impact of groupings within and around the labour movement on the emergence of the welfare state in the mid-20th century. *New* social welfare movements are partly distinguished by two characteristics. First 'they operate in and around an already established welfare state system to preserve, extend, deepen and improve service delivery' (Annetts et al, 2009, p 10). Second, they are united around 'a concern with the nitty-gritty of empowerment, representation, and ensuring the quality, availability and accountability of user-centred provision' (Williams, 1992, p 216). In some cases, their actions can be understood as a form of resistance to oppressive welfare state practices. Williams (1992, p 216) also suggests that 'they have the capacity to combine particularistic interests with universal values', as discussed in Chapter Seven.

User involvement and participation in decision-making about welfare services are at the heart of the demands of new social welfare movements. Their actions represent a new participatory 'praxis of social citizenship' in claiming social rights and a determination to wrest the interpretation of needs from the hands of professionals (Lustiger-Thaler and Shragge, 1993, p 167; see also Croft and Beresford, 1992). According to a group of social work educators, the innovative approaches to meeting service user needs that have developed as a result of these demands mean that 'social work needs to engage with, and learn from, these movements in ways that will allow partnerships to form and new knowledge bases and curricula to develop' (Jones et al, 2006, p 2).

The disabled people's movement

The disabled people's movement has been in the vanguard of contemporary social welfare movements: 'Disabled People's Movements have developed on a global scale' since the late 20th century (Mayo, 2000, p 58). The use of the plural indicates that the umbrella term 'disabled people's movement' or 'disability movement' can be understood to bring together a number of separate movements including those of deaf people, mental health service users/survivors and people with learning disabilities, as well as people with visible physical impairments. Not all members of these groups necessarily consider themselves members of the disabled people's movement. The position of the mental health service users/survivors movement, in particular, has been the subject of debate (Sayce, 2000).

And many members of what is often termed 'the Deaf community' 'see themselves as a linguistic minority rather than as having an impairment' (Lloyd and Riddell, 2002, p 310). Nevertheless, the common experience of discrimination, exclusion and barriers to participation, recognised in the UK disability discrimination legislation, has led to calls for different service user groups to make common cause.

Beckett has explored the nature of the disability movement. She suggests that, despite the movement's heterogeneity, it is united by 'an overall vision of the world as "disabling"' (2006b, p 747). This vision reflects the 'social' model of disability, which locates the source of disability not in individual impairment but in society's failure to accommodate the needs of disabled people and to dismantle exclusionary barriers (Barnes, 2002). This is a good example of how a social movement has achieved the reconstruction of a social problem (see Chapter Five). The social model of disability has been a cornerstone of the disabled people's movement. However, some feminist disabled activists and theorists have tempered their support for the social model with criticism of the way in which it disembodies disabled people so that, for instance, the pain some disabled people experience is glossed over. More generally, feminists have challenged the marginalisation of women and their concerns within the disabled people's movement.

The other cornerstone of the disabled people's movement has been the belief that disabled people should be able to speak for themselves rather than have non-disabled professionals speak for them. This has been expressed in demands for user-involvement and control and the slogan 'Nothing about us, without us'. According to Jane Campbell (2008), a leading British disability activist, who was the first chair of the Equality and Human Rights Commission's Disability Committee, this slogan describes 'our politics of disability identity'. She made this claim in a public lecture about the disability movement, extracts from which are reproduced in *Box 9.2*.

Box 9.2: Jane Campbell (2008) on the disability movement

The political movements on race or gender liberation certainly influenced the disability movement, but our journey was different as well as equal!

Simply by breaking away from those who spoke on our behalf, and finding a space where we could beg the question: Why are we excluded from society? And how can we break in? we found the key that unlocked some of the fundamental principles of the Social Model of Disability that became the unique hallmark of our struggle.

Campbell quotes a letter published in *The Guardian* on 20 September 1972 from Paul Hunt. It referred to how 'severely physically handicapped people find themselves isolated in unsuitable institutions where their views are ignored and they are subject to authoritarian and often cruel regimes'. As a result of this letter, the Union of the Physically Impaired Against Segregation was formed and the social model of disability developed.

> The social model played a crucial role in enhancing the collective consciousness of disabled people ... It gave disabled people a framework to distinguish between organisations, policies, laws and ideas which were emancipatory, and those which were oppressive or inadequate. Most importantly, the social model enabled the identification of a political strategy, namely barrier removal ... The second impact of the social model was on the identity of disabled people themselves ... We challenged society's misrecognition of our identity, casting off flawed, incomplete, tragic, brave, vulnerable and victim, and demanding the creation of a society in which all disabled people could participate fully as equal citizens.

> In recent years, what had been separate movements of people with a learning disability, people with mental health conditions and more recently people with neurological conditions have both demanded recognition within and come together with the mainstream disability movement. But of course disabled people face more than oppression and disadvantage linked to their different impairments and health conditions. Many have to struggle against other forms of oppression including ageism, racism, sexism, and heterosexism ... Many of us will identify with different bits of our identity at different times.

> We have emerged as a fully fledged civil rights movement ... Without transformative public services which enable disabled people the choice and control over their lives needed to participate fully, we will never overcome our social inequality. We will continue to be viewed as vulnerable people in need of care, instead of active valued citizens, in charge of our own lives. But I do not believe it is the politics of identity and recognition which will win the redistribution required to secure the services we seek. This requires a different sort of politics, a politics of participation and consensus ... Redressing injustice still requires a politics of recognition, but this should no longer be reduced to a question of group identity or allegiance: rather, it requires a politics aimed at overcoming the barriers which prevent all individuals, families and communities participating as full members of society; it requires a politics aimed at overcoming the misrecognition they individually face.

> As we gain equal rights, so we have equal responsibilities. It is our duty to take part in the building of society ... [We] are ready to move on to the next phase of our liberation as multifaceted human beings contributing to the broad enterprise of equality and human rights for all.
>
> The disability movement has demonstrated 'how to transform the state from an instrument of paternalism to an agency of empowerment that gives people greater choice and control over their lives.' 'The ideas of the disability movement' including 'equality legislation based on accommodating difference rather than ignoring it' form 'the blueprint for the next stages of promoting equality and human rights overall.
>
> **Question:** These extracts from Campbell's lecture illustrate a number of the theoretical themes that we have explored. Can you identify what they are?

Paul Hunt's letter, quoted by Campbell, clarifies how a major impetus for the emergence of the disability movement was the segregation of many disabled people in authoritarian institutions and the oppression and lack of autonomy they suffered. Humiliating rituals and petty restrictions were a means of disciplining inmates and regulating their lives (Borsay, 2005). 'Families and professionals spoke on behalf of disabled people, who were expected to be grateful and thought to be incapable' (Shakespeare, 2005, p 159). Disabled people thus represented the quintessential 'deferential welfare subjects' (see Introduction). The disability movement's rejection of such institutions represented a challenge to the microphysics of power, identified by Foucault and discussed in Chapter Four (see Borsay, 2005; Beckett, 2006b). Unequal power relations between disabled and non-disabled people continue to be an important factor in disabled people's experiences of targeted violence and hostility (Sin et al, 2009).

Resistance, citizenship and freedom

The disabled people's movement can be interpreted as a movement of resistance against oppressive and exclusionary institutions and practices (Peters et al, 2009). Individual service users may also engage 'in forms of subversion and resistance to institutionalised relations and practices of social subordination' (Lewis, 2009, p 266). The disability movement has also resisted dominant social constructions of disability and professional interpretations of disabled people's needs (see Chapters Five and Six). Dominant social constructions have equated disability with dependency and incapacity and have presented disabled people as, in Campbell's (2008) words, 'flawed, incomplete, tragic, brave, vulnerable and victim'. The social model of disability has challenged such constructions through its naming of disability as a set of oppressive and exclusionary mechanisms rather than an individual condition (Hughes, 1998b; Fawcett, 2000). It has also framed the disability movement's interventions in the politics of needs interpretation through its questioning of professional forms of expertise (see Chapter Six). According to Mike Oliver, a disability theorist and activist, it is 'rights to appropriate welfare services to meet their own self-defined needs that disabled people are demanding, not to have their needs defined and met by others' (1996, p 75). Indeed, as Oliver's statement implies, the challenge has been to the whole notion of needs-based welfare, with its implications of paternalistic professional gate-keeping to rationed resources. Instead members of the disabled people's movement have fought for 'welfare services based upon the idea of citizenship' and in particular citizenship rights (Oliver, 1996, p 75).

Disability theorists and activists, such as Mike Oliver, have drawn heavily on the language of (exclusion from) citizenship to frame their analysis and demands (see also Borsay, 2005). In her lecture, Campbell describes the disability movement as a 'civil rights movement' demanding full participation as 'equal citizens' and contributing to the achievement of 'human rights overall' (***Box 9.2***). Beckett rests her case for 'stronger links between citizenship and social movement theorizing' on her study of the disability movement in particular (2006a, p 88; 2006b). She also argues that citizenship theory can be enriched by taking better account of the experience of disability and the varying positions taken by members of the disability movement: 'Theorising on citizenship without considering "disability" is perilous for the very "particular" position of, and views held by, disabled people reveal both strengths and weaknesses in some of the dominant accounts/models of citizenship' (Beckett, 2005, p 420).

Although the language of liberty and freedom has not generally been vocalised as explicitly as that of citizenship by members of the disabled people's movement, it is implicit in the demands for 'greater choice and control over their lives' mentioned by Campbell (***Box 9.2***). It is implicit too in resistance to the social construction of disabled people as dependent and lacking in autonomy, which undermines their citizenship. From the demands to be freed from oppressive and authoritarian institutions to campaigns for independent living and direct payments to enable them to manage their own care, the desire for autonomy and the freedom to control their own lives has been an important impetus behind disabled people's struggles. However, Tom Shakespeare, a disability theorist and activist, has pointed to some of the dangers of the movement's 'espousal of values such as independence, freedom and choice' and campaigns for 'direct payments to enable individuals to make their own choices ... Many disabled people will not be able to take advantage of the freedom to choose and compete' (2005, p 163).

Equal and different

Shakespeare also draws attention to the limitations of narrowly conceived equality politics. It is common to characterise the 'international disabled people's movement [as] concerned with the ongoing struggle for equality' (Barnes, 2002, p 315). At the same time, however, 'unlike other oppressions, the challenge of disability is not just to treat people equally and fairly: we are obligated to take additional steps to ensure that needs are met and participation is assured' (Shakespeare, 2005, p 162). In other words, Shakespeare is calling for equitable treatment (see Chapter Eight).

There is a further tension, common to new social movements, between the 'struggle for equality' and the desire of some disabled people to be recognised as different. This is an example of the tension between the universal and the particular, discussed in Chapter Seven. Many leading members of the disability movement, as well as struggling for equality, have emphasised a 'different' positive disability identity and culture, summed up in the notion of 'disability pride' (see **Box 9.3**).

Box 9.3: Disability pride and difference

In a discussion of an emergent disability arts movement, Colin Cameron writes:

> Through coming into contact with the disabled people's movement and the social model, each of us is now able to say, with pride, 'This is who I am.' ... Through the development of a culture of resistance that is disability arts, disabled people have developed a discourse that rejects personal tragedy narratives and that identifies impairment as part of human experience to be celebrated. A recent outcome from the disability arts movement, a development that builds upon the social model, is an affirmative model which re-defines impairment as: 'physical, sensory or intellectual difference to be expected and respected within a diverse society '... At the same time, the affirmative model retains a social model definition of disability. Thus, people with impairments can affirm their personal and social identities as people with impairments, and as disabled people, recognizing that their opportunities and rights to participate as equals within mainstream society are restricted by socially imposed barriers. (2007, p 507-8)

Not all members of the disability movement, however, emphasise their difference or want to be seen as different. One study of mental health service user/community groups, for instance, found that 'service users' struggles were often underpinned by the principle of equal moral worth and common humanity' (Lewis, 2009, p 269). According to Beckett, 'there is a growing understanding that many disabled people have rejected the ideals being proposed as the basis of a solidarity/group consciousness because they consider it to be problematic to speak of "disability pride" and the "celebration of difference" in relation to lives affected by impairments that are painful, debilitating or even fatal' (2005, p 414). Her research with members of six UK disability organisations run by disabled people found that most of them prioritised the dismantling of continued structural barriers to equal participation over identity issues. She concludes: 'whilst all disabled people are keen to achieve recognition and respect, they are not all seeking to be recognized as having essentially *different* identities from those of non-disabled people, or as being part of a *different* culture, but rather, as equal *persons*' (2006a, p 176, emphasis in original).

Beckett's reference to 'recognition and respect' is indicative of how, whether or not the emphasis is on difference or equality, the disabled people's movement is forging a social justice politics of recognition. At the same time, as Campbell makes clear in her lecture (***Box 9.2***), it is also seeking redistribution. Drawing on Fraser's articulation of the politics of social justice, Shakespeare explains that 'the social movement of disabled people is about the politics of recognition, as well as the politics of redistribution. Disabled people suffer socio-economic injustices, such as marginalisation and deprivation, as well as cultural injustices, such as non-recognition and disrespect' (2005, p 164; see also Goodlad and Riddell, 2005; Witcher, 2005; Lewis, 2009). Derogatory language about disabled people is still all too common (Birrell, 2009). However, 'pejorative terms such as "cripple", "spastic", etc. are also being revalued and utilised in challenging ways by disabled people' as a form of resistance (Fawcett, 2000, p 26).

Moreover, misrecognition and disrespect are sometimes expressed through physical violence (Sin et al, 2009). It has been argued that physical and verbal violence against disabled people constitutes a hate crime 'motivated by contempt, hatred or hostility' (Quarmby, 2008, p 8). Hate crime represents 'an extreme articulation of the prejudice and discrimination disabled people face on a day-to-day basis', which in turn 'has been given the name "disablism"' (Quarmby, 2008, p 8). Disablism has been defined as 'discriminatory, oppressive or abusive behaviour arising from the belief that disabled people are inferior to others' (Quarmby, 2008, p 8).

The assertion that there should be 'nothing about us, without us' exemplifies the third dimension of Fraser's conceptualisation of social justice:

political representation. Recognition, redistribution and representation are all demanded by the disabled people's movement in order to achieve the parity of participation necessary to achieve social justice (see ***Box 8.8***).

The global social justice movement

As we saw in Chapter Eight, social justice is now being articulated in global terms. What was originally called the anti-globalisation movement is increasingly known as the 'global social justice movement', as mentioned earlier in this chapter. As Annetts et al put it: 'the anti-globalisation movement so-called is not anti-globalisation per se, but instead seeks to build and articulate alternative globalisations founded on ideas of social justice, eco-welfare and equity, that another globalisation might be possible!' (2009, p 226). It is a globalisation where 'welfare and need come first' (Annetts et al, 2009, p 232).

The movement is also sometimes represented as a movement for global citizenship, contesting 'the meaning of citizenship' within global capitalism, and as representing new forms of 'global solidarity and resistance', which represent 'globalisation from below' (Annetts et al, 2009, pp 245, 232, 233). The global social justice movement is 'driven by a concern with social justice, citizenship and human rights, security, environmental concerns, gender, "race", ethnic and cultural equality, and opposition to war and oppression, inequality, poverty and social harms' (Annetts et al, 2009, p 233).

Despite the name, there is not a single 'global justice movement'. Instead, a number of social justice movements are now organising across national borders at a global level, often spearheaded by movements in the global South (O'Nions, 2009). They cut across the distinction sometimes drawn between 'old' and 'new' social movements and their struggles represent differing mixes of demands for redistribution, recognition and representation. Some are, for instance, fighting global poverty or for social justice for asylum-seekers, refugees and migrant workers. National social justice movements are uniting across borders. For example, according to Peter Tatchell (2009), 'the struggle for LGBT [lesbian, gay, bisexual and transgendered] liberation has gone global', opposing homophobia and discrimination and claiming equality and sexual rights as human rights. Other global movements are fighting for environmental justice. An example is Climate Justice Now, 'a coalition of social movements and NGOs [non-governmental organisations] working to ensure that justice is at the heart of the world's response to global warming' (O'Nions, 2009, p 36).

As the examples illustrate, global social justice movements are, like national movements, deploying some of the concepts discussed in this volume in their struggles to change the world. Returning to the quotation from Marx which heads this chapter, I hope that this volume will have helped to equip you not only to interpret the world but also, should you wish, to change it.

Summary

- This chapter reinforces a key theme of the book: the relevance and value of theory to the practice of social policy.
- It uses the example of social movements to illuminate the ways in which theory can provide a mobilising and analytical tool for people who come together to try to change the world. In turn, the actions of social movements can inform theory.
- As well as providing a brief overview of the main characteristics of social movements generally, the chapter illustrates how new social movements, social welfare movements, the disability movement and the global justice movement all draw on or exemplify a number of the theoretical perspectives that we have explored.

Further reading

There is a large literature on social movements. I am simply recommending two volumes that are particularly valuable for social policy students and that best illustrate the theme of this chapter. The more general is **Annetts et al (2009)**. This provides an introduction to social movements together with a number of case studies of social welfare movements. **Beckett (2006a)** focuses on the disability movement in the context of a discussion of citizenship and of social movements more broadly.

references

Adebowale, M. (2008) 'Understanding environmental justice', in G. Craig, T. Burchardt and D. Gordon (eds) *Social Justice and Public Policy*, Bristol: The Policy Press, pp 251-75.

Aers, R. (2008) 'The one that got away', *Society Guardian*, 17 December, pp 1-2.

Ahmad, W. and Craig, G. (2003) '"Race" and social welfare', in P. Alcock, A. Erskine and M. May (eds) *The Student's Companion to Social Policy* (2nd edn), Oxford: Blackwell.

Alcock, P., Erskine, A. and May, M. (eds) (2002) *The Blackwell Dictionary of Social Policy*, Oxford: Blackwell.

Alcock, P., Glennerster, H., Oakley, A. and Sinfield, A. (eds) (2001) *Welfare and Wellbeing: Richard Titmuss's Contribution to Social Policy*, Bristol: The Policy Press.

Alcock, P., May, M. and Rowlingson, K. (eds) (2008) *The Student's Companion to Social Policy* (3rd edn), Oxford: Blackwell.

Aldridge, S. (2001) *Social Mobility: A Discussion Paper*, London: Cabinet Office.

Amin, A. (ed) (1994) *Post-Fordism: A Reader*, Oxford: Blackwell.

Annetts, J., Law, A., McNeish, W. and Mooney, G. (2009) *Understanding Social Welfare Movements*, Bristol: The Policy Press.

Anthias, F. and Yuval-Davis, N. (1993) *Racialized Boundaries*, London and New York: Routledge.

Arai, L. (2009) 'What a difference a decade makes: rethinking teenage pregnancy as a social problem', *Social Policy and Society*, vol 8, no 2, pp 171-83.

Bacchi, C. (1999) *Women, Policy and Politics*, London: Sage.

Baker, J., Lynch, K., Cantillon, S. and Walsh, J. (2004) *Equality. From Theory to Action*, Basingstoke: Palgrave.

Baldock, J. (1999) 'Culture: the missing variable in understanding social policy?', *Social Policy and Administration*, vol 33, no 4, pp 458-73.

Ball, S. J. (1998) 'Performativity and fragmentation in "postmodern schooling"', in J. Carter (ed) *Postmodernity and the Fragmentation of Welfare*, London and New York: Routledge, pp 187-203.

Barber, B. (2007) 'Invisible hand has to be led by us all', *The Times Higher*, 25 May, p 14.

Barker, P. (1996) 'Living as equals', in P. Barker (ed) *Living as Equals*, Oxford: Oxford University Press, pp 1-8.

Barnes, C. (2002) 'Introduction: disability, policy and politics', *Policy and Politics*, vol 30, no 1, pp 311-18.

Barrett, M. (1992) 'Words and things', in M. Barrett and A. Phillips (eds) *Destabilizing Theory*, Cambridge: Polity Press, pp 201-19.

Barry, N. (1999) 'Neo-classicism, the new right and British social welfare', in R. Page and R. Silburn (eds) *British Social Welfare in the 20th Century*, Basingstoke: Macmillan, pp 55-79.

Bartels, L. M. (2008) *Unequal Democracy*, New York: Russell Sage Foundation.

Bartley, M. (2006) *Capability and Resilience: Beating the Odds*, London: UCL.

Bauman, Z. (2005) *Work, Consumerism and the New Poor* (2nd edn), Maidenhead: Open University Press.

Beck, U. and Beck-Gernsheim, E. (2002) *Individualization*, London: Sage.

Beck, W., van der Maesen, L., Thomése, F. and Walker, A. (2001) *Social Quality: A Vision for Europe*, The Hague/London/Boston: Kluwer Law International.

Beckett, A. E. (2005) 'Reconsidering citizenship in the light of the concerns of the UK disability movement', *Citizenship Studies*, vol 9, no 4, pp 405-21.

Beckett, A. E. (2006a) *Citizenship and Vulnerability*, Basingstoke: Palgrave.

Beckett, A. E. (2006b) 'Understanding social movements: theorising the disability movement in conditions of late modernity', *The Sociological Review*, vol 54, no 4, pp 734-52.

Béland, D. and Waddan, A. (2007) 'Conservative ideas and social policy in the United States', *Social Policy and Administration*, vol 41, no 7, pp 768-86.

Bellamy, R., Castiglione, D. and Santoro, E. (eds) (2004) *Lineages of European Citizenship*, Basingstoke: Palgrave.

Beresford, P. (2008) 'Whose personalisation?', *Soundings*, no 40, pp 8-17.

Berger, P. and Luckmann, T. (1967) *The Social Construction of Reality*, Harmondsworth: Penguin.

Beveridge, W. (1942) *Social Insurance and Allied Services*, ('the Beveridge Report'), Cmnd 6404, London: HMSO.

Bhavnani, K. (2001) 'Introduction', in K. Bhavnani (ed) *Feminism and Race*, Oxford: Oxford University Press, pp 1-13.

BIHR, Joseph Rowntree Foundation, Amnesty International, Oxfam (2008) *Human Rights and Tackling UK Poverty*, Report of roundtable meeting 17 January 2008, London: British Institute of Human Rights.

Birrell, I. (2009) 'Mind your language: words can cause terrible damage', *The Independent*, 6 November.

Blair, T. (1997) 'Why we must help those excluded from society', *The Independent*, 8 December.

Blair, T. (1998) *The Third Way: New Politics for the New Century*, London: Fabian Society.

Blair, T. (1999) 'Beveridge revisited. A welfare state for the 21st century', in R. Walker (ed) *Ending Child Poverty*, Bristol: The Policy Press, pp 7-18.

Blair, T. (2004) Speech to IPPR and Demos, London: University of London, 11 October.

Blair, T. (2006) *PM's Respect Action Plan*, Speech, London: 10 Downing Street, January.

Blair, T. and Schröder, G. (1999) 'Europe: the third way/die neue mitte', *The Spokesman*, no 66, pp 27-37.

Blakemore, K and Griggs, E. (2007) *Social Policy. An Introduction* (3rd edn), Maidenhead: Open University Press.

Blunkett, D. (2006) *A Ladder out of Poverty: from State Dependence to Self-reliance*, London: Resolution Foundation.

Boardman, B. (1999) *Equity and the Environment*, London: Catalyst and Friends of the Earth.

Bonnett, A. (1997) 'Constructions of whiteness in European and American anti-racism', in P. Werbner and T. Modood (eds) *Debating Cultural Hybridity*, London and New Jersey: Zed Books, pp 173-92.

Bonoli, G. and Powell, M. (2004) 'One third way or several?', in J. Lewis and R. Surender (eds) *Welfare State Change. Towards a Third Way?*, Oxford: Oxford University Press, pp 47-66.

Borsay, A. (2005) *Disability and Social Policy in Britain since 1750*, Basingstoke: Palgrave.

Bottero, W. (2009) 'Class in the 21st century', in K. P. Sveinsson (ed) *Who Cares about the White Working Class?*, London: Runnymede, pp 7-15.

Bradshaw, J. (1972) 'The concept of social need', *New Society*, 30 March, pp 640-3.

Brent, J. (2009) *Searching for Community*, Bristol: The Policy Press.

Brighouse, H. and Swift, A. (2008) 'Social justice and the family', in G. Craig, T. Burchardt and D. Gordon (eds) *Social Justice and Public Policy*, Bristol: The Policy Press, pp 139-56.

Brown, G. (2007) *Liberty*, speech, London: University of Westminster, 25 October.

Bryson, V. (1999) *Feminist Debates*, Basingstoke: Macmillan.

Bryson, V. (2007) 'Time', in G. Blakeley and V. Bryson (eds) *The Impact of Feminism on Political Concepts and Debates*, Manchester: Manchester University Press, pp 161-77.

Bryson, V. (2008) *Gender and the Politics of Time*, Bristol: The Policy Press.

Bulmer, M. and Solomos, J. (1999) 'Introduction', in M. Bulmer and J. Solomos (eds) *Ethnic and Racial Studies Today*, London and New York: Routledge, pp 1-12.

Burchardt, T. and Craig, G. (2008) 'Introduction', in G. Craig, T. Burchardt and D. Gordon (eds) *Social Justice and Public Policy*, Bristol: The Policy Press, pp 1-15.

Burr, V. (2003) *Social Constructionism* (2nd edn), London and New York: Routledge.

Burrows, R. and Loader, B. (eds) (1994) *Towards a Post-Fordist Welfare State?*, London and New York: Routledge.

Cahill, M. (1999) 'Sustainability: the twenty first century challenge for social policy,' in H. Dean and R. Woods (eds) *Social Policy Review 11*, Social Policy Association and University of Luton, pp 90-106.

Cahill, M. (2001) *The Environment and Social Policy*, London and New York: Routledge.

Cahill, M. (2007) 'The environment and green social policy,', in J. Baldock, N. Manning and S. Vickerstaff (eds) *Social Policy* (3rd edn), Oxford: Oxford University Press, pp 574-600.

Cahill, M. (2008) 'Green perspectives', in P. Alcock, M. May and K. Rowlingson (eds) *The Student's Companion to Social Policy* (3rd edn), Oxford: Blackwell, pp 106-12.

Cahill, M. and Fitzpatrick, T. (2001) 'Editorial introduction', *Social Policy and Administration*, vol 35, no 5, pp 469-71, published also as M. Cahill and T. Fitzpatrick (eds) (2002) *Environmental Issues and Social Welfare*, Oxford: Blackwell.

Cameron, C. (2007) 'Whose problem? Disability narratives and available identities', *Community Development Journal*, vol 42, no 4, pp 501-11.

Cameron, D. (2006) *From state welfare to social enterprise*, The Scarman Lecture, London: Institute of Education, 24 November.

Cameron, D. (2008a) 'We are the champions of progressive ideals', *The Independent*, 9 May.

Cameron, D. (2008b) *Living within our means*, Speech, Birmingham, 19 May.

Cameron, D. (2009a) 'A Lib Dem Tory movement will vanquish Labour', *The Observer*, 20 September.

Cameron, D. (2009b) *The Big Society*, The Hugo Young Lecture. London, 10 November.

Campbell, J. (2008) *Fighting for a Slice or for a Bigger Cake?*, Lecture, Cambridge: St John's College, 29 April (www.equalityhumanrights.com).

Carabine, J. (1998) 'New horizons? New insights? Postmodernising social policy and the case of sexuality', in J. Carter (ed) *Postmodernity and the Fragmentation of Welfare*, London and New York: Routledge, pp 121-35.

Carpenter, M. (2009a) 'A third wave, not "a third way". New Labour, human rights and mental health in historical context', *Social Policy and Society*, vol 8, no 2, pp 215-30.

Carpenter, M. (2009b) 'The capabilities approach and critical social policy: lessons from the majority world?', *Critical Social Policy*, vol 29, no 3, pp 351-73.

Carter, J. (ed) (1998a) *Postmodernity and the Fragmentation of Welfare*, London and New York: Routledge.

Carter, J. (1998b) 'Preludes, introduction and meanings', in J. Carter (ed) *Postmodernity and the Fragmentation of Welfare*, London and New York: Routledge, pp 1-12.

Carter, J. (1998c) 'Studying social policy after modernity', in J. Carter (ed) *Postmodernity and the Fragmentation of Welfare*, London and New York: Routledge, pp 15-30.

Carter, J. and Rayner, M. (1996) 'The curious case of post-Fordism and welfare', *Journal of Social Policy*, vol 25, no 3, pp 347-67.

Charles, N. (2000) *Feminism, the State and Social Policy*, Basingstoke: Macmillan.

Churchill, H. (2007) 'New Labour versus lone mothers', discourses of parental responsibility and children's needs', *Critical Policy Analysis*, vol 1, no 2, pp 170-83.

Clark, C. (2008) 'Introduction to themed section:"Care or control? Gypsies, travellers and the state"', *Social Policy and Society*, vol 7, no 1, pp 65-71.

Clark, N. (2008) 'The European left', *New Statesman*, 8 December, pp 34-5.

Clarke, J. (1999) 'Coming to terms with culture', in H. Dean and R. Woods (eds) *Social Policy Review 11*, Luton: Social Policy Association and University of Luton, pp 71-89.

Clarke, J. (2001a) 'Social constructionism', in E. McLaughlin and J. Muncie (eds) *The Sage Dictionary of Criminology*, London: Sage, pp 266-8.

Clarke, J. (2001b) 'Social problems: sociological perspectives', in M. May, R. Page and E. Brunsdon (eds) *Understanding Social Problems*, Oxford: Blackwell, pp 3-15.

Clarke, J. (2004) *Changing Welfare, Changing States*, London: Sage.

Clarke, J. (2005) 'Welfare states as nation states: some conceptual reflections', *Social Policy and Society*, vol 4, no 4, pp 407-15.

Clarke, J. (2008) 'Managing and delivering welfare', in P. Alcock, M. May and K. Rowlingson (eds) *The Student's Companion to Social Policy* (2nd edn), Oxford: Blackwell, pp 243-50.

Clarke, J. and Cochrane, A. (1998) 'The social construction of social problems', in E. Saraga (ed) *Embodying the Social*, London and New York: Routledge, pp 13-42.

Clarke, J. and Langan, M. (1998) 'Review', in M. Langan (ed) *Welfare: Needs, Rights and Risks*, London and New York: Routledge, pp 259-71.

Clarke, J. and Newman, J. (1997) *The Managerial State*, London: Sage.

Clarke, J., Newman, J., Smith, N., Vidler, D., Westmorland, L. (2007) *Creating Citizen-Consumers*, London: Sage.

Clayton, M. and Williams, A. (eds) (2004) *Social Justice*, Oxford: Blackwell.

Coatman, C. (2009) 'Watching the watchers', *Red Pepper*, June/July, pp 18-19.

Cochrane, A. (1993) 'Comparative approaches and social policy', in A. Cochrane and J. Clarke (eds) *Comparing Welfare States*, London: Sage, pp 1-18.

Cohen, E. F. (2006) 'Foucault, Michel (1926-1984)', in B. S. Turner (ed) *The Cambridge Dictionary of Sociology*, Cambridge: Cambridge University Press, pp 212-14.

Cohen, G. A. (1997) 'Back to Socialist basics', in J. Franklin (ed) *Equality*, London: Institute for Public Policy Research, pp 29-47.

Cohen, P. (1997) 'Beyond the community romance', *Soundings*, no 5, pp 29-51.

Cohen, S. (1985) *Visions of Social Control*, Cambridge: Polity Press.

Collins, P. and Reeves, R. (2008) 'Liberalism or die', *Prospect*, June, pp 12-13.

Commission on Social Justice (1993) *The Justice Gap*, London: Institute for Public Policy Research.

Commission on Social Justice (1994) *Social Justice: Strategies for National Renewal*, London: Vintage.

Considine, M. (1999) 'Markets, networks and the new welfare state: employment assistance reforms in Australia', *Journal of Social Policy*, vol 28, no 2, pp 181-203.

Coote, A. and Franklin, J. (2009) *Green Well Fair. Three Economies for Social Justice*, London: new economics foundation.

Craig, G. (2007a) 'Community capacity building: something old, something new…?', *Critical Social Policy*, vol 27, no 3, pp 335-59.

Craig, G. (2007b) 'Cunning, unprincipled, loathsome. The racist tail wags the welfare dog', *Journal of Social Policy*, vol 36, no 4, pp 605-23.

Craig, G. (2008) 'The limits of compromise? Social justice, 'race', and multiculturalism', in G. Craig, T. Burchardt and D. Gordon (eds) *Social Justice and Public Policy*, Bristol: The Policy Press, pp 231-49.

Craig, G., Burchardt, T. and Gordon, D. (eds) (2008) *Social Justice and Public Policy*, Bristol: The Policy Press.

Croft, S. and Beresford, P. (1992) 'The politics of participation', *Critical Social Policy*, no 35, pp 20-44.

Cudworth, E., Hall, T. and McGovern, J. (2007) *The Modern State*, Edinburgh: Edinburgh University Press.

Culley, L. and Demaine, J. (2006) 'Race and ethnicity in United Kingdom public policy: education and health', in E. Rata and R. Openshaw (eds) *Public Policy and Ethnicity*, Basingstoke: Palgrave, pp 128-41.

Dahl, R. A. (2006) *On Political Equality*, New Haven and London: Yale University Press.

Dawnay, E. and Shah, H. (2005) *Behavioural Economics. Seven Principles for Policy-Makers*, London: new economics foundation.

Dawson, K. (2007) Briefing 2: Supervised Community Treatment, London: Mind (www.mind.org.uk/information/Legal/MHAlegalbriefing2.htm).

Deacon, A. (2002) *Perspectives on Welfare*, Buckingham: Open University Press.

Deacon, A. (2004) 'Different interpretation of agency within welfare debates', *Social Policy and Society*, vol 3, no 4, pp 447-55.

Deacon, A. and Mann, K. (1999) 'Agency, modernity and social policy', *Journal of Social Policy*, vol 28, no 3, pp 413-35.

Deacon, B. (2005) 'The governance and politics of global social policy', *Social Policy and Society*, vol 4, no 4, pp 437-45.

Deacon, B. with Halse, M. and Stubbs, P. (1997) *Global Social Policy*, London: Sage.

Deakin, N. and Wright, A. (1995) 'Tawney', in V. George and R. Page (eds) *Modern Thinkers on Welfare*, Hemel Hempstead: Harvester Wheatsheaf, pp 133-48.

Dean, H. (1988/9) 'Disciplinary partitioning and the privatisation of social security', *Critical Social Policy*, no 24, pp 74-82.

Dean, H. (1995) 'Offe', in V. George and R. Page (eds) *Modern Thinkers on Welfare*, Hemel Hempstead: Harvester Wheatsheaf, pp 217-33.

Dean, H. (1996) *Welfare Law and Citizenship*, Hemel Hempstead: Harvester Wheatsheaf.

Dean, H. (2002) *Welfare Rights and Social Policy*, Harlow: Prentice Hall.

Dean, H. (ed) (2004) *The Ethics of Welfare. Human Rights, Dependency and Responsibility*, Bristol: The Policy Press.

Dean, H. (2006) *Social Policy*, Cambridge: Polity Press.

Dean, H. (2008) 'Social policy and human rights: re-thinking the engagement', *Social Policy and Society*, vol 7, no 1, pp 1-12.

Dean, H. (2009) 'Critiquing capabilities', *Critical Social Policy*, vol 29, no 2, pp 261-78.

Dean, H. (2010) *Understanding Human Needs*, Bristol: The Policy Press.

Dean, H. and Taylor-Gooby, P. (1992) *Dependency Culture*, Hemel Hempstead: Harvester Wheatsheaf.

Dench, G. (ed) (2006) *The Rise and Rise of Meritocracy*, Oxford: Blackwell.

Department for Social Security (1998) *New Ambitions for Our Country: A new contract for welfare*, London: The Stationery Office.

Department for Work and Pensions (2008) *Raising Expectations and Increasing Support. Reforming Welfare for the Future*, London: The Stationery Office.

Department of Health (2003) *Fair Access to Care Services. Guidance on Eligibility Criteria for Adult Social Care*, London: Department of Health.

Diamond, P. and Giddens, A. (2005) 'The new egalitarianism: economic inequality in the UK', in A. Giddens and P. Diamond (eds) *The New Egalitarianism*, Cambridge: Polity Press, pp 101-19.

Dobson, A. (2003) *Citizenship and the Environment*, Oxford: Oxford University Press.

Dominelli, L. (2006) *Women and Community Action* (2nd edn), Bristol: The Policy Press.

Donald, A. and Mottershaw, E. (2009) *Poverty, Inequality and Human Rights*, York: Joseph Rowntree Foundation.

Donzelot, J. (1980) *The Policing of Families*, London: Hutchinson.

Dornan, P. and Hudson, J. (2003) 'Welfare governance in the surveillance society', *Social Policy and Administration*, vol 37, no 5, pp 468-82.

Dower, N. (2003) *An Introduction to Global Citizenship*, Edinburgh: Edinburgh University Press.

Doyal, L. and Gough, I. (1984) 'A theory of human need', *Critical Social Policy* 10, pp 6-38.

Doyal, L. and Gough, I. (1991) *A Theory of Human Need*, Basingstoke: Macmillan.

Driver, S. and Martell, L. (1997) 'New Labour's communitarianisms', *Critical Social Policy* vol 17, no 3, pp 27-46.

Driver, S. and Martell, L. (1998) *New Labour. Politics after Thatcherism*, Cambridge: Polity Press.

Driver, S. and Martell, L. (2002) *Blair's Britain*, Cambridge: Polity Press.

Drover, G. and Kerans, P. (1993) 'New approaches to welfare theory: foundations', in G. Drover and P. Kerans (eds) *New Approaches to Welfare Theory*, Cheltenham: Edward Elgar, pp 3-30.

Duncan, S. (2007) 'What's the problem with teenage parents? And what's the problem with policy?', *Critical Social Policy*, vol 27, no 3, pp 307-34.

Duncan, S. and Edwards, R. (1999) *Lone Mothers, Paid Work and Gendered Moral Rationalities*, Basingstoke: Macmillan.

Dwyer, P. (2004) *Understanding Social Citizenship*, Bristol: The Policy Press (2nd edn published 2010).

EHRC (2009a) *Equality Measurement Framework*. Press release and briefing, 23 July (www.equalityhumanrights.com).

EHRC (2009b) *Human Rights Enquiry. Executive Summary*. London: Equality and Human Rights Commission.

EHRC (2009c) *Our Human Rights Strategy and Programme of Action 2009-2012*, London: Equality and Human Rights Commission.

Ehrenreich, B. (2001) *Nickel and Dimed*, New York: Owl Books.

Ehrenreich, B. (2002) 'Preface', to R. Albeda and A. Withorn (eds) *Lost Ground*. Cambridge, MA: South End Press, pp vii–x.

Ellison, N. (2008) 'Neo-liberalism', in P. Alcock, M. May and K. Rowlingson (eds) *The Student's Companion to Social Policy* (3rd edn), Oxford: Blackwell, pp 61–8.

Etzioni, A. (2006) 'Communitarianism', in B. S. Turner (ed) *The Cambridge Dictionary of Sociology*, Cambridge: Cambridge University Press, pp 81–3.

Evans, R. and Becker, S. (2009) *Children Caring for Parents with HIV and AIDS*, Bristol: The Policy Press.

Fabian Commission on Life Chances and Child Poverty (2006) *Narrowing the Gap*, London: Fabian Society.

Fairclough, N. (2000) *New Labour, New Language?*, London and New York: Routledge.

Faulks, K. (1998) *Citizenship in Modern Britain*, Edinburgh: Edinburgh University Press.

Faulks, K. (2000) *Citizenship*, London and New York: Routledge.

Fawcett, B. (2000) *Feminist Perspectives on Disability*, Harlow: Prentice Hall.

Fawcett, B. and Featherstone, B. (1998) 'Quality assurance and evaluation in social work in a postmodern era', in J. Carter (ed) *Postmodernity and the Fragmentation of Welfare*, London and New York: Routledge, pp 67–82.

Featherstone, B. (2004) *Family Life and Family Support. A Feminist Analysis*, Basingstoke: Palgrave.

Featherstone, B. (2009) *Contemporary Fathering*, Bristol: The Policy Press.

Feeley, M. M. and Simon, J. (2003) 'The new penology', in E. McLaughlin, J. Muncie, and G. Hughes (eds) *Criminological Perspectives. Essential Readings* (2nd ed), London: Sage, pp 434–46.

Ferguson, I., Lavalette, M., Mooney, G. (2002) *Rethinking Welfare. A Critical Perspective*, London: Sage.

Ferris, J. (1991) 'Green politics and the future of welfare', in N. Manning (ed) *Social Policy Review 1990-91*, Harlow: Longman, pp 9–23.

Field, F. (1996) *Stakeholder Welfare*, London: Institute for Economic Affairs Health and Welfare Unit.

Field, F. (1997) *Reforming Welfare*, London: Social Market Foundation.

Finlayson, A. (2003) *Making Sense of New Labour*, London: Lawrence & Wishart.

Finlayson, A. (2007) 'Making sense of David Cameron', *Public Policy Research*, vol 14, no 1, pp 3–10.

Finlayson, A. and Martin, J. (2006) 'Poststructuralism', in C. Hay, M. Lister and D. Marsh (eds) *The State. Theories and Issues*, Basingstoke: Palgrave, pp 155–71.

Fitzpatrick, T. (1998) 'The implications of ecological thought for social welfare', *Critical Social Policy*, vol 18, no 1, pp 5-26.

Fitzpatrick, T. (1999) 'New welfare associations: an alternative model of well-being', in T. Jordan and A. Lent (eds) *Storming the Millenium*, London; Lawrence & Wishart, pp 156-171.

Fitzpatrick, T. (2001) *Welfare Theory: An Introduction*, Basingstoke: Palgrave.

Fitzpatrick, T. (2003) 'Environmentalism and social policy', in N. Ellison and C. Pierson (eds) *Developments in British Social Policy 2*, Basingstoke: Palgrave, pp 317-332.

Fitzpatrick, T. (2005) *New Theories of Welfare*, Basingstoke: Palgrave.

Fitzpatrick, T. (2011: forthcoming) *Understanding Environmental Policy*, Bristol: The Policy Press.

Flint, J. (2009) 'Subversive subjects and conditional, earned and denied citizenship', in M. Barnes and D. Prior (eds) *Subversive Citizens*, Bristol: The Policy Press, pp 83-98.

Foley, J., Grayling, T. and Dixon, M. (2005) 'Sustainability and social justice', in N. Pearce and W. Paxton (eds) *Social Justice*, London: Politico's, pp 178-98.

Foucault, M. (1965) *Madness and Civilization*, London: Tavistock.

Foucault, M. (1977) *Discipline and Punish*, London: Penguin.

Foucault, M. (1978) *The History of Sexuality*, London: Penguin.

Foucault, M. (1980) *Power/Knowledge. Selected Interviews and Other Writings 1972-1997*, edited by C. Gordon, New York: Pantheon.

Foucault, M. (2003) 'The carceral', in E. McLaughlin, J. Muncie, and G. Hughes (eds) *Criminological Perspectives. Essential Readings* (2nd edn), London: Sage, pp 417-23.

Fraser, N. (1987) 'Women, welfare and the politics of needs interpretation', *Hypatia*, vol 2, no 1, pp 103-19.

Fraser, N. (1989) *Unruly Practices*, Cambridge: Polity Press.

Fraser, N. (1997) *Justice Interruptus*, London and New York: Routledge.

Fraser, N. (2008) *Scales of Justice*, Cambridge: Polity Press.

Fraser, N. and Gordon, L. (1994) '"Dependency" demystified. Inscriptions of power in a keyword of the welfare state', *Social Politics*, vol 1, no 1, pp 4-31.

Fraser, N. and Nicholson, L. J. (1990) 'Social criticism without philosophy: an encounter between feminism and postmodernism', in L. J. Nicholson (ed) *Feminism/Postmodernism*, New York and London: Routledge, pp 19-37.

Fremeaux, I. (2005) 'New Labour's appropriation of the concept of community: a critique', *Community Development Journal*, vol 40, no 3, pp 265-74.

Gamble, A. (1988) *The Free Economy and the Strong State*, Basingstoke: Macmillan.

Gamble, A. and Wright, T. (2004) 'Introduction', in A. Gamble and T. Wright (eds) *Restating the State?*, Oxford: Blackwell, pp 1-10.

Garboden, M. (2009) 'It's hard to prove need', *Community Care*, 29 October, p 20.

Garner, S. (2009) 'Home truths: the white working class and the racialization of social housing' in K. P. Sveinsson (ed) *Who Cares about the White Working Class?*, London: Runnymede, pp 45-50.

George, V. and Page, R. (1995) 'Marxists', in V. George and R. Page (eds) *Modern Thinkers on Welfare*, Hemel Hempstead: Harvester Wheatsheaf, pp 199-200.

George, V. and Wilding, P. (1994) *Welfare and Ideology*, Hemel Hempstead: Harvester Wheatsheaf.

Giddens, A. (1991) *Modernity and Self-Identity*, Cambridge: Polity Press.

Giddens, A. (1998) *The Third Way*, Cambridge: Polity Press.

Gillies, V. (2007) *Marginalised Mothers*, London and New York: Routledge.

Gilliom, J. (2001) *Overseers of the Poor*, Chicago and London: University of Chicago Press.

Ginsburg, N. (1979) *Class, Capital and Social Policy*, Basingstoke: Macmillan.

Ginsburg, N. (1998) 'Postmodernism and social Europe', in J. Carter (ed) *Postmodernity and the Fragmentation of Welfare*, London and New York: Routledge, pp 267-77.

Glennerster, H. (1999) 'A third way?', in H. Dean and R. Woods (eds) *Social Policy Review 11*, Luton: Social Policy Association and University of Luton, pp 28-44.

Glennerster, H. (2003) *Understanding the Finance of Welfare*, Bristol: The Policy Press.

Goldsmith, Lord (2008) *Citizenship: Our Common Bond*, London: Ministry of Justice.

Goodlad, R. and Riddell, S. (2005) 'Social justice and disabled people: principles and challenges', *Social Policy and Society*, vol 4, no 1, pp 45-54.

Goodwin, B. (2007) *Using Political Ideas* (5th edn), Chichester: John Wiley and Sons.

Gordon, D., Adelman, L., Ashworth, K., Bradshaw, J., Levitas, R., Middleton, S., Pantazis, C., Patsios, D., Payne, S., Townsend, P. and Williams, J. (2000) *Poverty and Social Exclusion in Britain*, York: Joseph Rowntree Foundation.

Gordon, L. (1990) 'The new feminist scholarship on the welfare state', in L. Gordon (ed) *Women, the State and Welfare*, Madison, WI: University of Wisconsin Press, pp 9-35.

Gough, I. (1995) 'O'Connor', in V. George and R. Page (eds) *Modern Thinkers on Welfare*, Hemel Hempstead: Harvester Wheatsheaf, pp 201-33.

Gough, I. (1998) 'What are human needs?', in J. Franklin (ed) *Social Policy and Social Justice*, Cambridge: Polity Press, pp 50-6.

Gough, I. (2000) *Global Capital, Human Needs and Social Policies*, Basingstoke: Palgrave.

Graham, H. (2004) 'The role of theory in relation to the ESRC Health Inequalities Programme', in S. Becker and A. Bryman (eds) *Understanding Research for Social Policy and Practice*, Bristol: The Policy Press, pp 80-3.

Graham, S. and Wood, D. (2003) 'Digitizing surveillance: categorization, space, inequality', *Critical Social Policy*, vol 23, no 2, pp 227-48.

Gray, J. (2007) 'Maggie's boy', *New Statesman*, 7 May, pp 48-50.

Green, D. (2003) 'The neo-liberal perspective', in P. Alcock, M. May and K. Rowlingson (eds) *The Student's Companion to Social Policy* (2nd edn), Oxford: Blackwell, pp 71-7.

Green New Deal Group (2008) *A Green New Deal*, London: new economics foundation.

Grice, A. (2009) 'Cameron has yet to earn the love of the Conservative Party', *The Independent*, 24 October.

Griggs, J. and Bennett, F. (2009) *Rights and Responsibilities in the Social Security System*, Occasional Paper No 6, London: Social Security Advisory Committee.

Gupta, R. (2003a) 'Some recurring themes: Southall Black Sisters 1979-2003 – and still going strong', in R. Gupta (ed) *From Homebreakers to Jailbreakers*, London and New York: Zed Books, pp 1-27.

Gupta, R. (ed) (2003b) *From Homebreakers to Jailbreakers. Southall Black Sisters*, London and New York: Zed Books.

Hall, S. (2003) 'New Labour's double shuffle', *Soundings*, no 24, pp 10-24.

Hall, S. and Held, D. (1989) 'Citizens and citizenship', in S. Hall and M. Jacques (eds) *New Times*, London: Lawrence & Wishart, pp 173-88.

Hall, S. and Jacques, M. (1989) *New Times. The Changing Face of Politics in the 1990s*, London: Lawrence & Wishart.

Hall, T. and Williamson, H. (1999) *Citizenship and Community*, Leicester: Youth Work Press.

Hallett, C. (1996) 'Social policy: continuities and change', in C. Hallett (ed) *Women and Social Policy*, Hemel Hempstead: Harvester Wheatsheaf, pp 1-14.

Halpern, D. and Bates, C. (2004) *Personal Responsibility and Changing Behaviour: the state of knowledge and its implications for public policy*, London: Strategy Unit.

Hampson, T. (2008) 'Drop the word "chav"', *Fabian Review*, vol 120, no 2, p 19.

Harris, P. (1999) 'Public welfare and liberal governance', in A. Peterson, I. Barns, J. Dudley and P. Harris (eds) *Poststructuralism, Citizenship and Social Policy*, London and New York: Routledge, pp 25-64.

Hartsock, N. (1990) 'Foucault on power. A theory for women?', in L. J. Nicholson (ed) *Feminism/Postmodernism*, New York and London: Routledge, pp 157-75.

Harvey, D. (1993) 'Class relations, social justice and the politics of difference', in J. Squires (ed) *Principled Positions*, London: Lawrence & Wishart, pp 85-120.

Hastings, A. (1998) 'Constructing linguistic structures and social practices: a discursive approach to social policy analysis', *Journal of Social Policy*, vol 27, no 2, pp 191-211.

Hattersley, R. (1987) *Choose Freedom*, London: Michael Joseph.

Hay, C. (2004) 'Re-stating politics, re-politicising the state: neoliberalism, economic imperatives and the rise of the competitive state', in A. Gamble and T. Wright (eds) *Restating the State?*, Oxford: Blackwell, pp 38-50.

Hay, C., Lister, M., Marsh, D. (eds) (2006) *The State. Theories and Issues*, Basingstoke: Palgrave.

Hayek, F.A. (1976) *Law, Legislation and Liberty*, vol 2, London/New York, NY: Routledge.

Heng, S. (2007) 'Unhappy gatekeepers', *Community Care*, 8 November, p 10.

Henman, P. and Adler, M. (2003) 'Information technology and the governance of social security', *Critical Social Policy*, vol 23, no 2, pp 139-64.

Henman, P. and Marston, G. (2008) 'The social division of welfare surveillance', *Journal of Social Policy*, vol 37, no 2, pp 187-205.

Hensher, P. and Younge, G. (2006) 'Does the right to freedom of speech justify printing the Danish cartoons?', *The Guardian*, 4 February.

Hernes, H. M. (1987) *Welfare State and Woman Power*, Oslo: Norwegian University Press.

Hewitt, M. (1992) *Welfare Ideology and Need*, Hemel Hempstead: Harvester Wheatsheaf.

Hewitt, M. (1998) 'Social policy and human need', in N. Ellison and C. Pierson (eds) *Developments in British Social Policy*, Basingstoke: Palgrave.

Heywood, A. (1994) *Political Ideas and Concepts. An Introduction*, Basingstoke: Macmillan.

Hickman, R. (2009) *In Pursuit of Egalitarianism and Why Social Mobility Cannot Get Us There*, London: Compass.

Hier, S. P. and Greenberg, J. (eds) (2007) *The Surveillance Studies Reader*, Maidenhead: Open University Press.

Higgins, J. (1980) 'Social control theories of social policy', *Journal of Social Policy*, vol 9, no 1, pp 1-23.

Hillman, M. (2007) 'An inconvenient man. Matthew Taylor interviews Mayer Hillman', *Fabian Review*, vol 119, no 1, pp 8-10.

Hillyard, P. and Watson, S. (1996) 'Postmodern social policy: a contradiction in terms', *Journal of Social Policy*, vol 25, no 3, pp 321-46.

Hindmoor, A. (2006) 'Public choice', in C. Hay, M. Lister and D. Marsh (eds) *The State. Theories and Issues*, Basingstoke: Palgrave, pp 79-97.

Hobson, B. and Lister, R. (2002) 'Citizenship', in B. Hobson, J. Lewis and B. Siim (eds) *Contested Concepts in Gender and Social Politics*, Cheltenham: Edward Elgar, pp 23-54.

Hobson, B., Lewis, J., and Siim, B. (eds) (2002) *Contested Concepts in Social Politics*, Cheltenham: Edward Elgar.

Hoffman, J. (2004) *Citizenship Beyond the State*, London: Sage.

Hoggett, P. (1997a) 'Contested communities', in P. Hoggett (ed) *Contested Communities*, Bristol: The Policy Press, pp 3-16.

Hoggett, P. (1997b) *Contested Communities*, Bristol: The Policy Press.

Hoggett, P. (2001) 'Agency, rationality and social policy', *Journal of Social Policy*, 30 (1), pp 37-56.

Hoggett, P. and Thompson, S. (1998) 'The delivery of welfare. The associationist vision', in J. Carter (ed) *Postmodernity and the Fragmentation of Welfare*, London and New York: Routledge, pp 237-51.

Holden, C. (2005) 'Social policy and political economy: a tale of (at least) two disciplines', *Social Policy and Society*, vol 4, no 2, pp 173-81.

Honneth, A. (2003) 'Redistribution as recognition', in N. Fraser and A. Honneth, *Redistribution or Recognition? A Philosophical Exchange*, London and New York: Verso, pp 110-97.

Huby, M. (1998) *Social Policy and the Environment*, Buckingham: Open University Press.

Hughes, G. (ed) (1998a) *Imagining Welfare Futures*, London and New York: Routledge.

Hughes, G. (1998b) 'A suitable case for treatment?', Constructions of disability', in E. Saraga (ed) *Embodying the Social*, London and New York: Routledge, pp 43-90.

Hughes, G. and Lewis, G. (eds) (1998) *Unsettling Welfare*, London and New York: Routledge.

Hughes, G. and Mooney, G. (1998) 'Community', in G. Hughes (ed) *Imagining Welfare Futures*, London and New York: Routledge, pp 55-102.

Hunter, S. (2003) 'A critical analysis of approaches to the concept of social identity in social policy', *Critical Social Policy*, vol 22, no 3, pp 322-44.

Hutton, J. (2006) *The Active Welfare State: Matching Rights with Responsibilities*, Speech, London: Work Foundation, 16 January.

Ignatieff, M. (1990) *The Needs of Strangers*, London: The Hogarth Press.

Irving, Z. (2008) 'Gender and work', in D. Richardson and V. Robinson (eds) *Introducing Gender and Women's Studies*, (3rd edn), Basingstoke: Palgrave, pp 160-83.

Irving, Z., Yeates, N., and Young, P. (2005) 'What can global perspectives contribute to curriculum development in social policy?', *Social Policy and Society*, vol 4, no 4, pp 475-84.

Jackson, B. and Segal, P. (2004) *Why Inequality Matters*, London: Catalyst.

Jacobs, M. (1999) *Environmental Modernisation. The New Labour Agenda*, London: Fabian Society.

Jaggar, A. (1994) 'Introduction: Living with contradictions', in A. Jaggar (ed) *Living with Contradictions. Controversies in Feminist Social Ethics*, Boulder, CO: Westview Press, pp 1-12.

James, O. (2008) 'We have a constant hunger for more but curbing our desires might make us happier', *The Guardian*, 15 October.

Jameson, H. (2008) 'Live longer under Labour', *Fabian Review*, vol 120, no 1, pp 4-6.

Jessop, B. (1994a) 'Post-Fordism and the state', in A. Amin (ed) *Post-Fordism: A Reader*, Oxford: Blackwell, pp 251-79.

Jessop, B. (1994b) 'The transition to post-Fordism and the Schumpeterian workfare state', in R. Burrows and B. Loader (eds) *Towards a Post-Fordist Welfare State?*, London and New York: Routledge, pp 13-37.

Jessop, B. (2000) 'From the KWNS to the SWPR', in G. Lewis, S. Gewirtz and J. Clarke (eds) *Rethinking Social Policy*, London: Sage, pp 171-84.

John, P., Smith, G. and Stoker, G. (2009) 'Nudge, nudge, think, think. Two strategies for changing civic behaviour', *The Political Quarterly*, vol 80, no 3, pp 361-70.

Johnson, N. (2004) 'The Human Rights Act 1998: A bridge between citizenship and justice?', *Social Policy and Society*, vol 3, no 2, pp 113-21.

Joint Committee on Human Rights (2008) *A Bill of Rights for the UK*, HC150/HL165, London: The Stationery Office.

Jones, C. and Novak, T. (1999) *Poverty, Welfare and the Disciplinary State*, London and New York: Routledge.

Jones, C., Ferguson, I., Lavalette, M. Penketh, L. (2006) *Social Work and Social Justice: A Manifesto for a New Engaged Practice* (www.socmag.net/?p=177).

Jones, P. (1994) *Rights*, Basingstoke: Macmillan.

Jones, T. and Edwards, S. (2009) *The Climate Debt Crisis*, London: Jubilee Debt Campaign/World Development Movement.

Jordan, B. (1998) *The New Politics of Welfare*, London: Sage.

Jordan, B. (2006) *Social Policy for the Twenty-First Century*, Cambridge: Polity Press.

Joseph, K. and Sumption, J. (1979) *Equality*, London: John Murray.

Kabeer, N. (2005) 'Introduction', in N. Kabeer (ed) *Inclusive Citizenship*, London and New York: Zed Books, pp 1-27.

Kantola, J. (2006) 'Feminism', in C. Hay, M. Lister and D. Marsh (eds) *The State. Theories and Issues*, Basingstoke: Palgrave, pp 118-34.

Katwala, S. (2009) 'In Maggie's shadow', *Public Policy Research*, vol 16, no 1, pp 3-13.

Kendall, J. (2008) 'Voluntary welfare', in P. Alcock, M. May and K. Rowlingson (eds) *The Student's Companion to Social Policy* (3rd edn), Oxford: Blackwell, pp 212-18.

Kiernan, K., Land, H. and Lewis, J. (1998) *Lone Motherhood in 20th Century Britain*, Oxford: Oxford University Press.

Killeen, D. (2008) *Is poverty in the UK a denial of people's human rights?* Viewpoint, York: Joseph Rowntree Foundation.

King, D. S. (1987) *The New Right. Politics, Markets and Citizenship*, Basingstoke: Macmillan.

Klug, B. (2007) 'No one has the right to speak for British Jews on Israel and Zionism', *The Guardian*, 5 February.

Klug, F. (2006) 'Enlightened values', *The Guardian*, 18 February.

Kremer, M. (2007) *How Welfare States Care*, Amsterdam: Amsterdam University Press.

Kretsedemas, P. (2008) 'Redefining "race" in North America', *Current Sociology*, vol 56, no 6, pp 826-44.

Kundnani, A. (2009) 'Trust made meaningless', *The Guardian*, 19 October.

Kymlicka, W. (1995) 'Liberalism', in T. Honderich (ed) *The Oxford Companion to Philosophy*, Oxford: Oxford University Press, pp 483-5.

Land, H. (2008) 'Altruism, reciprocity and obligation', in P. Alcock, M. May and K. Rowlingson (eds) *The Student's Companion to Social Policy* (3rd edn), Oxford: Blackwell, pp 50-7.

Langan, M. (1998a) *Welfare: Needs, Rights and Risks*, London and New York: Routledge.

Langan, M. (1998b) 'The contested concept of need', in M. Langan (ed) *Welfare: Needs, Rights and Risks*, London and New York: Routledge, pp 3-33.

Langan, M. and Clarke, J. (1994) 'Managing the mixed economy of care', in J. Clarke, A. Cochrane and E. McLaughlin (eds) *Managing Social Policy*, London: Sage, pp 73-93.

Lavalette, M. (1997) 'Marx and the Marxist critique of welfare', in M. Lavalette and A. Pratt (eds) *Social Policy. A Conceptual and Theoretical Introduction*, London: Sage, pp 50-79.

Lavender, B. (2009) 'American healthcare is in truth already rationed', *The Guardian*, 17 August.

Law, I. (1996) *Racism, Ethnicity and Social Policy*, Hemel Hempstead: Prentice Hall.

Law, I. (2009) 'Racism, ethnicity, migration and social security', in J. Millar (ed) *Understanding Social Security* (2nd edn), Bristol: The Policy Press, pp 75-92.

Lawlor, E., Kersley, H. and Steed, S. (2009) *A bit rich: Calculating the real value to society of different professions*, London: new economics foundation.

Lawson, N. (2006) 'Freedom and security: the case for liberal socialism', in N. Lawson, E. Vaizey, J. Browne (eds) *Freedom: Three Perspectives on the Meaning of Liberty in the 21st Century*, London: Centre Forum, pp 5-23.

Lawson, N. (2009) *All Consuming*, London: Penguin.

Lee, P. and Raban, C. (1988) *Welfare Theory and Social Policy – Reform or Revolution?*, London: Sage.

Le Grand, J. (1997) 'Knights, knaves and pawns. Human behaviour and social policy', *Journal of Social Policy*, vol 28, no 3, pp 413-35.

Le Grand, J. (2003) *Motivation, Agency and Public Policy*, Oxford: Oxford University Press.

Leira, A. and Saraceno, C. (2000) 'Care: actors, relationships and contexts', in B. Hobson, J. Lewis and B. Siim (eds) *Contested Concepts in Gender and Social Politics*, Cheltenham: Edward Elgar, pp 55-83.

Lekhi, R. and Newell, P. (2006) 'Environmental justice, law and accountability', in P. Newell and J. Wheeler (eds) *Rights, Resources and the Politics of Accountability*, London and New York, Zed Books.

Leonard, P. (1997) *Postmodern Welfare*, London: Sage.

Levitas, R. (2004) 'Shuffling back to equality', *Soundings*, no 26, pp 59-72.

Levitas, R. (2005) *The Inclusive Society?* (2nd edn), Basingstoke: Palgrave.

Lewis, G. (ed) (1998a) *Forming Nation, Framing Welfare*, London and New York: Routledge.

Lewis, G. (1998b) 'Review', in G. Lewis (ed) *Forming Nation, Framing Welfare*, London and New York: Routledge, pp 265-85.

Lewis, G. (1998c) '"Growing apart at the seams": the crisis of the welfare state', in G. Hughes and G. Lewis (eds) *Unsettling Welfare*, London and New York: Routledge, pp 39-79.

Lewis, G. (1998d) 'Welfare and the social construction of "race"', in E. Saraga (ed) *Embodying the Social*, London and New York: Routledge.

Lewis, G. (2003) 'Difference and social policy', in N. Ellison and C. Pierson (eds) *Developments in British Social Policy 2*, Basingstoke: Palgrave, pp 90-106.

Lewis, G. (ed) (2004) *Citizenship, Personal Lives and Social Policy*, Bristol: The Policy Press.

Lewis, J. (2000) 'Gender and welfare regimes', in G. Lewis, S. Gewirtz and J. Clarke (eds) *Rethinking Social Policy*, London: Sage, pp 22-36.

Lewis, J. (2004) 'Individualization and the need for new forms of family solidarity', in T. Knijn and A. Komter (eds) *Solidarity Between the Sexes and the Generations*, Cheltenham, UK and Northampton, MA: Edward Elgar.

Lewis, J. (2005) 'New Labour's approach to the voluntary sector', *Social Policy and Society*, vol 4, no 2, pp 121-31.

Lewis, J. and Bennett, F. (2004) 'Introduction to themed section on Gender and Individualisation', *Social Policy and Society*, vol 3, no 1, pp 143-5.

Lewis, J. and Giullari, S. (2005) 'The adult worker model family, gender equality and care', *Economy and Society*, vol 34, no 1, pp 76-104.

Lewis, J. and Surender, R. (eds) (2004) *Welfare State Change. Towards a Third Way?*, Oxford: Oxford University Press.

Lewis, L. (2009) 'Politics of recognition: what can a human rights perspective contribute to understanding users' experiences of involvement in mental health services?', *Social Policy and Society*, vol 8, no 2, pp 257-74.

Lewis, O. (1967) *La Vida*, London: Secker & Warburg.

Liddiard, M. (2007) 'Social need and patterns of inequality', in J. Baldock, N. Manning, S. Vickerstaff (eds) *Social Policy* (3rd edn), Oxford: Oxford University Press, pp 120-43.

Lister, R. (1990) *The Exclusive Society: Citizenship and the Poor*, London: Child Poverty Action Group.

Lister, R. (1996) 'Introduction: in search of the "underclass"', in R. Lister (ed) *Charles Murray and the 'Underclass': The Developing Debate*, London: Institute of Economic Affairs Health and Welfare Unit, pp 1-16.

Lister, R. (2000) 'Gender and the analysis of social policy', in G. Lewis, S. Gewirtz and J. Clarke (eds) *Rethinking Social Policy*, London: Sage, pp 22-36.

Lister, R. (2002) 'Sexual citizenship', in E. F. Isin and B. S. Turner (eds) *Handbook of Citizenship Studies*, London: Sage, pp 191-207.

Lister, R. (2003a) *Citizenship: Feminist Perspectives* (2nd edn), Basingstoke: Palgrave.

Lister, R. (2003b) 'Investing in the citizen-workers of the future: transformations in citizenship and the state under New Labour', *Social Policy and Administration*, vol 37, no 5, pp 427-443.

Lister, R. (2004a) *Poverty*, Cambridge: Polity Press.

Lister, R. (2004b) 'The third way's social investment state', in J. Lewis and R. Surender (eds) *Welfare State Change. Towards a Third Way?*, Oxford: Oxford University Press, pp 157-181.

Lister, R. (2006) 'Ladder of opportunity or engine of inequality?', in G. Dench (ed) *The Rise and Rise of Meritocracy*, Oxford: Blackwell, pp 232-36.

Lister, R. (2007a) 'Inclusive citizenship: realizing the potential', *Citizenship Studies*, vol 11, no 1, pp 49-61.

Lister, R. (2007b) 'The real egalitarianism? Social justice after Blair', in G. Hassan (ed) *After Blair*, London: Lawrence & Wishart, pp 146-59.

Lister, R. (2007c) '(Mis)recognition, social inequality and social justice: A critical social policy perspective', in T. Lovell (ed) *(Mis)recognition, Social Inequality and Social Justice: Nancy Fraser and Pierre Bourdieu*, London and New York: Routledge, pp 157-76.

Lister, R. (2007d) 'Social justice: meanings and politics', *The Journal of Poverty and Social Justice*, vol 15, no 2, 113-25.

Lister, R. (2007e) in G. Blakeley and V. Bryson (eds) *The Impact of Feminism on Political Concepts and Debates*, Manchester: Manchester University Press, pp 57-72.

Lister, R. (2008a) 'Citizenship and access to welfare', in P. Alcock, M. May and K. Rowlingson (eds) *The Student's Companion to Social Policy* (3rd edn), Oxford: Blackwell, pp 233-40.

Lister, R. (2008b) 'Recognition and voice: the challenge for social justice', in G. Craig, T. Burchardt and D. Gordon (eds) *Social Justice and Public Policy*, Bristol: The Policy Press, pp 105-22.

Lister, R. (2009a) 'A Nordic nirvana?', Gender, citizenship and social justice in the Nordic welfare states', *Social Politics*, vol 16, no 2, pp 242-78.

Lister, R. (2009b) 'Poor citizenship: social rights, poverty and democracy in the late 20th century and early 21st century', in A. Kessler-Harris and M. Vaudagna (eds) *Democracy and Social Rights in the Two Wests*, Turin: Otto Editore, pp 43-65.

Lister, R., Smith, N., Middleton, S. and Cox, L. (2003) 'Young people talk about citizenship: empirical perspectives on theoretical and political debates', *Citizenship Studies*, vol 7, no 2, pp 235-53.

Lister, R., Williams, F., Anttonen, A., Bussemaker, J., Gerhard, U., Heinen, J., Johansson, S., Leira, A., Siim, B. and Tobío, C. with Gavanas, A. (2007) *Gendering Citizenship in Western Europe*, Bristol: The Policy Press.

Lloyd, L. and Riddell, S. (2002) 'Editorial', *Policy and Politics*, vol 30, no 1, pp 309-10.

Loader, B. D. (1998) 'Welfare direct', in J. Carter (ed) *Postmodernity and the Fragmentation of Welfare*, London and New York: Routledge, pp 220-33.

Lowe, R. (1993) *The Welfare State in Britain since 1945*, Basingstoke: Macmillan.

Lukes, S. (1974/2005) *Power. A Radical View*, Basingstoke: Palgrave.

Lupton, D. (1999) *Risk*, London and New York: Routledge.

Lustiger-Thaler, H. and Shragge, E. (1993) 'Social movements and social welfare: the political problem of needs', in G. Drover and P. Kerans (eds) *New Approaches to Welfare Theory*, Cheltenham: Edward Elgar, pp 161-76.

Lyon, D. (2001) *The Surveillance Society*, Buckingham: Open University Press.

Lyon, D. (2007a) 'Everyday surveillance: personal data and social classifications', in S. P. Hier and J. Greenberg (eds) *The Surveillance Studies Reader*, Maidenhead: Open University Press, pp 136-46.

Lyon, D. (2007b) 'Resisting surveillance', in S. P. Hier and J. Greenberg (eds) *The Surveillance Studies Reader*, Maidenhead: Open University Press, pp 368-77.

Macpherson, W. (1999) *The Stephen Lawrence Inquiry: The Report of an Inquiry by Sir William Macpherson of Cluny*, London: The Stationery Office.

Mandle, J. (2006) *Global Justice*, Cambridge: Polity Press.

Mann, K. (1994) *The Making of an English 'Underclass'?* Buckingham: Open University Press.

Mann, K. (1998) 'Lamppost modernism. Traditional and critical social policy?', *Critical Social Policy*, vol 18, no 1, pp 77–102.

Manning, N. (2007) 'Social needs, social problems, social welfare and well-being', in P. Alcock, M. May and K. Rowlingson (eds) *The Student's Companion to Social Policy* (3rd edn), Oxford: Blackwell, pp 26–33.

Marcuse, H. (1964) *One Dimensional Man*, London: Routledge and Kegan Paul.

Margo, J., Sodha, S. and Vance, R. (2007) 'Conclusion', in J. Margo (ed) *Beyond Liberty*, London: Institute for Public Policy Research, pp 235-53.

Marquand, D. (2006) 'New Statesman essay', *New Statesman*, 16 January, pp 34-7.

Marquand, D. (2007) 'A man without history', *New Statesman*, 7 May, pp 36-8.

Marquand, D. (2008) 'Labour has got Cameron wrong: this is no crypto-Thatcherite but a whig', *The Guardian*, 29 August.

Marshall, T. H. (1950) *Citizenship and Social Class*, Cambridge: Cambridge University Press.

Marsland, D. (1996) *Welfare or Welfare State?*, Basingstoke: Macmillan.

Marx, K. (1852/2007) *Eighteenth Brumaire of Louis Bonaparte*, Charleston SC: BiblioBazaar.

Marx, K. (1875) *Critique of the Gotha Programme*, Marxists Internet Archive (www.marxists.org/archive/marx/).

Marx, K. (1888) *Theses on Feuerbach*, Marxists Internet Archive (www.marxists.org/archive/marx/).

Marx, K. (1976) *Capital. A Critique of Political Economy*, translated by B. Foulkes, Harmondsworth: Penguin.

Maslow, A. (1943) 'A theory of human motivation', *Psychological Review*, no 50, pp 370-90.

Mason, D. (2000) *Race and Ethnicity in Modern Britain* (2nd edn), Oxford: Oxford University Press.

Max-Neef, M., Elizalde, A., Hopenhayne, M. (1989) 'Human scale development', *Development Dialogue*, no 1, pp 7–80.

Mayo, M. (2000) *Culture, Communities, Identities*, Basingstoke: Palgrave.

McDonald, C. and Marston, G. (2005) 'Workfare and welfare', *Critical Social Policy*, vol 25, no 3, pp 374-401.

McHugh, N. A. (2007) *Feminist Philosophies A-Z*, Edinburgh: Edinburgh University Press.

McKee, K. (2009) 'Post-Foucauldian governmentality: what does it offer social policy analysis?', *Critical Social Policy*, vol 29, no 3, pp 465-86.

McNay, L. (1994) *Foucault. A Critical Introduction*, Cambridge: Polity Press.

McVeigh, R. (2008), 'The "final solution": reformism, ethnicity denial and the politics of anti-travellerism in Ireland', *Social Policy and Society*, vol 7, no 1, pp 91-102.

Mead, L. (1986) *Beyond Entitlement: The Social Obligations of Citizenship*, New York: The Free Press.

Mead, L. (1997) 'Rejoinder', in A. Deacon (ed) *From Welfare to Work*, London: Institute for Economic Affairs Health and Welfare Unit, pp 127-33.

Mepham, D. (2005) 'Social justice in a shrinking world', in N. Pearce and W. Paxton (eds) *Social Justice*, London: Politico's, pp 133-57.

Michaelson, J., Abdallah, S., Steuer, N., Thompson, S. and Marks, N. (2009) *National Accounts of Well-being*, London: new economics foundation.

Miliband, D. (1999) 'This is the modern world', *Fabian Review*, no 111, pp 11-13.

Miliband, E. (2005) 'Does inequality matter?', in A. Giddens and P. Diamond (eds) *The New Egalitarianism*, Cambridge: Polity Press, pp 39-51.

Miliband, R. (1977) *Marxism and Politics*, Oxford: Oxford University Press.

Miller, D. (1997) 'What kind of equality should the Left pursue?', in J. Franklin (ed) *Equality*, London: Institute for Public Policy Research, pp 83-99.

Miller, D. (1999) *Principles of Social Justice*, Cambridge MA and London: Harvard University Press.

Miller, D. (2005) in N. Pearce and W. Paxton (eds) 'What is social justice?' *Social Justice*, London: Politico's, pp 3-20.

Miller, S. (1995) 'Plant' in V. George and R. Page (eds) *Modern Thinkers on Welfare*, Hemel Hempstead: Harvester Wheatsheaf, pp 166-79.

Mills, C. W. (1979) *The Sociological Imagination*, Oxford: Oxford University Press.

Ministry for Justice (2009) *Rights and Responsibilities: Developing Our Constitutional Framework*, London: The Stationery Office.

Modood, T. (1998) 'Racial equality: Colour, culture and justice', in J. Franklin (ed) *Social Policy and Social Justice*, Cambridge: Polity Press, pp 167-181.

Mooney, G. (2008) 'Explaining poverty, social exclusion and inequality: towards a structural approach', in T. Ridge and S. Wright (eds) *Understanding Inequality, Poverty and Wealth*, Bristol: The Policy Press.

Mooney, G., Scott, G. and Mulvey, G. (2008) 'The "Celtic Lion" and social policy: some thoughts on the SNP and social welfare', *Critical Social Policy*, vol 28, no 3, pp 378-94.

Morgan, A. (2005) 'Governmentality vs. choice in contemporary special education', *Critical Social Policy*, vol 25, no 3, pp 325-48.

Morris, J. (2005) *Citizenship and Disabled People*, London: Disability Rights Commission.

Morris, L. (1996) 'Dangerous classes: neglected aspects of the underclass debate', in E. Mingione (ed) *Urban Poverty and the Underclass: A Reader*, Oxford: Blackwell.

Morris, L. (1998) 'Legitimate membership of the welfare community', in M. Langan (ed) *Welfare: Needs, Rights and Risks*, London and New York: Routledge, pp 215-57.

Mouffe, C. (1992) 'Democracy and the political community', in C. Mouffe (ed) *Dimensions of Radical Democracy*, London and New York: Verso, pp 225-39.

Mount, F. (2008) *Five Types of Inequality*, Viewpoint, York: Joseph Rowntree Foundation.

Muir, R. (2007) *The New Identity Politics*, London: Institute for Public Policy Research.

Murray, C. (1996) 'The emerging British underclass', in R. Lister (ed) *Charles Murray and the 'Underclass': The Developing Debate*, London: Institute of Economic Affairs Health and Welfare Unit, pp 23-53.

Nasir, S. (1996) '"Race", gender and social policy', in C. Hallett (ed) *Women and Social Policy*, Hemel Hempstead: Harvester Wheatsheaf, pp 15-30.

National Equality Panel (2010) *An Anatomy of Economic Inequality in the UK*, London: Government Equalities Office/Centre for Analysis of Social Exclusion, London School of Economics and Political Science.

Needham, C. (2008) 'Choice in public services. "No choice but to choose!"', in M. Powell (ed) *Modernising the Welfare State*, Bristol: The Policy Press, pp 179-97.

nef (new economics foundation) (2008) *The Wealth of Time*, London: nef.

Newman, J. and Yeates, N. (2008a) 'Making social justice: ideas, struggles and responses', in J. Newman and N. Yeates (eds) *Social Justice. Welfare, Crime and Society*, Maidenhead: Open University Press, pp 1-28.

Newman, J. and Yeates, N. (2008b) 'Conclusion', in J. Newman and N. Yeates (eds) *Social Justice. Welfare, Crime and Society*, Maidenhead: Open University Press, pp 163-79.

Newman, J. and Yeates, N. (eds) (2008c) *Social Justice. Welfare, Crime and Society*, Maidenhead: Open University Press.

Nicholson, L. J. (1990) 'Introduction', in L. J. Nicholson (ed) *Feminism/Postmodernism*, New York and London: Routledge, pp 1-16.

Nixon, J. and Hunter, C. (2009) 'Disciplining women: anti-social behaviour and the governance of conduct', in A. Millie (ed) *Securing Respect*, Bristol: The Policy Press, pp 119-38.

Nixon, J. and Prior, D. (2009) 'Disciplining difference – introduction', *Social Policy and Society,* vol 9, no 1, pp 71-5.

Noble, M., Magasela, W. and van Niekerk, R. (2007) 'Social policy in South Africa', *Policy World,* Autumn, pp 10-11.

Novak, M. (1987) *The New Consensus on Family and Welfare,* Washington DC: American Enterprise Institute.

Novak, T. (1988) *Poverty and the State,* Milton Keynes: Open University Press.

Novak, T. (1997) 'Poverty and the "underclass"', in M. Lavalette and A. Pratt (eds) *Social Policy: A Conceptual and Theoretical Introduction,* London: Sage, pp 214-27.

Nozick, R. (1974) *Anarchy, State and Utopia,* Oxford: Blackwell.

Nussbaum, M. (1995) *Women and Human Development,* Cambridge: Cambridge University Press.

O'Brien, M. and Penna, S. (1998) *Theorising Welfare,* London: Sage.

O'Connor, J. (1973) *The Fiscal Crisis of the State,* New York: St Martin's Press.

O'Malley, P. (2001) 'Governmentality', in E. McLaughlin and J. Muncie (eds) *The Sage Dictionary of Criminology,* London: Sage, pp 134-5.

O'Neill, O. (2006) 'A right to offend?', *The Guardian,* 13 February.

O'Nions, J. (2009) 'Our friends in the South', *Red Pepper,* February/March, pp 33-7.

Obama, B. (2007) *Dreams from My Father,* Edinburgh: Canongate Books.

Offe, C. (1982) 'Some contradictions of the modern welfare state', *Critical Social Policy,* vol 2, no 2, pp 7-16.

Oldfield, A. (1990) *Citizenship and Community, Civic Republicanism and the Modern World,* London and New York: Routledge.

Oliver, M. (1996) *Understanding Disability: From Theory to Practice,* Basingstoke: Macmillan.

Osborne, G. (2008) *On fairness,* Speech, London: Demos, 20 August.

Parekh, B. (2006) *Rethinking Multiculturalism* (2nd edn), Basingstoke: Palgrave.

Pascall, G. (1997) *Social Policy: A New Feminist Analysis,* London and New York: Routledge.

Paterson, M., Doran, P. and Barry, J. (2006) 'Green theory', in C. Hay, M. Lister and D. Marsh (eds) *The State. Theories and Issues,* Basingstoke: Palgrave, pp 135-54.

Pearce, N. and Paxton, W. (eds) (2005) *Social Justice,* London: Politico's.

Penketh, L. and Ali, Y. (1997) 'Racism and social welfare', in M. Lavalette and A. Pratt (eds) *Social Policy. A Conceptual and Theoretical Introduction,* London: Sage, pp 101-20.

Penna, S. and O'Brien, M. (1996) 'Postmodernism and social policy: a small step forwards?', *Journal of Social Policy,* vol 25, no 1, pp 39-61.

Peters, S., Gabel, S. and Symeonidou, S. (2009) 'Resistance, transformation and the politics of hope: imagining a way forward for the disabled people's movement', *Disability and Society*, vol 24, no 5, pp 543-56.

Pfau-Effinger, B. (1998) 'Gender cultures and the gender arrangement – a theoretical framework for cross-national gender research', *Innovation*, vol 11, no 2, pp 147-66.

Pfau-Effinger, B. (2005) 'Culture and welfare state policies: reflections on a complex interrelation', *Journal of Social Policy*, vol 34, no 1, pp 3-20.

Phillips, A. (1999) *Which Equalities Matter?*, Cambridge: Polity Press.

Piachaud, D. (2008a) 'Freedom to be a child: commercial pressure on children', *Social Policy and Society*, vol 7, no 4, pp 445-56.

Piachaud, D. (2008b) 'Social justice and public policy: a social policy perspective', in G. Craig, T. Burchardt and D. Gordon (eds) *Social Justice and Public Policy*, Bristol: The Policy Press, pp 33-51.

Pierson, C. (1994) 'Continuity and discontinuity in the emergence of the "post-Fordist" welfare state', in R. Burrows and B. Loader (eds) *Towards a Post-Fordist Welfare State?*, London and New York: Routledge, pp 95-113.

Pierson, C. (1996) *The Modern State*, London and New York: Routledge.

Pilkington, A. (2003) *Racial Disadvantage and Ethnic Diversity in Britain*, Basingstoke: Palgrave.

Pinker, R. (2008) 'The Conservative tradition', in P. Alcock, M. May and K. Rowlingson (eds) *The Student's Companion to Social Policy* (3rd edn), Oxford: Blackwell, pp 69-76.

Plant, R. (1988) *Citizenship, Rights and Socialism*, London: Fabian Society.

Plant, R. (1990) 'Citizenship and rights', in R. Plant and N. Barry, *Citizenship and Rights in Thatcher's Britain: Two Views*, London: Institute for Economic Affairs Health and Welfare Unit, pp 1-32.

Plant, R. (1996) 'Social democracy', in D. Marquand and A. Sheldon (eds) *The Ideas that Shaped Post-War Britain*, London: Fontana Press, pp 165-94.

Plant, R. (2004) 'Neo-liberalism and the theory of the state', in A. Gamble and T. Wright (eds) *Restating the State?*, Oxford: Blackwell, pp 24-37.

Plant, R., Lesser, H. and Taylor-Gooby, P. (1980) *Political Philosophy and Social Welfare*, London and New York: Routledge.

Platt, L. (2007) *Poverty and Ethnicity in the UK*, Bristol: The Policy Press.

Platt, L. (2008) '"Race" and social welfare', in P. Alcock, M. May and K. Rowlingson (eds) *The Student's Companion to Social Policy* (3rd edn), Oxford: Blackwell, pp 369-377.

Pogge, T. (2004) 'Justice across borders', in M. Clayton and A. Williams (eds) *Social Justice*, Oxford: Blackwell, pp 264-85.

Preston, J. (2007) 'All shades of a wide white world, *The Times Higher*, 19 October, p 14.

Pringle, R. and Watson, S. (1992) '"Women's interests" and the post-structuralist state', in M. Barrett and A. Phillips (eds) *Destabilizing Theory*, Cambridge: Polity Press, pp 53-73.

Prior, D. (2009) 'Policy, power and the potential for counter agency', in M. Barnes and D. Prior (eds) *Subversive Citizens*, Bristol: The Policy Press, pp 17-32.

Prowse, M. (1999) 'A private problem', *Prospect*, October, pp 36-40.

Purnell, J. (2008) *Ready to Work. Skilled for Work*, Speech, London: 28 January.

Purnell, J. (2009) 'Labour still has one life left', *New Statesman,* 19 October, p 29.

QAAHE (2007) *Benchmarking Statement for Social Policy and Administration*, Gloucester: Quality Assurance Agency for Higher Education.

Quarmby, K. (2008) *Getting Away with Murder. Disabled People's Experiences of Hate Crime in the UK*, London: Scope.

Radford, L. (2001) 'Domestic violence', in M. May, R. Page and E. Brunsdon (eds) *Understanding Social Problems*, Oxford: Blackwell, pp 70-83.

Rae, D. (1981) *Equalities*, Cambridge MA: Harvard University Press.

Ramazanoglu, C. (1993) 'Introduction', in C. Ramazanoglu (ed) *Up against Foucault*. London and New York: Routledge, pp 1-25.

Ratcliffe, P. (2004) *'Race', Ethnicity and Difference*, Maidenhead: Open University Press.

Rawls, J. (1972) *A Theory of Justice*, Oxford: Clarendon Press.

Reeves, R. (2008) 'This is David Cameron', *Public Policy Research*, vol 15, no 2, pp 63-7.

Reeves, R. (2009) 'We'll win when we become New Labour', *New Statesman,* 5 October, pp 41.

Richards, S. (2009) 'Size should not be everything in Cameron's vision of a modern state', *The Independent*, 13 November.

Richardson, D. (2000) 'Constructing sexual citizenship', *Critical Social Policy*, vol 20, no 1, pp 105-35.

Ridge, T. (2002) *Childhood Poverty and Social Exclusion*, Bristol: The Policy Press.

Robins, J. (2009) 'A radical alternative to prison', *Red Pepper*, October/November, pp 36-7.

Roche, M. (1992) *Rethinking Citizenship*, Cambridge: Polity Press.

Rodger, J. J. (1996) *Family Life and Social Control*, Basingstoke: Macmillan.

Rodger, J. J. (2000) *From a Welfare State to a Welfare Society*, Basingstoke: Macmillan.

Rogers, B. and Muir, R. (2007) *The Power of Belonging*, London: Institute for Public Policy Research.

Rummery, K. (2007) 'Caring, citizenship and New Labour: dilemmas and contradictions for disabled and older women', in C. Annesley, F. Gains and K. Rummery (eds) *Women and New Labour*, Bristol: The Policy Press.

Rustin, M. (2008) 'New Labour and the theory of globalization', *Critical Social Policy*, vol 28, no 3, pp 273-82.

Sandel, M. J. (2009) *Justice. What is the Right Thing to Do?*, London: Allen Lane.

Sandvoss, C. (2006) 'Social constructionism', in B. S. Turner (ed) *The Cambridge Dictionary of Sociology*, Cambridge: Cambridge University Press, pp 569-71.

Saraga, E. (ed) (1998a) *Embodying the Social*, London and New York: Routledge.

Saraga, E. (1998b) 'Review', in E. Saraga (ed) *Embodying the Social*, London and New York: Routledge, pp 189-206.

Sardar, Z. (2008) 'Who are the British Asians?', *New Statesman*, 29 September, pp 32-3.

Saunders, P. (1996) *Unequal but Fair?*, London: Institute for Economic Affairs Health and Welfare Unit.

Sayce, L. (2000) *From Psychiatric Patient to Citizen*, Basingstoke: Macmillan.

Sen, A. (1985) *Commodities and Capabilities*, Amsterdam: Elsevier Science Publishers.

Sen, A. (1992) *Inequality Reexamined*, Oxford: Clarendon Press.

Sen, A. (1999) *Development as Freedom*, Oxford: Oxford University Press.

Sen, A. (2006) *Identity and Violence*, London: Penguin.

Sen, A. (2009) *The Idea of Justice*, London: Allen Lane.

Shah, N. and Marks, N. (2004) *A Well-being Manifesto for a Flourishing Society*, London: new economics foundation.

Shakespeare, T. (2005) 'Disabling politics? Beyond identity', *Soundings*, no 30, pp 156-65.

Shaw, M. (2007) 'Community development and the politics of community', *Community Development Journal*, vol 43, no 1, pp 24-36.

Shteir, R. (2006) 'The shame of America', *The Guardian*, 8 August.

Silver, H. (1994) 'Social exclusion and social solidarity', *International Labour Review*, vol 133, no 5-6, pp 531-78.

Sin, C. H., Hedges, A., Cook, C., Mguni, N. and Comber, N. (2009) *Disabled People's Experiences of Targeted Violence and Hostility*, London: Office for Public Management.

Skillen, T. (1995) 'The Social Justice Commission: community and the new welfare state', in J. Baldock and M. May (eds) *Social Policy Review 7*, Canterbury: Social Policy Association, pp 77-94.

Smart, C. (1996) 'Deconstructing motherhood', in E. B. Silva (ed) *Good Enough Mothering?*, London and New York: Routledge.

Smith, D. M. (2005) *On the Margins of Inclusion*, Bristol: The Policy Press.

Smith, N., Lister, R., Middleton, S. and Cox, L. (2005) 'Young people as real citizens: towards an inclusionary understanding of citizenship', *Journal of Youth Studies*, vol 8, no 4, pp 425-43.

Social Policy and Society (2005) Themed section: Transnational Social Policy, vol 4, no 4.

Social Policy and Society (2009) Themed section: Disciplining Difference, vol 9, no 1.

Soper, K. (1993) 'Review: A theory of human need', *New Left Review*, no 197, pp 113-28.

Spector, M. and Kitsuse, J. I. (2001) *Constructing Social Problems*, New Brunswick, NJ: Transaction Publishers.

Spicker, P. (1993) 'Needs as claims', *Social Policy and Administration*, vol 27, no 1, pp 7-17.

Spicker, P. (2006) *Liberty, Equality, Fraternity*, Bristol: The Policy Press.

Squires, J. (1993) 'Introduction', in J. Squires (ed) *Principled Positions*, London: Lawrence & Wishart, pp 1-13.

Squires, P. (1990) *Anti-Social Policy: Welfare, Ideology and the Disciplinary State*, Hemel Hempstead: Harvester Wheatsheaf.

Squires, P. (2006) 'New Labour and the politics of anti-social behaviour', *Critical Social Policy*, vol 26, no 1, pp 144-68.

Sriskandarajah, D. (2005) 'Outsiders on the inside: towards socially just migration policies', in N. Pearce and W. Paxton (eds) *Social Justice*, London: Politico's, pp 158-77.

Stevens, S. (2009a) 'Beware the label', *Community Care*, 26 February, p 10.

Stevens, S. (2009b) 'Outcomes 1, needs 0', *Community Care*, 29 October, p 10.

Stone, L. and Muir, R. (2007) *Who Are We? Identities in Britain*, London: Institute for Public Policy Research.

Sullivan, M. (1999) 'Democratic socialism and social policy', in R. Page and R. Silburn (eds) *British Social Welfare in the 20th Century*, Basingstoke: Macmillan, pp 105-30.

Sveinsson, K. P. (2009) 'Introduction: the white working class and multiculturalism', in K. P. Sveinsson (ed) *Who Cares about the White Working Class?*, London: Runnymede, pp 3-6.

Sykes, R. (2008) 'Globalization and social policy', in P. Alcock, M. May and K. Rowlingson (eds) *The Student's Companion to Social Policy* (3rd edn), Oxford: Blackwell, pp 430-37.

Sykes, R., Palier, B. and Prior, P. M. (2001) *Globalization and European Welfare States*, Basingstoke: Palgrave.

Tao, J. and Drover, G. (1997) 'Chinese and Western notions of need', *Critical Social Policy*, vol 17, no 1, pp 5-25.

Tatchell, P. (2009) *The Global Struggle for Queer Freedom*, Lincoln: The Activists', Caroline Benn Memorial Lecture, 13 October (www.petertatchell.net/).

Tawney, R. H. (1931/1964) *Equality*, London: George Allen & Unwin.

Taylor, A. (2008) 'Food for thought', *Community Care*, 28 February, pp 20-1.

Taylor, D. (1998) 'Social identity and social policy', *Journal of Social Policy*, vol 27, no 3, pp 329-50.

Taylor-Gooby, P. (1994) 'Postmodernism and social policy. A great leap backwards', *Journal of Social Policy*, vol 23, no 3, pp 385-404.

Taylor-Gooby, P. (1997) 'In defence of second-best theory: state, class and capital in social policy', *Journal of Social Policy*, vol 26, no 2, pp 171-92.

Taylor-Gooby, P. (2009) *Reframing Social Citizenship*, Oxford: Oxford University Press.

Thaler, R.H. and Sunstein, C.R. (2009) *Nudge*, New York and London: Penguin Books.

Thatcher, M. (1996) 'Foreword', in D. Marsland *Welfare or Welfare State?*, Basingstoke: Macmillan, pp ix-x.

Therborn, G. (2009) 'The killing fields of inequality', *Soundings*, no 42, pp 20-32.

Thompson, S. and Hoggett, P. (1996) 'Universalism, selectivism and particularism', *Critical Social Policy*, vol 16, no 1, pp 21-43.

Titmuss, R. M. (1968) *Commitment to Welfare*, London: George Allen & Unwin.

Titmuss, R. M. (1971) *The Gift Relationship*, London: Allen & Unwin.

Titmuss, R. M. (1974) *Social Policy*, London: Allen & Unwin.

Tomlinson, J. (1995) 'Hayek', in V. George and R. Page (eds) *Modern Thinkers on Welfare*, Hemel Hempstead: Harvester Wheatsheaf, pp 17-30.

Toynbee, P. and Walker, D. (2008) *Unjust Rewards*, London: Granta.

Vale, D., Watts, B. and Franklin, J. (2009) *The Receding Tide: Understanding Unmet Needs in a Harsher Economic Climate*, London: The Young Foundation.

Van Oorschot, W. (2007) 'Culture and social policy: a developing field of study', *International Journal of Social Welfare*, no 16, pp 129-39.

Vizard, P. and Burchardt, T. (2007) *Developing a Capability List*, CASEpaper 121, London: Centre for Analysis of Social Exclusion.

Voet, R. (1998) *Feminism and Citizenship*, London: Sage.

Wacquant, L. (2009) *Punishing the Poor*, Durham NC and London: Duke University Press.

Walker, A. (1997) 'Introduction. The strategy of inequality', in A. Walker and C. Walker (eds) *Britain Divided*, London: Child Poverty Action Group, pp 1-13.

Walzer, M. (1983) *Spheres of Justice*, New York: Basic Books.

Warde, A. (1994) 'Consumers, consumption and post-Fordism', in R. Burrows and B. Loader (eds) *Towards a Post-Fordist Welfare State?*, London and New York: Routledge, pp 223-38.

Watson, S. (2000) 'Foucault and the study of social policy', in G. Lewis, S. Gewirtz and J. Clarke (eds) *Rethinking Social Policy*, London: Sage, pp 66-77.

Webb, S. (2007) 'Free to be fair or fair to be free? Liberalism and social justice', in J. Margo (ed) *Beyond Liberty*, London: Institute for Public Policy Research, pp 133-43.

Weeks, J. (1996) 'The idea of a sexual community', *Soundings*, no 2, pp 71-84.

Weeks, J. (1998) 'The sexual citizen', *Theory, Culture & Society*, 15 (3-4), pp 35-42.

Wetherell, M. (2008) 'Speaking to power. Tony Blair, complex multicultures and fragile white English identities', *Critical Social Policy*, vol 28, no 3, pp 299-319.

Wetherly, P. (1996) 'Basic needs and social policies', *Critical Social Policy*, vol 16, no 1, pp 45-65.

White, S. (1996) 'Regulating mental health and motherhood in contemporary welfare services', *Critical Social Policy*, vol 16, no 1, pp 67-94.

White, S. (ed) (2001) *New Labour. The Progressive Future?* Basingstoke: Palgrave.

White, S. (2002) 'Must liberty and equality conflict?', *Renewal*, vol 10, no 1, pp 27-38.

White, S. (2003) *The Civic Minimum*, Oxford: Oxford University Press.

White, S. (2004) 'Welfare philosophy and the third way', in J. Lewis and R. Surender (eds) *Welfare State Change. Towards a Third Way?*, Oxford: Oxford University Press, pp 25-46.

White, S. (2007) *Equality*, Cambridge: Polity Press.

White, S. (2009) 'Thinking the future', *New Statesman*, 7 September, pp 20-2.

White, S. and Cooke, G. (2007) 'Taking responsibility: a fair welfare contract', in J. Bennett and G. Cooke (eds) *It's All About You: Citizen-centred Welfare*, London: Institute for Public Policy Research.

Wilding, P. (1995) 'Titmuss', in V. George and R. Page (eds) *Modern Thinkers on Welfare*, Hemel Hempstead: Harvester Wheatsheaf, pp 149-65.

Wilkinson, R. and Pickett, K. (2009) *The Spirit Level*, London: Allen Lane.

Williams, F. (1989) *Social Policy: A Critical Introduction*, Cambridge: Polity Press.

Williams, F. (1992) 'Somewhere over the rainbow: universality and diversity in social policy', in N. Manning and R. Page (eds) *Social Policy Review 4*, Great Britain: Social Policy Association, pp 200-19.

Williams, F. (1994) 'Social relations, welfare and the post-Fordism debate', in R. Burrows and B. Loader (eds) *Towards a Post-Fordist Welfare State?*, London and New York: Routledge, pp 49-73.

Williams, F. (1995) 'Race/ethnicity, gender and class in welfare states: a framework for comparative analysis', *Social Politics*, vol 2, no 2, pp 127-59.

Williams, F. (1999) 'Good-enough principles for welfare', *Journal of Social Policy*, vol 28, no 4, pp 667-87.

Williams, F. (2005) 'New Labour's family policy', in M. Powell, L. Bauld and K. Clarke (eds) *Social Policy Review 17*, Bristol: The Policy Press, pp 289-302.

Williams, F. (2008) 'Culture and nationhood', in P. Alcock, M. May and K. Rowlingson (eds) *The Student's Companion to Social Policy* (3rd edn), Oxford: Blackwell, pp 159-165.

Williamson, H. (1997) 'Status zero youth and "the underclass". Some considerations', in R. MacDonald (ed) *Youth, the 'Underclass', and Social Exclusion*, London and New York: Routledge, pp 70-82.

Wills, M. (2009) 'Language and the politics of liberty and security', *Public Policy Research*, vol 16, no 1, pp 34-7.

Wilson, E. (1977) *Women and the Welfare State*, London: Tavistock.

Wilson, H. and Huntingdon, A. (2006) 'Deviant (m)others: the construction of teenage motherhood in contemporary discourse', *Journal of Social Policy*, vol 35, no 1, pp 59-76.

Witcher, S. (2005) 'Mainstreaming equality: the implications for disabled people', *Social Policy and Society*, vol 4, no 1, pp 55-64.

Wright, G. and Magasela, W. (2007) 'Poverty debates in South Africa', *Policy World*, Autumn, pp 12-13.

Yeates, N. (1999) 'Social politics and policy in an era of globalization. Critical reflections', *Social Policy and Administration*, vol 33, no 4, pp 372-93.

Yeates, N. (2001) *Globalization and Social Policy*, London: Sage.

Yeates, N. (2002) 'Globalization and social policy', *Global Social Policy*, vol 2, no 1, pp 69-91.

Yeates, N. (2005) 'A global political economy of care', *Social Policy and Society*, vol 4, no 2, pp 227-34.

Yeates, N. (ed) (2008) *Understanding Global Social Policy*, Bristol: The Policy Press.

Young Foundation (2009) *Sinking and Swimming. Understanding Britain's Unmet Needs*, London: Young Foundation.

Young, I. M. (1990) *Justice and the Politics of Difference*, Princeton, NJ: Princeton University Press.

Young, M. (1961) *The Rise of the Meritocracy*, Harmondsworth: Penguin.

Young, M. (2001) 'Down with meritocracy', *The Guardian*, 29 June.

Younge, G. (2005) 'We do not always choose our identity – sometimes it's imposed', in M. Bunting (ed) *Islam, Race and Being British*, London: *The Guardian*, pp 31-2.

INDEX

Note: page numbers followed by *n* refer to notes.